CRUISING GUIDE TO COASTAL SOUTH CAROLINA

CRUISING GUIDE TO COASTAL SOUTH CAROLINA

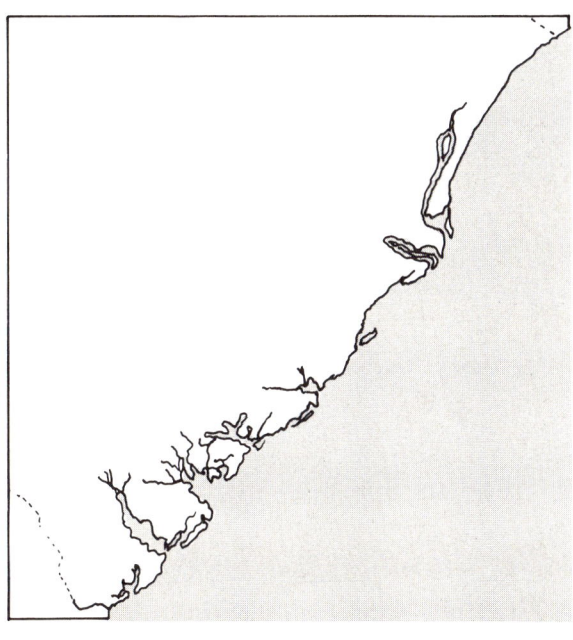

By Claiborne S. Young

With invaluable historical contributions by the South Carolina Sea Grant Consortium

JOHN F. BLAIR, Publisher
Winston-Salem, North Carolina

LEE COUNTY LIBRARY
107 Hawkins Ave.
Sanford, NC 27330

Copyright © 1985 by Claiborne S. Young
Printed in the United States of America
All Rights Reserved

Design by Virginia Ingram
Cover photograph by Bernard Carpenter

Black and white photographs by the author
 and his first mate unless otherwise noted
Composition by Graphic Composition, Inc.
Manufactured by Donnelley Printing Company

Library of Congress Cataloging in Publication Data

Young, Claiborne S. (Claiborne Sellars), 1951–
   Cruising guide to coastal South Carolina.

   Includes index.
   1. Yachts and yachting—South Carolina—Guide-books.
2. Intracoastal waterways—South Carolina—Guide-books.
3. Inland navigation—South Carolina—Guide-books.
4. South Carolina—Description and travel—1981-   —
Guide-books. I. South Carolina Sea Grant Consortium.
II. Title.
GV815.Y68 1985   797.1'09757   85-11278
ISBN 0-89587-045-2 (pbk.)

This book is dedicated

to my partner in life

Karen Ann

without whose loving help

as research assistant,

navigator, and proofreader

this guide would not

have been possible

Contents

Acknowledgments ix
Introduction xi

I   Little River to Georgetown   3
    ICW to Waccamaw River   3
    Waccamaw River   11
II   Georgetown   29
    Georgetown   30
    Pee Dee River   43
    Black River   45
    Winyah Bay   48
III   Winyah Bay to Charleston   53
    Minim Canal to McClellanville   53
    McClellanville to Charleston Harbor   67
IV   Charleston   81
    Charleston   81
    Charleston Harbor   96
    Cooper River   106
    Wando River   118
    Ashley River   121
V   Wappoo Creek to South Edisto River   125
    ICW to Stono River   126
    Stono River   128
    ICW to North Edisto River   136
    Toogoodoo Creek   140
    North Edisto River   142
    ICW to South Edisto River   156

VI   South Edisto River to St. Helena Sound   159
    South Edisto River   160
    Upper South Edisto River   161
    ICW and South Edisto River   162
    Lower South Edisto River   165
    Ashepoo River   171
    Rock Creek   175
VII   St. Helena Sound to Beaufort   179
    St. Helena Sound   180
    Morgan River   182
    Harbor-Story River Area   188
    Combahee River   197
    New Chehaw River   198
    Old Chehaw River   200
    Bull River   202
    ICW to Beaufort   206
VIII   Beaufort   213
    Beaufort   214
IX   Beaufort River to Georgia   233
    Beaufort River   233
    Port Royal Sound Area   239
    ICW to Cooper River   249
    ICW through Calibogue Sound   250
    Mackay Creek   258
    May River   260
    ICW to Savannah River   262

Acknowledgments

First and foremost I want to thank my first mate, Karen, without whose help as an experienced navigator, research assistant, and partner this book would not have been possible. Very special thanks also go to the South Carolina Sea Grant Consortium for their many invaluable historical contributions. Rhett Wilson, Jack Keenar, and Margaret Wilson deserve particular recognition for their tireless efforts to make the most reliable historical data available to this writer. Without their aid many of the historical sketches here presented could not have appeared in this guide.

Very special thanks go also to Andy and Meri Lightbourne and to Robert and Susan Kernodle for their many tireless hours of proofreading. To my research assistants—Earle Williams, John Horne, Vick and Debbie Harllee, and Kerry Horne—goes my heartfelt gratitude for their efforts to help me complete the seemingly endless research necessary to put this guide together.

I gratefully acknowledge the aid of the May Memorial Library of Burlington, North Carolina, the South Carolina State Library, and the South Caroliniana Library for their aid in helping me to accumulate the vast body of information needed for this project. Special mention should also be made of the long-suffering efforts of research assistant Earle Williams to acquire all this data and forward it to me.

Many thanks go to Herbert Berle for all his assistance in securing long-term berths. I would also like to acknowledge the assistance of Belle Isle, Ashley, and Buzzards Roost marinas, who aided me repeatedly with valuable information and much-needed assistance. To the Georgetown and Beaufort chambers of commerce also goes a special note of thanks for their ready assistance and for permission to reproduce their tour maps of the Georgetown and Beaufort historical districts.

To the following publishers, I extend my gratitude for permission to quote from the works listed: the Georgetown Rice Museum, *No Heir to Take Its Place* by Dennis Lawson (1972); South Carolina Federal Bank, *A Brief History of Beaufort* by John Duffy (1976); and the University of South Carolina Press, *Charleston in the Age of the Pinckneys* by George C. Rogers, Jr. (1980). Thanks are also due to author Nell S. Graydon for permission to quote from her two books, *Tales of Edisto* (Sandlapper Publishing, 1955) and *Tales of Beaufort* (Beaufort Book Shop, 1963); to Mrs. J. Stevenson Bolick for the use of material from *Ghosts from the Coasts* by her late husband, J. Stevenson Bolick; and to Edith Bannister Dowling for the use of her poem, "For This Your Land" (previously published in *One for Sorrow, Two for Joy*, © 1967, and *A Patchwork of Poems about South Carolina*, © 1970).

Finally, I express my most heartfelt thanks to Mr. John F. Blair and his fine staff for their enthusiastic support and encouragement during this project. I am indeed fortunate to have such a fine and caring publisher.

Introduction

"To know the coast (of South Carolina) is to love it." Of the many coastal visitors and residents who have no doubt expressed this sentiment at one time or another, writer James Henry Rice, Jr., was perhaps the most inclined to eloquence. Describing the region in his 1925 *Glories of the Carolina Coast,* Rice speaks of "vast avenues of live oaks and magnolias flanked by towering pines, whose crowns are masses of wisteria dropping purple blooms and at whose feet azaleas bloom . . . I think of winding rivers and pictured shores; of tillandsia, streaming from the trees, groves alive with birds, the haunting silence of deep woods where wild creatures revel . . . and I feel pity for people with toy houses and tiny yards . . . . "

Without a doubt the coast of South Carolina is about as close to a cruising paradise as pleasure boaters are ever likely to find. The possibilities are endless. At times, your greatest problem will be to choose between the various intriguing alternatives.

The beauty and the diversity of coastal South Carolina's waters are undeniable. Whether viewing the silent cypress swamps of Waccamaw River, the huge grass savannahs of Santee Delta that seem to extend beyond the horizon, or the tall, mysterious oaks of the southern Sea Islands, the visitor to this enchanting land will come away enriched by his experience.

In addition to the breathtaking natural scenery so aptly described by Mr. Rice, there are also many historical sites readily visible from the water. These include lovely plantation homes that have never lost that vague flavor of the Old South, sleepy villages such as McClellanville, and the vast harbors of Charleston and Beaufort. The cruising boater who is not captivated by the very special qualities of coastal South Carolina must possess truly numbed sensibilities.

The sidewaters of the South Carolina coast offer a huge selection of overnight anchorages. Many of these are quite isolated, which can make for memorable evenings spent under the stars. Sometimes it's possible to drop the hook within sight of a historic plantation home. It is a very special experience to watch the sun set over these grand old homeplaces. (Remember, however, that most of these plantations are privately owned. Please don't abuse your privilege by trespassing.) Anchoring on the waters of coastal South Carolina need never be dull or repetitive.

Marina facilities are numerous and of good reputation. The vast majority of South Carolina's marinas cater to transient boaters and are eager to serve the cruiser. I was impressed time and time again by the friendly greetings and offers of assistance from the various facilities I visited. This friendly attitude seems to prevail in both large and small marinas. The cruising boater can approach most of South Carolina's facilities with confidence.

Moving from north to south, the geography of coastal South Carolina presents many striking contrasts. The northerly section, which runs from the North Carolina line to Winyah

Bay, exhibits high banks and is pierced by only a few minor inlets. This section includes the Myrtle Beach area, usually seen by the boater from the none-too-attractive Pine Island Cut Canal, and the lovely Waccamaw River, which resembles a ghostly primeval cypress swamp.

Winyah Bay provides the first reliable access to the sea below Cape Fear. The old port town of Georgetown sits at the strategic confluence of the bay and four major rivers.

South of Winyah Bay the coast begins to change. The land quickly drops to the seemingly endless grass savannahs of the Santee Delta. The marsh grass dominates much of the shoreline from Winyah Bay to Charleston Harbor. A few minor Sea Islands border the ocean in this section, but they are surrounded by relatively small, mostly shallow streams. Inlets are shoal and dangerous.

The "Holy City" of Charleston sits astride one of the finest natural harbors on the East Coast of the United States. The tidal Cooper, Wando, and Ashley rivers extend far inland from the port city and provide many additional cruising opportunities.

Moving south from Charleston, the nature of the coast quickly changes yet again. This is the land of the fabled South Carolina Sea Islands. These historic land masses form an irregular, broken chain that shields the mainland from the Atlantic. They are surrounded by a bewildering maze of rivers, creeks, and inlets. There are also three large sounds. Along with Winyah Bay to the north, St. Helena, Port Royal, and Calibogue sounds share the distinction of being the largest water bodies in all of South Carolina.

The coast of South Carolina presents a wide array of attractions waiting to greet the cruising boater. Perhaps the greatest single attraction is the coastal native. Born in a tradition of hospitality that is known and respected worldwide, he will greet you with a word of cheer in his own inimitable accent. Like most people who have lived to and depended upon themselves for many years, the coastal South Carolinian does not take kindly to strangers telling him how something can be done better. He is likely to inform you that it has worked this way just fine for many generations. On the other hand, if you approach the coastal resident with respect and a genuine interest in his past, you will be welcomed into the heart of that special land that is coastal South Carolina.

Another attraction well worth your notice is the many fine restaurants dotting the South Carolina coast. This is "deep fried" seafood country, and this special cuisine has been perfected in the South Carolina Low Country. The preparation of fowl is another specialty of the area. Duck, quail, turkey, and chicken are often prepared in sauces whose recipe has been handed down from generation to generation.

This tradition of fine food has its roots deep in the past. In his memorable book, *Charleston in the Age of the Pinckneys*, George C. Rogers, Jr., explains that these recipes might have come "from a French grandmother or a Santo Domingan grandmother or a German passing through Charleston . . . it was some combination of Old World culinary arts with the New World staples." I am pleased to report that the tradition of eclectic cuisine and fine dining is alive and well today on the coast of South Carolina.

It is not this guide's purpose to discuss the many angling opportunities of coastal South Carolina, but it is certainly worth noting that both saltwater and freshwater fish are readily taken all along the coast. The upper reaches of Cooper River have long been known for bass and bream fishing. If you are interested in trying your luck, I suggest you find a friendly local native and engage him in a conversation about what's been biting lately. Judging from my observations during research, your efforts are more than likely to meet with success.

Certainly South Carolina's three important coastal cities, Georgetown, Charleston, and Beaufort, rank as major attractions for passing boaters. All three towns offer a wide variety of historical attractions and numerous facilities for the cruising boater. Each has its own special charms, beckoning the passing cruiser to stop for a few days or even a week to explore and gain a sense of the past. I highly recommend that you heed this call.

The major Sea Islands south of Charleston are another significant cruising attraction. Here and there, beautifully restored plantation homes gaze serenely out upon rivers and creeks they have watched over for more than a hundred years. Cruising amid the old oaks and moss-draped cypress of the islands, it is not difficult to imagine that time has somehow lost its course and you have strayed into a far-removed era. Few will remain unmoved by the faded grandeur of the South Carolina Sea Islands.

Within the last several decades, developers have transformed several of the Sea Islands into plush seaside resorts. Many consider these to be one of the coast's principal attractions. Happily, some of this development has been carefully managed to coexist with the fragile coastal ecosystem. Others, unfortunately, have not followed this wise course of action. Many of these luxurious retreats do not offer facilities for transient boaters. Hilton Head Island, to the south, is a major exception. Boasting six marinas, the island eagerly waits to greet the visiting cruiser.

Many boaters in South Carolina waters will be fortunate enough to experience some entertaining moments courtesy of a group of remarkable creatures. Large schools of bottlenose dolphins, or porpoises, can often be seen at play along the coast's rivers and creeks. These beautiful creatures add their unique and amusing charm to the waters of the South Carolina coast.

Within the body of this guide I have endeavored to relate all the information the cruising boater may need to take full advantage of coastal South Carolina's splendid cruising potential. I have paid particular attention to anchorages, marina facilities, and danger areas. All the navigational information necessary for a successful cruise has been included. In the guide, these data have been screened in gray for ready identification. Each and every water body, large and small, has been personally visited and sounded for the latest depth information. However, remember that bottom configurations do change. The cruising boater should always be equipped with the latest charts and "Notices to Mariners" before leaving the dock.

This guide is not a navigational primer, and I am assuming that you have a working knowledge of piloting and coastal navigation. If you don't, you should acquire these skills before tackling these waters.

The inland waters of coastal South Carolina are mostly deep and well marked. Many smaller sidewaters hold good depths from shore to shore and do not require aids to navigation. Thus, successful navigation of the state's waters is relatively simple.

You must not be lulled to sleep, however, by the generally forgiving nature of South Carolina waters. The unwary boater can still pile up on a hidden sandbar if he does not pay attention to his sounder. Always have the latest chart on hand to resolve quickly any questions that might arise. Observe all markers carefully and keep alert. I also advise you to study the navigational information contained within the body of this guide *before* your cruise. This basic planning will insure an enjoyable cruising experience.

Many South Carolina water bodies are well sheltered and seldom give rise to rough conditions. Others, such as Winyah Bay and Charleston Harbor, can produce a healthy chop when winds and tides are contrary. For the most part, however, your cruise of the state's waters will be quite pleasant as long as the fickle wind stays below 15 knots.

Boaters from the Middle Atlantic States will be struck by the tidal nature of South Carolina waters. Currents run swiftly indeed, and 7- to 8-foot tidal ranges are the norm. You will find that many marinas have floating docks to compensate for this phenomenon. If you do berth at fixed piers, leave plenty of slack in your lines.

Because the tidal ranges are so wide, I made every attempt to perform my soundings at low tide. Where that proved impossible, I compensated for higher tides, always leaning toward the conservative in my estimate. Nevertheless, if you enter waters just deep enough for your draft, feel your way in and watch the sounder closely.

Sailcraft and slow-moving trawlers must be alert for the side-setting effect of the swift tidal currents. Be sure to look to your stern as well as the course ahead to quickly note any slippage.

All boaters should have a well-functioning depth sounder on board before leaving the dock. This is one of the most basic safety instruments in any navigator's arsenal of aids. The cruiser who does not take this elementary precaution is asking for trouble. An accurate knotmeter/log is another instrument that will prove to be quite useful. While not as critical as a sounder, it is often just as important to know how far you have gone as to know what course you are following. On the other hand, Loran C is not a serious consideration for inland passage of South Carolina waters. Of course, if you plan to cruise offshore extensively, Loran C would be beneficial, but most inland coastal waters are not even charted with Loran position lines.

In this guide, lighted daybeacons are always called "flashing daybeacons." I feel this is a more descriptive term than the officially correct designation, "light," or the more colloquial expression "flasher." Also, to avoid confusion, daybeacons without lights are always referred to as "unlighted daybeacons." Similarly, lighted buoys are called "flashing buoys."

Autumn is the ideal cruising season for the South Carolina coast. From the middle of September all the way through November, coastal weather is usually at its best. Bright, shining days are frequent, usually with just enough wind for a good sail. Fall storms occasionally break this pattern of good weather, but they are usually of short duration. It always surprises me how many boaters never even visit the coast after Labor Day. Those who make this mistake will miss the most beautiful season the coast has to offer.

Summer is also a good time for cruising coastal South Carolina. However, heat and humidity during July and August can leave the air sticky and breathless. Fortunately, the frequent sea breezes do offer some relief. South Carolina is also noted for its afternoon thunderstorms, which can reach severe proportions from time to time. To avoid any last-minute surprises, it is a good idea to check the latest weather forecast before beginning your summer cruise.

Spring comes early to the South Carolina seashore. Warm-weather boating can often resume as early as the first of March. The trouble is that the spring weather is more than a little capricious. As seems to be true all along the eastern seaboard, weather from the first of March to the middle of May can range from beautiful, sun-draped days of light breezes to overcast days full of rain-driven gales. Be sure to include the latest weather update in your springtime cruising plans.

Many boaters continue their cruising through the colder winter months of December, January, and February. While freezes are possible, the visitor from northerly climes will be amazed by the mild character of coastal South Carolina winters. If you choose to join the ranks of these adventurous "frostbite" cruisers, be sure to dress warmly and check the forecast in case a hard freeze is due. Small craft should not leave the dock in weather where there might be a danger of capsizing. The cold waters could quickly bring on hypothermia. Otherwise, consider giving South Carolina winter cruising a try. It may not be for you, but on the other hand, it may prove to be a most enjoyable adventure.

In addition to the raw navigational data presented in this guide, I have included numerous historical sketches and coastal folktales to enrich your cruising experience. The state of South Carolina enjoys one of the richest historical heritages of all the American states, and the cruising boater must acquire some sense of South Carolina's colorful past if he is fully to enjoy his visit.

Founded as one of the original thirteen colonies, South Carolina was prominent in American affairs until the close of the Civil War. Because the colony was blessed from its beginnings with rich soil, natural harbors, and navigable rivers, South Carolina became an agricultural giant in the New World. The cultivation first of indigo, then of rice, and finally of Sea Island cotton brought almost unimaginable wealth to some planters and gave rise to a system of large plantations that characterized the South Carolina lifestyle and economic base until the coming of the Civil War.

It is not too much to say that South Carolina led the whole Southern region in that time of crisis and conflict. Little did the state's enthusiastic politicians realize that their policies would lead to the destruction of a society that had been built by many proud and struggling generations.

The Civil War decimated South Carolina as it did much of the South. Coastal South Carolina became an underutilized land of small farms and poor villages. Wilderness reclaimed many a field that had once waved with cotton or rice. The coast of South Carolina was a land whose greatness seemed locked in the past.

During this difficult period some were wise enough to see the coast's potential. In *Glories of the Carolina Coast,* written during the troubled twenties, James Rice states, "We must . . . remember also that the sixty years which have elapsed since the Confederate War are less by a third than the period of the coast's glory. Time is the test of enduring worth and when the rest of the State shows a record equal in producing men eminent for character, intellect and achievement, and, finally, equal in promoting human happiness, it will be time enough to institute a comparison."

Mr. Rice's faith has at last been justified in the twentieth century. The coming of large-scale tourism to coastal South Carolina has clearly breathed new life into the region. Many of the surviving plantations have been restored as vacation homes, and some of the Sea Islands have been carefully developed as multimillion dollar resorts. Yet, for all this welcome activity, nostalgia for the "old" way of life persists and at times is almost a tangible entity. This vague feeling of regret and sorrow seems to be the key to an understanding of a very special aura of romance and mystery that seems to bathe coastal South Carolina in its warm glow.

There are very few states indeed that can lay claim to such a colorful heritage. Today's South Carolinian is justly proud of his storied past. Thanks to the efforts of a number of excellent writers, many books on the history and folklore of the state are available today for anyone who wishes to partake of this rich tradition. The coastal visitor would do well to make the acquaintance of at least a part of this large body of literature before his trip. There is perhaps no surer way to get in touch with the spirit of the land and its people.

If by now you have detected a certain rampant enthusiasm for coastal South Carolina on the part of this writer, then you are on the right track. In my cruising experience I have never found any other waters that combine breathtaking natural scenery, historic character, and ease of navigation in such perfect measure. The coast of South Carolina sits shimmering in the summer sun, waiting to greet you. Boaters everywhere should rejoice in its promise. And just in case your boating appetite has not been sufficiently whetted, consider James Rice's unforgettable description of cruising down a South Carolina river.

"A summer trip along one of the coastal rivers will show the giant yuccas in flower and the magnolia, the royal woman of the Southern wood, with its creamy white blossoms laid on shining green leaves, the cypresses clad in vivid green and lilies floating on still waters while the wampee shows forth its blossoms—everywhere blooms run riot. On the uplands tall brooding pines sway in the wind and murmur things unutterable. Huge wood ibises stalk along the shore; redwings chatter and quarrel; rails cry in the reeds; coots and gallinules patter over the lily pads; the bald eagle soars, often a speck in the empyrean, while coppices are snow white with egrets; and nonpareils cling to grass stalks, eating seeds. All is life, life omnipresent—bird and beast, insect and flower, reptile and fish."

Good luck and good boating!

This Your Land

For this your land you have shown me I feel a familiar love:
Its water vistas, quiet marshes, dear sunshine, and hymnsong of trees,
These manly, majestic trees, with Gothic moss hanging and swaying
Like fairytale mermaid hair, in the soft shore breeze;
And the rustling, stiff-barked palmettoes; the brown marsh grasses,
Brown by the blue of wide rivers and flame of great skies
Of the sunsets we saw, together, before the red moon
And all the stars, and the darkness, took over with wonderful arms,
Here there is grandeur, and joy, and continuing peace.
Always the tides of the ocean, the wave-break and the return,
Promising, giving, always. Ah, the sounds of these waters
And all the choirs of the birds . . .
For these things, not contained, given thanks for, in words,
I feel a familiar love.

Edith Bannister Dowling

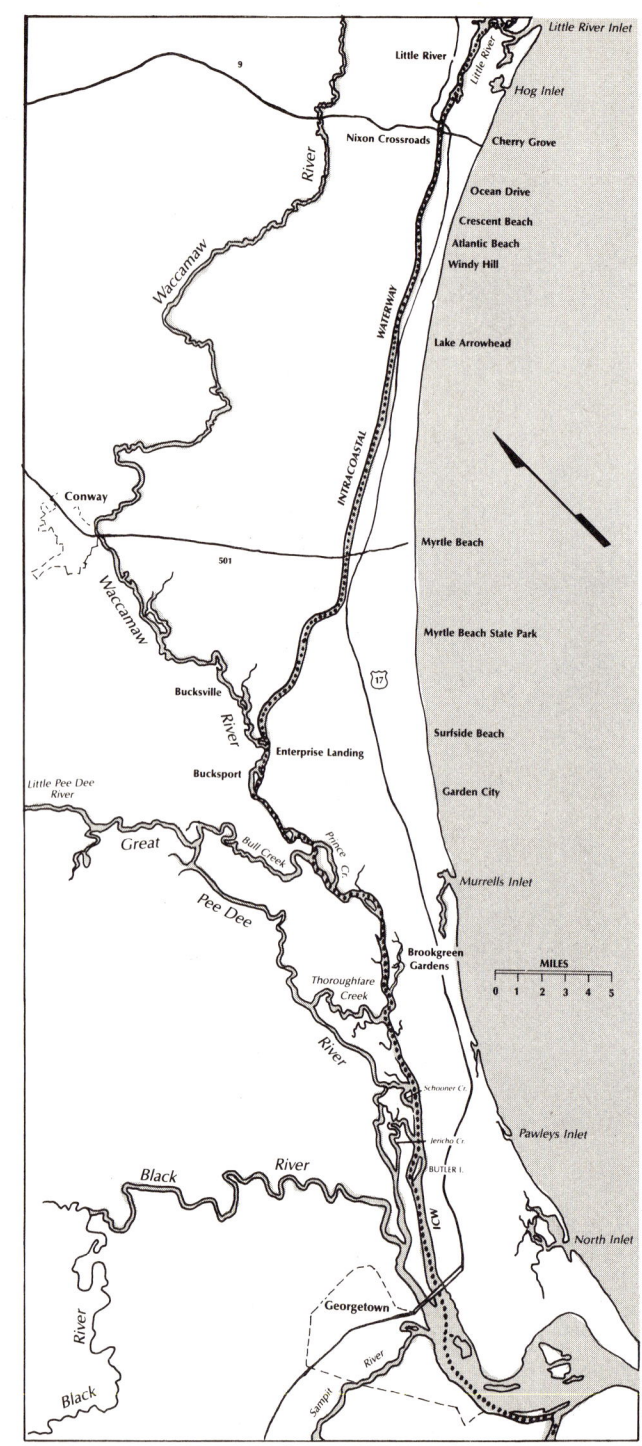

CHAPTER 1

Little River to Georgetown

The waters of northeastern South Carolina present a study in contrasts for the cruising boater. Little River, a part of the ICW for approximately 5 nautical miles, is a typical but undramatic section of the waterway. From the river the waterway enters a man-made canal known as Pine Island Cut. This is one of the least attractive sections of the entire ICW. Additionally, the presence of numerous underwater rock ledges gives good cause for concern. Fortunately, the canal eventually leads into Waccamaw River, considered by many to be one of the most beautiful sections of the ICW. Its reputation is richly deserved. The river winds its way lazily to the south for some 22 nautical miles until it finally intersects the headwaters of Winyah Bay near Mile 400 of the waterway.

Coastal South Carolina's northerly waters present an excellent opportunity for the cruising boater in a variety of settings. From gunkholing to historic cruising, the region has something for everyone. While a few sections may not warrant much of the boater's time, others beg to be explored and cruised. Take the time necessary for a full appreciation of the region.

Charts You will only need one chart to navigate this section of the South Carolina ICW: **11534** covers all South Carolina waters from the state line to Winyah Bay.

ICW to Waccamaw River

South Carolina's northernmost waters consist almost solely of the ICW's channel through Little River, followed by the manmade Pine Island Cut. Most of the route has treeless shores, often marred by visible evidence of dredging. This cut is, in this writer's opinion, one of the least enjoyable portions of the entire South Carolina ICW. Anchorages are very few and far between. Low-key facilities are available at the village of Little River, while the Myrtle Beach area to the south boasts several excellent marinas. Those who like a bustling, resort atmosphere will find Myrtle Beach, located to the east of the waterway, and the nearby "Grand Strand" communities worth their while. Otherwise, except for the excellent area marinas, most boaters will be glad to put this stretch behind them.

Little River Inlet

Moving north to south, Little River Inlet is the first South Carolina seaward cut available to the cruising boater. The inlet provides fairly reliable access to the open sea. Buoys and daybeacons are not charted, as they are frequently shifted to follow the ever-changing sands. Local knowledge, though not absolutely required, is certainly preferable before attempting the channel. If you are not familiar with the area, it might be a good idea to watch for a local craft putting out to sea and follow in his wake. You might also consider checking the current inlet conditions at one of Little River's marinas.

Calabash Creek

Calabash Creek, just to the east of the waterway's intersection with Little River Inlet, provides the first and one of the only opportunities for overnight anchorage on this section of the ICW. The eastern shore of the creek's upper branch provides good shelter and solid holding ground in 8 feet of water. The shoreline is in its natural state and no facilities are available on this section of the stream.

Calabash Creek leads north to the village of Calabash, barely within the borders of North Carolina. The channel has been newly dredged and marked within the last three years and currently carries minimum depths of 6 feet. There are no formal marinas on the Calabash waterfront, but the diplomatic boater may be able to negotiate dockage for the night at one of the many commercial docks.

Calabash has long been famous for its fried seafood. You may want to step ashore and test its reputation for yourself. Better hurry, though; locals declare that if one more restaurant is built, the entire town will sink into the ocean.

Historic Boundary House

As you pass flashing daybeacon #4, look to the north and you will see a golf course and a clubhouse. These mark the approximate site of the old Boundary House. This establishment served as a resting place for colonial travelers on the King's Highway between North and South Carolina.

Little River

The village of Little River offers the first facilities catering to the cruising boater traveling south on the ICW. Two marinas on the village waterfront welcome transients. Northside Marina, as its name implies, is the northernmost of the area facilities. It is a fairly new and rather small establishment. The marina offers limited overnight dockage with all power and water connections. Diesel fuel is available, but gasoline is not.

Little River Plantation Marina is the second facility encountered as you move south on the village waterfront. This marina welcomes the transient boater and provides fairly extensive overnight berths on a long fixed pier with all power and water connections. Gasoline and diesel fuel are readily available and some mechanical repairs can be arranged. There is an on-site restaurant, The Plantation Seafood House, which pleasantly overlooks the river. This writer highly recommends the combination fried seafood platter, an awesome mound of delectable shrimp, flounder, scallops, and oysters. Several other restaurants and a grocery store are a short walk away. Little River Plantation Marina can be unreservedly recommended for craft of almost any size.

There used to be a third facility on the waterfront, Little River Marina. While the docks are still very much in evidence and an Exxon sign is still visible, this establishment is now closed. If you are approaching from the south, be careful not to mistake the abandoned docks for the active area facilities.

Little River History The village of Little River is quite old. It was established before the Revolutionary War as a center of trade. Many of the original residents were from the northern colonies, and the community was first known as "Yankee Town." For many years logging was the mainstay of the local economy. Old piles still line the shore, marking the former sites of sawmills. As logging declined, commercial fishing assumed increasing importance. In recent times, sport fishing has become popular in Little River. Several fishing tournaments are held during the course of the year. Charter boats that put to sea from Little River Inlet are available for anglers.

Myrtle Beach Yacht Club at Coquina Harbor

South of Little River, Coquina Harbor soon appears on the northern shore. This large marina and condominium project is enclosed in a protected harbor that once served as a stone quarry. When developers connected the quarry to the ICW, they encountered a rather unique problem. A certain regulation prohibits joining any body of water that is deeper than the waterway channel to the ICW. Consequently, sand had to be pumped into the old quarry to raise its depths to that of the waterway. Minimum dockside and entrance depths of 12 feet are still held, however.

At the time of this writing, Coquina Harbor's piers were only half complete. Construction of the nearby condo project had just begun. Already, however, there are many slips available to the transient boater with gasoline, diesel fuel, and all power and water connections readily available. Mechanical repairs can be arranged, and there is a restaurant nearby. When complete, Coquina Harbor will be one of the largest facilities available to the South Carolina boater north of Charleston.

Nixon Crossroads

Two facilities are found near the small village of Nixon Crossroads. Just north of flashing daybeacon #20, Bella Marina, located on the waterway's northern shore, offers limited transient dockage, mechanical repairs, gasoline, and a well-stocked ships' store. Overnight berths feature floating docks with all power and water connections. Deep-draft boaters should be warned, however, that low tide dockside depths are only 5 feet. Bella Marina is open only from March 1 to December 31.

South of flashing daybeacon #20, Palmetto Shores Marina is located on the southern shore of the ICW. The marina is entered via a small creek, which maintains dead low tide depths of only 4 to 5 feet. Low tide dockside depths are around 5 to 6 feet. Transient boaters are welcomed here by a friendly management. However, there may not be appropriate slip space available for craft over 50 feet in length. Overnight berths feature floating docks with all power and water connections. Gasoline and diesel fuel are readily available. The marina offers both mechanical and below-the-waterline repairs. As you approach Palmetto Shores, don't be fooled by the large dock fronting onto the southern shore of the ICW. It has apparently been abandoned by the marina for some time.

For those boaters who want to sample the

resort life of the Myrtle Beach-Grand Strand area, Palmetto Shores is the northernmost starting point. You will need a courtesy or rental car, as the beach area is too far for walking.

Vereens Marina

About 1 nautical mile south of the Little River swing bridge, Vereens Marina is encountered on the southern shore. This is a modern, full-service facility that gladly accepts the transient boater. Dead low tide entrance depths run around 5 feet and dockside depths are 5 to 6 feet. Vessels drawing more than 4½ feet should call ahead on VHF channel 16 for the latest depth information. The marina's floating docks offer all power and water connections. Gasoline is available at a fuel dock just to port as you enter the marina complex. Diesel fuel can be purchased at a dock that fronts onto the southern shore of the waterway. Some mechanical repairs can be arranged.

Like Palmetto Shores, just to the north, Vereens offers the cruising boater access to the Grand Strand area. There are several golf courses and a restaurant within walking distance, but again, you will need a courtesy or rental car in order to visit the heart of the resort.

Hague Marina

Hague Marina is a well-managed, full-service facility sheltered in a loop on the waterway's southern shore some 2.4 nautical miles south of the Myrtle Beach swing and railroad bridge. Transient craft are gladly accepted. All power and water connections are available, as are gasoline and diesel fuel. Hague specializes in repairs, both above and below the waterline. If you are having mechanical or prop difficulty, it would be a good idea to put in here before proceeding on your way.

Hague Marina is the closest facility to the town of Myrtle Beach. Again, it will be necessary to obtain the use of a courtesy or rental car before visiting the resort.

Myrtle Beach–Horry County History Myrtle Beach and the adjacent Grand Strand communities, all within the confines of Horry County, have grown into South Carolina's most popular resort area. Thousands of tourists make the annual trek to these famous beaches. Such popularity, however, was not always the case.

In colonial days Horry County was one of the most sparsely populated areas of the state. Those who did settle here often migrated from the north and tended to establish a small farm culture, very unlike the large plantation system to the south, which spread from Charleston. Development was further impeded by the presence of vast swamps in the district.

It was not until 1899 that the strand received its first great boost. In that year a railroad was completed from Conway to Myrtle Beach. Originally built to transport crops grown in the area, it was later to have much greater impact.

In 1926, John Woodside of Greenville, S. C., and Col. Holmes B. Springs began an intensive promotional effort. The railroad brought crowds of vacationers to the strand. Myrtle Beach was incorporated in 1938 and has apparently never looked back. Its popularity has grown at a miraculous rate since World War II. Today, the visitor will find a bustling community crowded with motels, hotels, condos, restaurants, and amusements of all descriptions. There are also several very popular fishing piers along the beaches.

Boaters who prefer the quiet of an isolated anchorage may find the Grand Strand a bit robust. However, there is certainly no denying the resort's long-time popularity. As the saying goes, "All those people can't be wrong," so if you are so inclined, take the time to rent a car and explore the beach's many possibilities.

Enterprise Landing

The modern boater will note the small village of Enterprise Landing mostly as the northerly entrance to Waccamaw River. There is little left of the hustle and bustle when ferries plied the waters of the upper Waccamaw here. They provided the only reliable means of travel south from the Horry area. Certainly the construction of modern bridges has greatly facilitated transportation for all. As you pass, however, take a minute to reflect on the color of that era when travel was a real adventure, not just an everyday occurrence.

ICW to Waccamaw River Navigation

Navigation in this section of the South Carolina ICW is a fairly straightforward business of holding to the mid-width of the waterway. There are a few sections that require special attention, however, and these are detailed below.

Soon after crossing the state line you will approach the intersection of Little River Inlet, Calabash Creek, and the ICW. Be on watch for strong tidal currents. Slow-moving craft should be particularly alert for side-setting currents.

Little River Inlet Good depths are maintained in the Little River seaward cut as far south as the southeastern tip of Little River Neck. From this point the inlet is marked by uncharted nun and can buoys, which are frequently shifted in position to follow the shifting sands. As recommended earlier, if you are unfamiliar with the cut, you should try following a local craft or inquire about current conditions at one of the local marinas. Aside from these precautions, just take it slow and keep a wary eye on the sounder, and you should run the cut without any problem.

Calabash Creek To enter Calabash Creek, leave the ICW just before reaching unlighted daybeacon #2 by turning 90 degrees to the east. Favor the port shore a bit as you enter. A series of markers now leads to Calabash village. Point to pass unlighted daybeacon #2 to starboard and unlighted daybeacon #3 to your fairly immediate port. Past #3 the stream splits. Do not attempt the westerly fork. Instead, if you choose to continue upstream, enter the easterly branch by passing flashing daybeacon #4 to starboard.

Between #3 and #4 good depths of 8 feet or more run well in towards the eastern shore. This is a popular anchorage for waterway craft and you may be joined by several fellow boaters. Select a spot off the main channel and set the hook.

Good depths of 8 to 10 feet continue up the well-marked creek to Calabash village. Pass unlighted daybeacon #6 to starboard, unlighted daybeacon #7 to your immediate port, unlighted daybeacon #8 to starboard, and unlighted daybeacon #9 to port. Past #9 the dockage area of Calabash will open out to port. If you continue upstream, be sure to pass flashing daybeacon #10 to starboard. The first dock you will encounter is a long pier owned by Calabash Fishing Fleet. Try docking here, but check at the ticket office on the shore side of the pier. You may, for a modest fee, be able to arrange an overnight berth. These docks do have 20-amp power and water connections.

Pine Island Cut It is a navigationally simple run down the ICW through the Little River swing bridge, which opens on demand, to the beginning of Pine Island Cut. Running the canal itself, however, presents some problems. Often referred to as "the Rock Pile," the Pine Island cut hides numerous partially submerged rock shelves on both sides of the channel. Because of these hazards, extreme caution must be exercised in the canal, particularly in passing situations. It is most important to hold strictly to the mid-width when at all possible. This is often made difficult for slow-

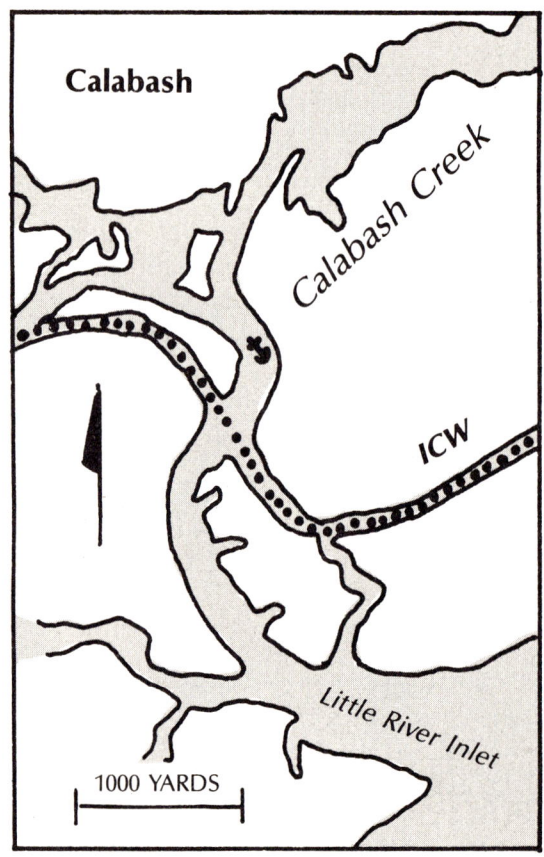

moving craft by the strong tidal currents that may be encountered in the canal. Don't allow your attention to wander; be alert at all times when running the cut.

When you do meet another vessel, slow down to idle speed and hope he does the same. The slow speed will allow you to pass each other closely without undue wake and without having to encroach on the channel's edge.

Overtaking another vessel also calls for special attention. Often this situation will

LITTLE RIVER TO GEORGETOWN

be the result of a powerboat having overtaken a sailing vessel. It is an excellent practice for the sailcraft to squeeze just a bit to the side of the mid-width and slow down as much as possible. The powerboat should then continue forward with just enough speed to pass the sailcraft. Failure to abide by this common-sense practice could result in some very frayed tempers and possible damage to both vessels.

As if the rock ledges were not problem enough, the canal is cursed with an abundant supply of flotsam. Floating logs and debris of all kinds abound, carried into the cut by the swift tidal currents. Keep a sharp watch for these hazards or bent shafts and props could be your unlucky reward.

On the ICW As you pass Standard Mile 350, watch the southern shore and you will soon spy a large golf course laid out along the banks. Some 3.5 nautical miles south of the Myrtle Beach Airport Vortac tower, clearly marked on chart 11534, you will pass under a cable car. This conveyance carries golfers across the waterway to a course located on the western shore. There is also a restaurant overlooking the canal at this point, but there is no dockage for boaters.

The Pine Island Cut meanders its way south through the Myrtle Beach combination railroad and fixed highway bridges. The railway span is usually open unless a train is due, and the highway bridge has a vertical clearance of 80 feet.

About one nautical mile south of the entrance to Hague Marina, the cruising boater will encounter the first South Carolina bridge to have restricted operating hours. The Socastee Bridge opens only on the hour and half hour from 7 A.M. to 10 A.M.

Sailcraft meets powerboat on Pine Island Cut

and from 2 P.M. to 6 P.M., Monday thru Friday, between May 31 and the next April 30. From May 1 to May 31 the bridge opens only on the hour and half hour between 10 A.M. and 2 P.M. At all other times the span opens on demand.

Just south of Socastee Bridge there is an indentation on the waterway's northern banks. Minimum depths of 8 feet can be held almost into shore, although there are some snags at the small cove's western tip. If you are desperate for anchorage and cannot proceed further, this area could serve as an emergency stop, but you will be exposed to the wake of all passing waterway traffic and the bottom is reportedly littered with stumps.

South of Socastee Bridge the land begins to change. Shores begin to rise and the banks become heavily wooded. You are now beginning your approach to Waccamaw River, and this scenery is just a taste of what is to come. At flashing daybeacon #27 the waterway intersects the beautiful Waccamaw.

Socastee Bridge on Pine Island Cut

Waccamaw River

The Waccamaw River has long been known as one of the loveliest sections of the entire Intracoastal Waterway. As one slowly cruises along its cool length, pondering the ancient cypress forests that line its shores, one can see how this reputation was acquired. Stop your engine for a moment and listen. There are very few houses along this section, and the silence of the swamps can be eerie. Watch the shoreline carefully and you may well catch sight of an alligator lying in the sun or slithering into the water. It is easy to imagine that one has somehow slipped into a time far removed, long before the age of automobiles and factories. This primeval character can lend to your cruise a feeling of adventure that is all too often absent in more developed areas.

Waccamaw River presents a multitude of possibilities for the cruising boater. Isolated, well-protected anchorages abound on the many deep creeks leading off the river. Some of these make fascinating side trips as well. Good marina facilities are found at Bucksport and Wachesaw. Tours of Brookgreen Gardens, one of the most lavish outdoor spectacles of flora in the Southeast, can be arranged from the latter facility. The upper Waccamaw, abandoned by the ICW, offers a most interesting side trip. Stretching some fifteen miles inland, the stream eventually leads the boater to the town of Conway, where a small but friendly marina is located. It is seldom indeed that the boater is presented with such a wide array of pleasurable choices in such a small span of distance.

Navigationally, the Waccamaw is a delight. Good depths run almost from shore to shore. Sidewaters are almost invariably deep and invite serious gunkholing. About the only hazard you need to watch for is the presence of flotsam. While not as great a problem here as in Pine Island Cut, floating logs and snags are encountered from time to time.

By now you have undoubtedly discerned that this writer has a great deal of enthusiasm for the Waccamaw. I believe that any serious cruising boater will have a similar reaction. Plan your cruise to allow ample time for full appreciation of this river's exceptional charms.

Waccamaw River History Waccamaw River was the site of many beautiful plantations before the Civil War. Sadly, only a few proud homes survive today. These vast farms were first based on the cultivation of indigo but later came to depend on the growing of rice. In the next chapter, the rice culture that dominated the lands around Georgetown will be discussed. For the moment we need only say that the plantations of the Waccamaw area were a part of this remarkably affluent era.

During the summer months, the planters usually fled their plantations and spent the summer at coastal retreats, not to return until the first hard frost. Believing that the dreaded malaria, or "swamp fever," arose from the nearby swamps, they sought the more "healthful" breezes of the ocean. Little did these proud aristocrats suspect that their real enemy was the ignoble mosquito and that the sea breezes merely helped to disperse the foe.

Some time before the first hot spell the entire household would be packed aboard a small fleet of pirogues. These were boats of various sizes made by hollowing out logs. As the slaves rowed the master and his family down the river, they would sing certain songs peculiar to each plantation. It is said that the knowledgeable native could recognize the origin of a particular party long before it passed, simply by listening to the slow and sad singing that came on before it. There are those who will tell you that on a quiet spring night one may still hear ghostly singing along the river's banks. Perhaps it is only the wind remembering the grandeur and tragedy of long-lost days.

Upper Waccamaw River

The adventurous boater can, if he so chooses, abandon the ICW at Enterprise Landing and follow the upper reaches of Waccamaw River for some 15 nautical miles to Conway. Most of the route is uncharted, but it is well marked, and the river holds depths of 8 to 20 feet as far as Conway. During daylight hours the stream's navigational difficulties are limited to a fair number of snags along the

Old warehouse on upper Waccamaw River at Conway

way. As the stream approaches Conway it remains consistently deep but narrows somewhat. Consequently, this side trip is not recommended for craft over 40 feet. You must also be able to clear one fixed bridge with 25 feet of vertical clearance. Be sure to read the Upper Waccamaw River navigation section presented later in this chapter before trying the cut.

The upper Waccamaw is well protected. The boater may choose to drop his hook almost anywhere along the stream. River traffic is light, so just select a likely spot and settle down for a peaceful evening.

At Conway a small marina provides limited overnight dockage with all power and water connections for just $3.00 a day. Gasoline is available, but the marina does not offer diesel fuel. This facility has minimum entrance depths of 6 feet with 9 to 10 feet of water at dockside. The cruising boater is fortunate to have such an excellent facility available to him so far from the beaten path.

For the most part the shoreline of the upper Waccamaw is in its natural state, though here and there you will find a few lightly developed areas. Just upstream of unlighted daybeacon #6, a few homes are visible on the western shore. These are all that is left of Bucksville, once the middle mill of Henry Buck's lumbering empire.

Conway History Conway was originally settled in 1734 as the town of Kingston. The name was changed in 1802 to honor Robert Conway, a hero of the Revolutionary War. Most of the village's early settlers were from North Carolina and Virginia. The dense swamps to the south made it difficult for settlers to migrate northward from Charleston. Since colonial days Conway has been a leading center of government and politics for this section of South Carolina. Today the visitor can still view a number of historic sites within walking distance of the marina. Ask at the office for directions.

Bucksville History In the mid–1800s Henry Buck emigrated to the Waccamaw area from New England with the intention of founding a great lumbering enterprise. Buck was apparently a man of enormous energy and resource. He did not waste any time in setting about his task and soon established three sawmills. The lower plant was at Bucksport on the Waccamaw, the second or middle mill was at Bucksville, and the third was at Bucksville Plantation, just upriver from unlighted daybeacon #8. The plantation house survives at this upper site. It is readily visible from the water. Look just to the right of the house and you will see an old brick chimney. This is all that remains of the once-busy sawmill.

By 1875 Buck was shipping large consignments of lumber to the north. His mills were busy, bustling places. Always looking for a new way to turn a profit, Buck decided to try his hand at shipbuilding. His intention was to compare the cost of building a ship on the Waccamaw with that incurred by the shipwrights of his native New England. The product of this experiment was a three-masted sailing ship, the *Henrietta*. Surprisingly, Buck's neighbors objected to his new enterprise. Bowing to their wishes, Buck built no more ships at the mills. The *Henrietta* survived for nineteen years and was finally sunk in a violent hurricane near Japan in 1894. Her long service is evidence of Henry Buck's remarkable craftsmanship, so typical of all his works.

The ICW and Waccamaw River

From Enterprise Landing the ICW follows the splendid Waccamaw for some 22 nautical miles south to the headwaters of Winyah Bay. Good facilities and a wide array of anchorages are available along the route.

Old chimney marking the site of Bucksville Plantation sawmill

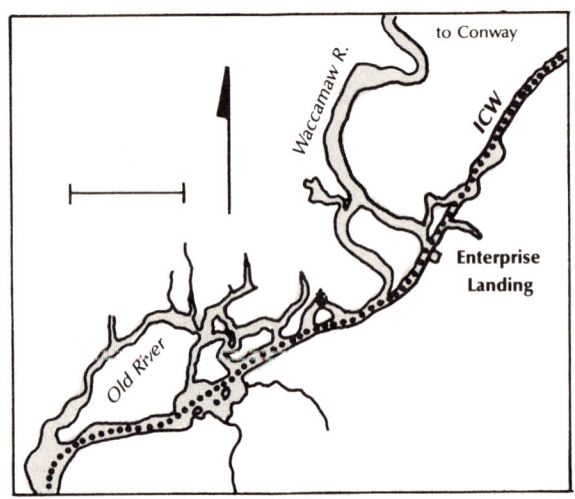

Island Anchorage

Just north of flashing daybeacon #29 a branch of the river splits off to the west and loops behind a small island. Minimum depths are 12 feet. The shoreline is in its natural state and no facilities are available in the area. This is a good overnight anchorage even though it lacks some of the adventurous opportunities of the creeks to the south. If it has been a long day and you have seen enough of what is around the next bend for the moment, don't hesitate to drop the hook here.

Old River

Old River is a rather small stream that splits off from the Waccamaw to the north near flashing daybeacon #36. Minimum depths are 12 feet, but there is not sufficient swing room for craft over 28 feet in length, and the southerly entrance is littered with snags. Better anchorages are to be found just to the south.

LITTLE RIVER TO GEORGETOWN

Bucksport Plantation Marina

Just south of flashing daybeacon #36, Bucksport Plantation Marina will come abeam on the western shore. This friendly facility welcomes the transient boater and provides overnight dockage with all power and water connections. Gasoline and diesel fuel are readily available, as are mechanical and below-the-waterline repairs. The well-stocked marina store can meet most of your grocery needs.

Bucksport Marina features its own on-site restaurant. This well-known eatery features a wide menu including seafood, steaks, and chicken. Because the windows front onto the river, you can watch the passing waterway traffic while you dine.

Take a moment to investigate the old house behind the marina store. It is one of the homes Henry Buck built to serve his needs at the lower mill. Sadly, the once-proud structure is now in poor condition. Perhaps in the near future some enterprising soul will undertake the task of restoring the old homeplace to its former glory.

Bucksport Plantation Marina

All in all, Bucksport Plantation Marina is an excellent facility for the cruising boater. You may be sure of a warm and hearty welcome, so if it's near the end of your cruising day and you are nearby, don't hesitate to stop for a pleasant evening.

Prince Creek

The northern entrance to Prince Creek is found just east of flashing daybeacon #44. The creek loops inland to the south and rejoins the Waccamaw at flashing daybeacon #53. The beautiful shoreline is entirely in its natural state, covered for the most part with tall cypress and hardwoods. No facilities are available in the area. Minimum depths are 12 feet for the creek's entire length, running to 30 feet in a few places. Boaters with craft over 30 feet in length will find the best swinging room near the northern and southern entrances. The creek gives adequate protection for heavy weather.

Prince Creek gives the cruising boater his first opportunity to experience the charms of an overnight anchorage on the enchanting Waccamaw south of Bucksport. A few other spots may offer more swinging room, but for natural beauty, Prince Creek need not take a back seat to any sidewater of Waccamaw River.

Bull Creek

Bull Creek is a major sidewater of the Waccamaw. It is one of the largest auxiliary streams on the river and provides what is unquestionably one of the finest anchorage opportunities north of Georgetown. The stream's considerable width gives plenty of swing

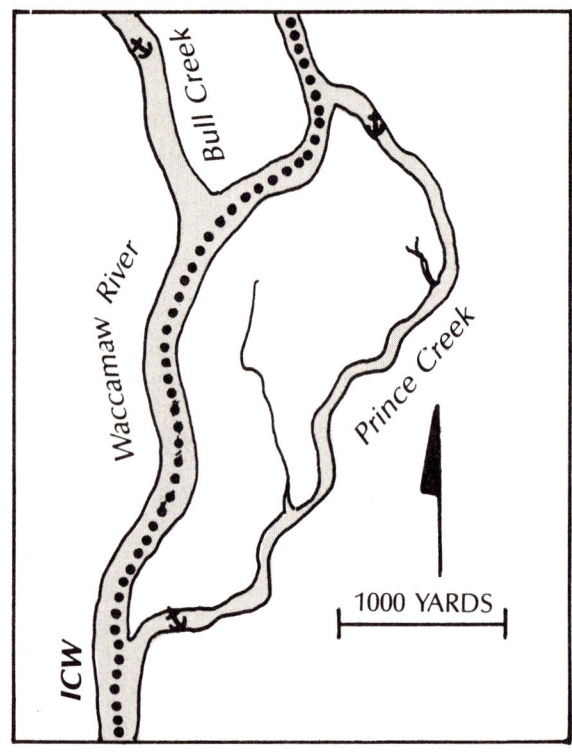

room for larger craft. Minimum depths of 14 feet are held far upstream. The shoreline is entirely undeveloped with high sandy banks in a few spots. The cypress and other hardwoods are lush along the banks. It is seldom that the cruising boater will find an overnight anchorage that combines so many fortunate qualities. There are no facilities on the creek, but even if you usually frequent marinas, consider spending a night on the tranquil waters of Bull Creek. You may find that it is an evening to remember.

Wachesaw Landing

Just south of flashing daybeacon #57 the cruising boater will come upon Wacca Wache

LITTLE RIVER TO GEORGETOWN 17

Marina at the small village of Wachesaw Landing. Wacca Wache provides overnight berths with all power and water connections for transients. Gasoline and diesel fuel are available, and mechanical and below-the-waterline repairs can be arranged. Minimum dockside depths are about 6 feet. Over and above these raw statistics, this writer could not help liking Wacca Wache. Walking into the small marina store was like stepping back some twenty years. I can well remember a soft drink machine, just like the one still in use here, at Southport Marina in my younger days. It is evident that folks are rarely in a rush around here. However, the entire staff is as friendly and helpful as can be.

Tours of Brookgreen Gardens, not far to the south, can be arranged at the marina. There is no longer any access by water to the gardens, so if you want to visit, you must make your reservations here. A large drydock facility for small craft is housed in a huge metal building behind the marina. For the landlubber, a tour boat leaves Wacca Wache several times a day for excursions along the Waccamaw River. Even the road leading to the marina has its charms. It is covered with a canopy of tall trees, giving cool shade to the old track.

Don't be in so great a hurry to reach Georgetown that you pass Wacca Wache Marina by without a thought. Few boaters who appreciate the slower pace of Low Country

ICW cruise ship on Waccamaw River

South Carolina will be disappointed with an overnight stop here.

Wachesaw Legend In his book *Ghosts From the Coast*, master storyteller J. Stevenson Bolick describes the Wachesaw area thus: "Those who love the romantic and the beautiful fall in love with the spot on sight. The verdant sub-tropical vegetation, the bright flowers and berries, the great live oaks with their pennants of Spanish moss waving lazily with the breeze, the towering pine forests, and the green, green grasses and marshes that change color with the changing seasons all add to a charm and loveliness hard to surpass. Many who stop here for a short visit find the place so much to their liking that they end up buying plantations, farms, or resort homes in the vicinity."

It is in this idyllic setting that one of the many ghostly tales of the upper South Carolina Low Country is set. In the 1920s, work was begun on a new home atop Wachesaw Bluff. This is the same house you may see today through the trees just south of the marina. The preliminary excavations unexpectedly revealed a number of human skulls and bones. Work was suspended and the Charleston museum was notified. Careful digging revealed many human skeletons, some of enormous size and others buried in huge urns. Also unearthed were many tools, weapons, and other artifacts from which it was possible to identify the remains as those of early Indian tribes. It may well have been that the Wachesaw area was an ancient burial ground for many different Indian peoples.

While the archeological work was going forward, an epidemic of diphtheria broke out in the area. Some said that the germs had been unearthed with the old remains. Others said that the scourge was the result of an Indian curse on those who disturbed the dead.

A related tale recounts the hair-raising experiences of a young man who worked at the digs. One night, so the story goes, he took home several arrowheads and spearheads that he had unearthed during the day. That night his sleep was troubled by a strange dream. He seemed to hear loud wailing coming from the direction of the burial ground. When he awoke, the strange sounds ceased, but for a long time he was too afraid to sleep again. When he finally dropped off, the strange dream was repeated.

The next night he dreamt that he saw an unusually large Indian warrior, dressed in full battle regalia, standing in the next room, sifting through the artifacts. As the restless nights passed, more and more warriors appeared to the unhappy man. Finally, on the sixth night, he was awakened by a violent thunderstorm. The lightning flashes revealed a blood-chilling scene with their phantom light. The warriors in the next room were fighting over the relics. Suddenly, to his horror, the wretched man realized that he was not dreaming this time. The strange spirits were actually present!

Too terrified to move, the young man huddled in his bed till dawn, when, as soon as he could persuade his frightened limbs to move, he rushed from the house and went in search of the museum officials. Finding them after a time, he immediately turned over his relics and went on to say that he never wanted to see the accursed articles again. That was the

LITTLE RIVER TO GEORGETOWN   19

last of his haunting. Perhaps the spirits of the ancient warriors were appeased at last.

If you think this tale a bit fanciful, you may be surprised to learn there are many in the South Carolina Low Country who believe it implicitly. The coastal ghost lore is quite old and not to be dismissed out of hand. Many of these tales have given more than one visitor a goose pimple or two.

Murrells Inlet and Pawleys Island

Murrells Inlet and Pawleys Island, to the east of Wachesaw Landing, are two very popular resort communities whose roots are deep in the past. While neither village is accessible by water from the ICW, you may want to consider securing the use of a courtesy or rental car for a visit. Murrells Inlet is famous for its many fine seafood restaurants, and Pawleys Island is one of the most frequently visited resorts between Myrtle Beach and Georgetown.

Both communities were originally summer retreats for the wealthy planters fleeing the Low Country's "fever season" of malaria. As you might well imagine, the long history of summer occupation by the romantic planter class has given rise to many legends. In *Ghosts from the Coast*, J. Stevenson Bolick has done a masterful job of relating several of these fascinating yarns. Similarly, Nancy

Litchfield Beach (*Courtesy of S. C. Department of Parks, Recreation & Tourism*)

Rhyne presents a number of very moving legends concerning the Pawleys Island-Murrells Inlet area in her two books, *Tales of the South Carolina Low Country* and *More Tales of the South Carolina Low Country*.

While little evidence remains today of the planters' occupation, these villages seem still to remember the grandeur of those lost days. If you have the chance to visit, take a few minutes to stroll along the beach and picture, if you can, the planter's wife and daughter dressed in their long white gowns, looking from their porches across the ever-moving sea. One cannot help wondering what their thoughts and dreams might have been.

Murrells Inlet Legend The natives of Murrells Inlet will tell you that they and their fathers before them have long known the origins of hurricanes. A very old legend holds that whenever a mermaid is captured and held captive at the inlet, a great storm begins to build in the south. Its strength increases, and unless the child of the sea is released, it sweeps with devastating fury upon Murrells' shores. Just such a storm is the setting for the legend of the phantom lights.

Tradition tells us that in the period following the American Revolution there lived an ambitious young man on the shores of Murrells Inlet. His dream was to acquire a sailing craft of his own to make coastal cruises and go on fishing expeditions. At last, after many years of being a ship's officer, he made his dream a reality. He purchased a beautiful schooner from a wealthy Georgetown rice planter and proudly sailed his new craft out of Winyah Bay with his whole family aboard. They took an extended ocean voyage and visited Wilmington, New Bern, Baltimore, and New York. Finally the new master brought his shining vessel to his own docks at Murrells Inlet. The boat caused quite a stir, and people came from miles around to admire the young captain's purchase. Some commented on the running lights, which were covered with thick Venetian glass in rich shades of ruby and emerald.

For a time all went well. The captain enjoyed a profitable cargo voyage and a suc-

Murrells Inlet (*Courtesy of S. C. Department of Parks, Recreation & Tourism*)

cessful fishing trip. Then came the September gale season. It was not long before a severe storm hit the coast. As the storm became more and more violent, the proud craft was driven relentlessly against its piling and began to suffer damage. The creek was too narrow for anchorage, so the master set sail with a few trusted hands with the intention of riding out the storm just offshore. Before leaving, the captain told his wife to keep a light burning in the window so he could maintain a bearing on the shore. Arriving offshore within sight of the beach, the crew set their anchor. As the wind rose, the anchor dragged repeatedly. Time and again, the anxious watchers ashore saw the distinctive running lights disappear, then reappear as the craft was masterfully piloted back towards the lighted window until the hook could again be set.

On the next day the storm reached the height of its violence. Whole trees were uprooted, and the tide was frighteningly high. As the long afternoon drew to a close, the watchers lost sight of the ship in a blinding rainstorm. When night fell, all ashore strained for a glimpse of the ship's lights, but they were nowhere to be seen.

As the great storm finally abated, search parties were launched, but no trace of the proud ship was ever found. The captain's saddened wife continued to place a lamp in her window every night. It became a symbol to her of the promise she had made to her husband to keep the light burning. One year to the day after the tragic event, the captain's wife happened to look out of her upstairs window and was startled to see lights on the ocean, bearing an amazing resemblance to those of the lost barque. Other family members were summoned, as were several neighbors. An anxious vigil was kept throughout the night. The lights were visible until just before dawn, but when it was daylight at last, not a ship was to be seen on the horizon.

Many will tell you that those desperate but beautiful lights may still be seen across the sea on September nights. Who can say? In the romance of Murrells Inlet, perhaps love is stronger than death.

Brookgreen Gardens

In the 1930s the fabulously rich Archer M. Huntington acquired several of the old plantations along Waccamaw Neck. Many of these had originally belonged to the prominent Alston family. (One plantation, The Oaks, was the home of ill-fated Theodosia Burr Alston, whose story will be presented in the next chapter.) When the properties were joined, Huntington began to construct a huge garden to serve as a setting for the artistic creations of his wife, sculptor Anna Hyatt Huntington. No expense was spared, and as the years passed, the beautiful gardens were counted among the great splendors of the southeast. Following Mr. Huntington's death, the gardens were left to the people of South Carolina. Now all who are inclined may enjoy this talented couple's amazing creation. The gardens remain a timeless monument to their determination and their love for the people of South Carolina.

Cow House Creek

The northern entrance of Cow House Creek makes off from the western shore of Waccamaw River just across from Wachesaw Landing. The stream holds minimum depths of 6 feet and provides very sheltered overnight anchorage for any craft of 38 feet or less. Larger boats may find the creek a bit small for adequate swinging room. The shoreline is in its natural state, and no facilities are available on the stream. While not the most attractive of all Waccamaw anchorages, the creek can certainly serve as a snug haven for the night.

Thoroughfare Creek

Thoroughfare Creek is a major sidewater of Waccamaw River and can lead the adventurous skipper into the waters of upper Pee Dee River. The creek itself is quite deep, holding 12-foot minimum depths until it joins the Pee Dee. The natural shoreline is particularly attractive and affords excellent protection. Once past the entrance to Guendalose Creek, a narrow but deep offshoot on the western shore of Thoroughfare Creek, the stream becomes wide enough to afford plenty of swinging room for large craft. The creek provides yet another excellent overnight anchorage opportunity for the boater traveling along Waccamaw River.

Hasty Point is found just across from the intersection of Thoroughfare Creek and Pee Dee River. Tradition claims that its name is derived from the "hasty" retreat of Francis Marion, the "Swamp Fox," during one of his many Revolutionary War campaigns.

For those boaters who can stand some 5-foot depths, it is possible to cruise south on the Pee Dee for a short distance until Exchange Plantation comes abeam on the western shore. One and one-half stories tall, the house can be identified by a prominent central dormer window. The plantation, which dates back to 1825, supposedly acquired its name because it was given in exchange for another plantation.

Further passage south or north on the Pee Dee is not recommended as depths become uncertain.

Waverly Creek

Waverly Creek is a small stream that enters the eastern bank of the Waccamaw south of flashing daybeacon #77. The creek maintains minimum depths of 6 feet but is too narrow for anchorage by all but small craft. A few private docks are located along the stream's banks.

In the years before the Civil War, a number of rice mills carried on their bustling trade along the creek's shores, forming a small community known as Waverly Mills. Though the land was subdivided after the demise of the rice industry and the old mills have disappeared entirely, the adventurous boater can follow the stream and catch sight of one period house that still stands. This venerable structure dates from 1871 and was apparently used by the owners of the rice mills. Watch to starboard for the roofline as you approach the eastern reaches of the creek.

Butler Creek

Butler Creek is a small stream on the river's western shore, just south of flashing daybeacon #78. The creek holds minimum depths of 6 feet, deepening to 13 feet in a few places. The undeveloped banks afford excellent protection, even in heavy weather. Craft under

LITTLE RIVER TO GEORGETOWN

35 feet can confidently drop the hook here for an undisturbed night.

Schooner Creek

Schooner Creek, found just below Butler Creek, is an offshoot of the lower Pee Dee River. The stream holds minimum depths of 6 feet for a good distance upstream and has enough swing room for craft under 38 feet. Protection is excellent. The shoreline is undeveloped, and no facilities are available. Be sure to read the navigational material on Butler and Schooner creeks presented later in this chapter before cruising either stream or attempting the small cut joining the two.

Jericho Creek

Jericho Creek makes into the Waccamaw's western banks just north of flashing daybeacon #83. This stream is an offshoot of the lower Pee Dee River and will be covered in the next chapter. For the moment we shall simply note that the creek is deep, well protected, and easily navigable all the way to the

Exchange Plantation on Pee Dee River

Pee Dee. It can serve as a good overnight anchorage for craft under 45 feet.

Butler Island

South of flashing daybeacon #83, Butler Island bisects Waccamaw River. The ICW continues down the eastern arm, but the western branch also maintains a wide, deep channel. Unfortunately, the area is too open for effective shelter in any but the lightest of airs. Unless you are in immediate need of anchorage, it would be better to make use of the many anchorages to the north.

Arcadia Plantation

As you begin your approach to flashing daybeacon #90, watch the eastern shore carefully. Soon you will spot a long canal flanked by a large collection of old piles. If you peer carefully up the cut's length, you may catch a quick glimpse of the Arcadia Plantation house. Don't attempt to cruise up the canal for a closer look. It is quite shoal.

Arcadia is actually a collection of several old plantations that were consolidated by the Emerson-Vanderbilt family in the early 1900s. One of Arcadia's former plantations, Clifton, had the distinction of entertaining George Washington on his tour of the Southern states following the American Revolution. Many of Arcadia's other plantations serve as settings for several popular legends. Interested readers should consult J. Stevenson Bolick's tale, "The Suicide Room," found in *Ghosts from the Coast.*

Waccamaw Navigation

Generally, navigation of Waccamaw River is a delightful process requiring only common-sense piloting. However, don't let the beautiful stream lull you into too great a sense of security. Snags and flotsam are encountered from time to time and there are a few shoal areas to be avoided. Have chart 11534 handy at all times and keep a sharp watch. Nighttime passage is not particularly recommended because of possible encounters with unseen snags.

Upper Waccamaw As stated earlier, depths remain consistently good on the upper Waccamaw as far as Conway. Most of the route is uncharted, but it is well marked and relatively easy to follow. As the river approaches Conway it begins to narrow a bit. For this reason the upper Waccamaw is not recommended for boats over 40 feet. Give points a wide berth and be on the lookout for flotsam and snags. Otherwise, armed with the navigational information presented in this guide, don't hesitate to take advantage of this fascinating side trip off the beaten path.

The boater has a choice of two routes to enter the upper Waccamaw from the ICW. A cut-through runs west from unlighted daybeacon #25 and intersects the river at unlighted daybeacon #2. This small channel maintains minimum depths of 8 feet but may be a bit narrow for larger craft. The main entrance breaks off to the north from unlighted daybeacon #1. Enter the stream on its mid-width.

The first navigational aid you will see will be unlighted daybeacon #2. Pass it to starboard and bear to port up the river's main branch. Unlighted daybeacon #3 marks a channel that cuts off a loop of the river. Good depths are maintained in the cut, so unless you want to explore the loop, continue straight through. Pass unlighted daybeacon #4 to starboard and bear off on the river's main branch to port. Pass unlighted daybeacon #5 to port and bear off to starboard. As you enter the branch marked by #5, you may see a small sign marked "Conway," with an arrow pointing up the cut, nailed on a shoreside tree. Pass unlighted daybeacon #6 to starboard and bend sharply to port. Soon you will encounter the small community of Bucksville along the port shore. Unlighted daybeacon #8 directs you into a port fork and should be passed to starboard.

After passing #8, watch the port shore and you will soon spy Bucksville Plantation House. The old chimney marking one of Henry Buck's sawmills can be seen just to the right of the house.

Pass unlighted daybeacon #10 to starboard and bear to port. At unlighted daybeacon #12, hold a straight course and pass the aid to starboard. Look behind as you continue upriver and you will see that this daybeacon marks a fork for southbound boaters. Pass unlighted daybeacon #14 to starboard. This aid marks an area of shallower water on the river's right bank. At unlighted daybeacon #16, bear off to port and pass the aid to starboard. Soon you will begin to come upon more developed areas, followed by an unmarked fork of the river. Take the port branch. As you begin to enter the outskirts of Conway you will spot the highrise Highway 501 bridge dead ahead. Continue on through and begin watching to port. Before long the marina at Conway will come abeam to port.

A small stream, whose entrance holds minimum depths of 6 feet, leads to the marina. Dockside depths are from 9 to 11 feet. There is a small park with its own docks to starboard, while the marina gas dock is to port. The marina office is located in the building marked "Firemens Clubhouse," to the left of the gas dock.

Upstream from the marina the river passes under another highrise highway bridge and soon forks. The port branch is blocked by a low-level fixed railroad bridge, and the starboard fork is cut off by an old swing railroad bridge that has obviously not operated for years.

On the ICW Flashing daybeacon #47 marks a shoal area and a large snag to its northern side. Pass #47 well to its westerly side. Flashing daybeacon #48 marks a similar area of shallow water on the river's western shore. Pass well to the east of #48.

Bull Creek To enter Bull Creek, favor the port shore a bit. Past the stream's mouth, good depths open out from shore to shore.

26 CRUISING GUIDE TO COASTAL SOUTH CAROLINA

Thoroughfare Creek Navigation of Thoroughfare Creek is a simple matter until the creek intersects the upper Pee Dee River. Minimum depths of 5 feet can be held moving south on the river as far as the area abeam of Exchange Plantation. Further passage to the south is not recommended, as depths become inconsistent. The northern branch of the Pee Dee soon leaves the chart and is unmarked. Consequently, this section is not recommended either.

Butler Creek Butler Creek maintains minimum depths of 6 feet until the cut-through to Schooner Creek comes abeam on the creek's southern shore. Do not cruise further upstream, as depths soon fall off. The cut to Schooner Creek holds surprising minimum depths of 8 feet but may be too narrow for larger craft.

Schooner Creek Navigation of Schooner Creek is straightforward until the creek's first sharp swing to starboard. As you round the bend, watch for a bad snag near the starboard shore. As shown on chart 11534, the creek eventually begins to widen as it joins the lower reaches of Pee Dee River. Do not approach this area, as 4-foot depths are encountered.

On the ICW Flashing daybeacon #90 marks an area of very shoal water. Pass #90 well to its easterly side.

South of #90 the waterway quickly begins its approach to Winyah Bay by passing under the Highway 17 highrise bridge. This is an area that calls for caution. The old remnants of a long-unused, low-level bridge still flank both sides of the river to the north of the highrise. Flashing daybeacon #92 and flashing daybeacon #93 mark the extreme edges of the old structure. If you should be making your passage at night, watch carefully for these two aids and pass between them.

During the spring months this area is often littered with fishing nets. If you spot any net lines as you are making your ap-

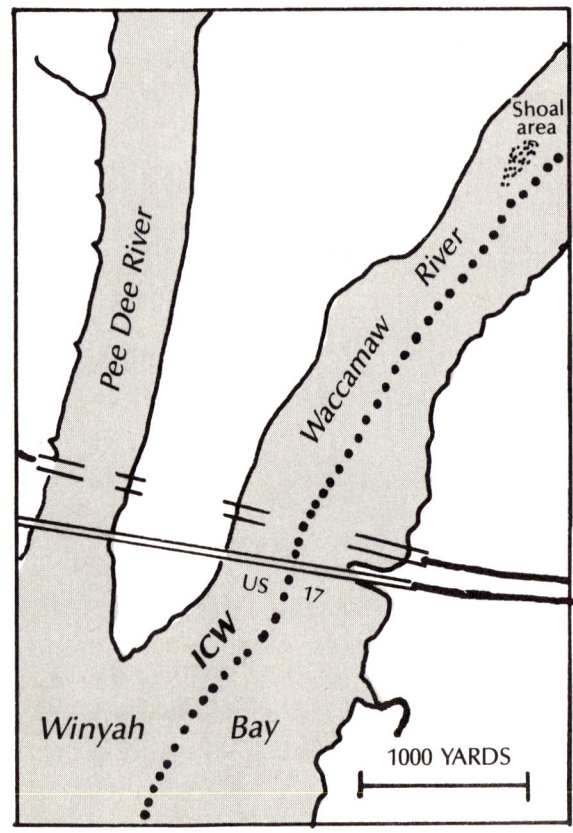

LITTLE RIVER TO GEORGETOWN 27

proach to Winyah Bay, slow down and proceed with caution.

It is a good idea to run compass courses when entering Winyah Bay until you are well south of the shallow water extending out from Waccamaw Point between the mouths of the Waccamaw and Great Pee Dee rivers.

Continued navigation of the ICW and other area rivers is presented in the next chapter.

Hobcaw Barony, resort home of Bernard Baruch

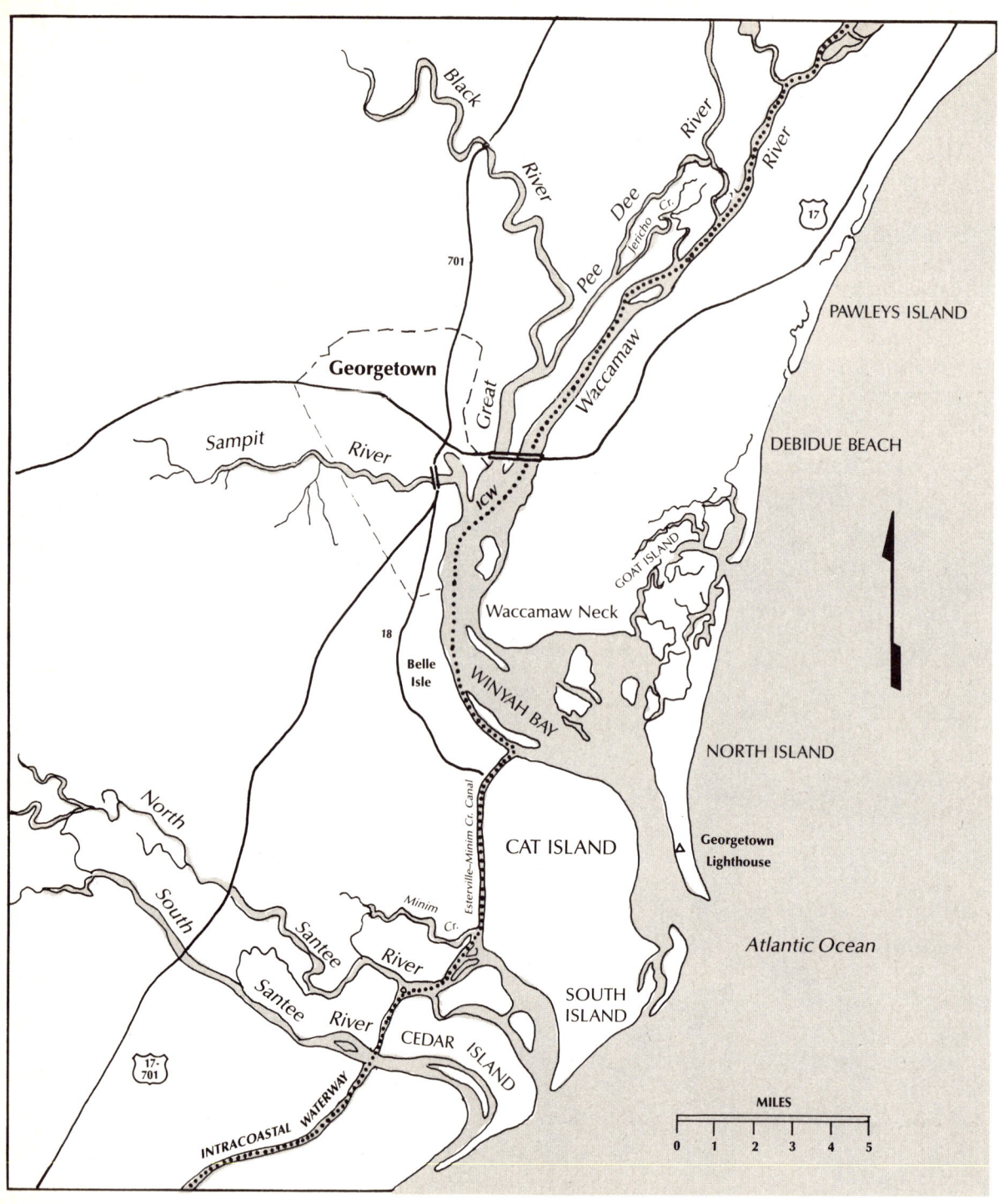

CHAPTER II

Georgetown

Sitting astride the confluence of Winyah Bay and Sampit River, present-day Georgetown constantly calls to mind its storied past. Long the most important South Carolina port north of Charleston, the town retains the character of bygone years. The cruising boater who makes Georgetown a port of call will find a quiet, beautiful, and historic town waiting to greet him.

Before the Civil War, Georgetown was the seat of a fabulously rich rice culture, still remembered with pride and romance. Go quietly as you pass, and perhaps you may still hear the delicate tinkle of crystal glasses at an elegant garden party or the hoofbeats of the master's horse as he rides to check his fields in the early morning mist. The heritage of the rice culture is an almost tangible entity here, and you cannot fully appreciate Georgetown and its surrounding streams without an understanding of this remarkable era.

Anyone who takes a few moments to study the charts will soon realize that Georgetown is ideally situated to take advantage of waterborne commerce. The waters of the Black, Pee Dee, Waccamaw, and Sampit rivers all converge at the port to form Winyah Bay. All of these waters together present a multitude of

Georgetown waterfront

cruising opportunities for the pleasure boater. The various streams—for the most part quite deep and easily navigable—offer many miles of isolated cruising and a host of overnight anchorage opportunities, as well as a fair share of delightful surprises. Just when you've decided that you are truly in the middle of nowhere, the next bend of the river or creek will reveal one of the fabulous plantation houses that has survived the trials of the years. It would take a very hard-bitten boater not to be smitten by the charms of Georgetown's rivers.

Winyah Bay provides reliable access to the open sea and cruising opportunities of its own. Good facilities are found on the southern shore, and a number of side trips to several historical sites are possible.

The Georgetown area offers the state's widest array of cruising opportunities north of Charleston. It's enough to set any true cruiser to dreaming. The boater who rushes by without making the acquaintance of Georgetown and its rivers will miss one of the greatest opportunities in all of South Carolina.

Charts You will need two NOAA charts to cover the waters in the Georgetown area: **11534** covers the ICW through Winyah Bay and south on the Minim-Esterville Creek Canal as well as the Pee Dee and Black rivers. **11532** details Winyah Bay including its inlet channel and the upper reaches of Sampit River.

Georgetown

What a delight it is to spend an evening, a week, or a month docked on the Georgetown waterfront. Snug in your slip, docked in the shadow of the Rice Museum's historic clock tower, you could be excused for forgetting that you are in the twentieth century. Fortunate indeed is the cruising boater who finds his way along Sampit River to Georgetown.

Most of Georgetown's facilities are located on the northern loop of Sampit River along the town's waterfront. While all these marinas are fairly small, they are quite friendly and cater to the transient boater.

Moving east to west, the first facility you will come upon is Hazzard's Marina. Dockside depths run around 8 to 9 feet. Transients are welcome. Overnight berths feature all power and water connections. Gasoline and diesel fuel are readily available, as are both mechanical and below-the-waterline repairs. As is the case with all the waterfront marinas, the historical district, the local chamber of commerce, and many shoreside businesses are only a short walk away.

Moving upstream, you will next find the Georgetown Exxon Marina. Some 7 to 10 feet of water is found at the docks. Berths with all power and water connections are readily available for transient boaters. Gasoline and diesel fuel can be purchased, and an "exchange library" is maintained for passing boaters at the marina office. Some mechanical

GEORGETOWN 31

repairs can be arranged. This is another of Georgetown's small but friendly marinas and can be unreservedly recommended.

Cathou's Boat Yard is found just beside the Exxon Marina. Some below-the-waterline repairs can be arranged here, but Cathou's greatest attraction is the fresh seafood that is often for sale. I was amused one evening to see a local citizen pounding on the shop's door, seemingly long after business hours. To my great surprise, the door swung open, an old yellow light was switched on, and flounder caught that same day was soon forthcoming.

The last marina on the waterfront is the Gulf Auto Marina. This is perhaps the largest of the facilities on the Sampit. Cruising boaters will find a warm welcome and transient berths with all power and water connections. Gasoline and diesel fuel are available, as are mechanical repairs.

The largest and most modern marina available in the Georgetown area is not located on the town waterfront. Georgetown Landing is found on the Pee Dee's western shore just south of the Highway 17 bridge. This fine facility boasts the most modern slips, on floating piers, with all power and water connections. Diesel fuel and gasoline are, of course, available. The marina can help you with mechanical repair problems, and some below-the-waterline repairs can be arranged. A large, well-stocked ships' store is maintained on the premises. The marina advertises the availability of a courtesy automobile for use by transients. The entire facility is en-

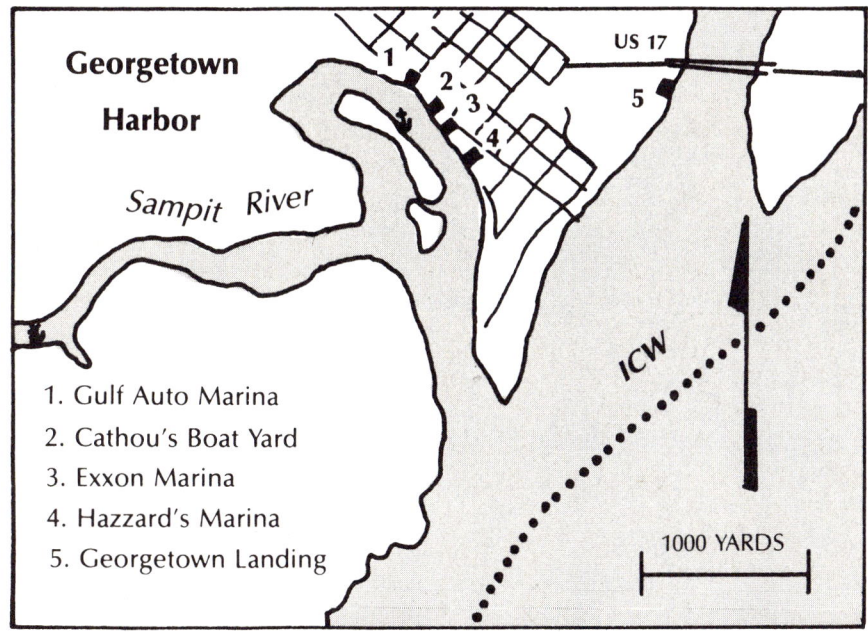

closed by an artificial, partially submerged breakwater composed of old automobile tires. Be careful when approaching the facility at night.

Lands End Restaurant is a part of Georgetown Landing and a very pleasant spot to rest after a long day of cruising. The restaurant looks out over the marina and Pee Dee River. It is quite a treat to sit at a table by the window and dine on the freshest of seafood while watching the daylight fade from the Pee Dee waters.

If you feel like a stroll, a short jaunt will bring you to one of Georgetown's finest eateries. Lafayette Restaurant is located on Highway 17, several blocks to the west of the bridge. Here the weary boater can dine on lobster and steak or the incomparable combination seafood platter. The she-crab soup is delectable, and the desserts are homemade. This writer highly recommends Lafayette for the famished cruiser.

Georgetown Historical District

The Georgetown historical district sits on some 220 acres of land and includes approximately forty-six historical buildings. It is bounded to the south by Sampit River, to the east by Meeting Street, to the north by Highway 17, and to the west by Wood Street. Begin your visit at the local chamber of commerce, where you can obtain complete information on the historical area. The staff is eager to help, and it is sometimes possible to arrange for a motorized tour.

The Georgetown Chamber of Commerce has graciously consented to the reproduction of their historical district map on the following page. A quick study of this excellent cartographical guide reveals many interesting homes and buildings worthy of exploration. Only a few of this writer's favorites can be mentioned here. It would be well worth your time, however, to take full advantage of the splendid historical sightseeing that the district affords.

Prince George Episcopal Church, Winyah, is located on the corner of Broad and Highmarket streets. The congregation dates from 1721, but the building was finished in 1750. As this writer viewed the cracked brick and

Georgetown Rice Museum

GEORGETOWN 33

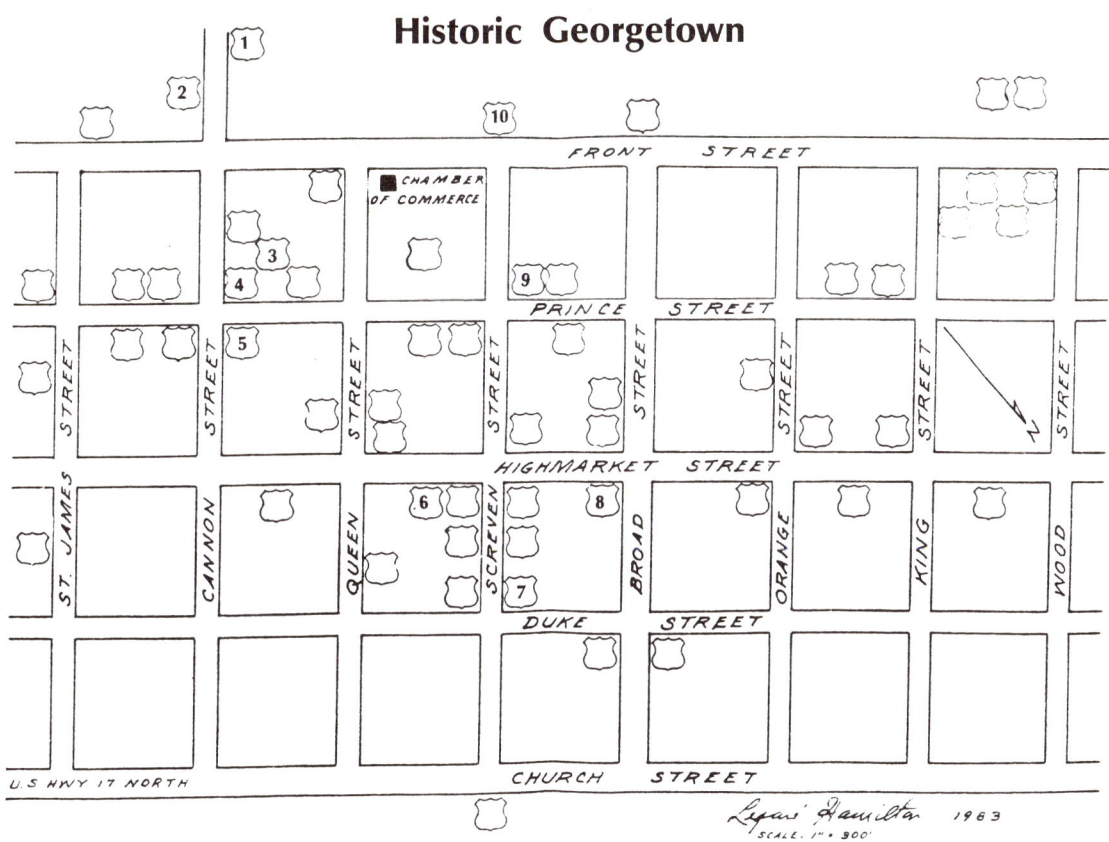

1. Heriot-Tarbox House. (c. 1740)
2. Red Store-Tarbox Warehouse.
3. Winyah Indigo Society-Betancourt House.
4. Winyah Indigo Society Hall. (c. 1857)
5. Morgan-Ginsler House. (c. 1825)
6. Waterman-Kaminski House. (c. 1770)
7. Henning-Miller House. (c. 1800)
8. Prince George Episcopal Church, Winyah. (c. 1750)
9. Georgetown County Court House. (c. 1824)
10. The Rice Museum. (c. 1835)

Note: Only the numbered locations are discussed in this guide. Consult a complete map for other historic sites.

mortar, the old church seemed to exude an almost tangible atmosphere of age. Stroll through the graveyard to the left of the church. It affords an excellent view of the tower, added in 1824, and among its interesting headstones are many dating from the 1700s. Finally, take a moment to go inside. The doors are usually open and respectful visitors are welcome. Standing amid the old-style box pews, one can almost picture the planters and their wives dressed in their best Sunday broadcloth and taffeta, listening soberly to the long sermon.

The Henning-Miller House, circa 1800, is located at the corner of Duke and Screven streets. Like many Georgetonian homes, this fine old building has its ghost story. The spirit, however, is most helpful. Tradition claims that during the British occupation of Georgetown, an officer staying at the house fell to his death on the main stairway. He is said to have lost his footing during a nightly alarm. It is whispered that to this day his ghost will firmly grasp the shoulder of anyone who might trip on the stairs, saving that person from a fall.

The charming Waterman-Kaminski House is located at 620 Highmarket Street. This old home, circa 1770, was the scene of not one, but two tragedies. There is the sad story of a young boy who pined away at an early age. His thin little spirit is well known. The upstairs room opening onto the central dormer was the scene of another sort of tragedy. An old tale speaks of a young girl who was in love with a sea captain, but discovered her lover to be untrue. Heartbroken, she took her own life in the upstairs room. On summer nights her ghost is said to appear in the dormer window, patiently watching for the return of her faithless lover's ship.

The Winyah Indigo Society Hall is located on the corner of Prince and Cannon streets. Organized in 1740 as a social club for wealthy planters, the Indigo Society eventually established a free school, founded a library, and served as both a business and social organization. The society survives to this day and still meets on a regular basis.

Just across the street from the Society Hall

Prince George Episcopal Church

is the Morgan-Ginsler House. This building was used during the Civil War as a hospital for Union soldiers. It is said that strange noises have been heard from time to time in the dining room. There are those who claim that the ghostly noises are the sounds of Satan driving back the souls of the unfortunate soldiers who died there to relive their last few moments of misery on earth. This writer has a deep suspicion that a Southern sympathizer was the originator of this tale.

Two of Georgetown's historical points of interest can be found at the foot of Cannon Street fronting onto Sampit River. To the left is the Red Store-Tarbox Warehouse. In 1812, Theodosia Burr Alston, daughter of politician Aaron Burr, sailed fom the warehouse docks on an ill-fated voyage to New York. The ship on which she sailed ran into a fierce gale off the coast of the Carolinas and was apparently lost at sea or wrecked somewhere on the coast. Although there has been much specu-

Interior of Prince George Episcopal Church

lation about her fate (one compelling version of her story is found in Charles H. Whedbee's *Legends of the Outer Banks and Tar Heel Tidewater),* nobody really knows what happened to Theodosia.

Across the street from the warehouse is the Heriot-Tarbox House, one of the loveliest homes in Georgetown and the setting for what may well be the area's most touching legend.

Legend of the Heriot-Tarbox House Some years before the Civil War, a wealthy family lived in this beautiful homeplace by the river. They had only one child, a daughter, on whom they showered all their love and attention. The girl was closely guarded by her parents to insure a proper upbringing. She grew into a great beauty and was known by all the town's citizens for her gracious manners and shy nature.

The young enchantress was very fond of pets and always kept several dogs of rare pedigree. One day as she was throwing a ball into the yard to see which dog was the swiftest retriever, a young officer from a ship docked at her father's warehouse happened to walk by and was captivated by the girl's loveliness. He retrieved one of the balls that had fallen nearby and carried it up the broad steps to the shy maiden. Perhaps it was love at first sight. Before long the two began to see each other on a regular basis, and their relationship blossomed with the passing of the days.

The young woman's tutor became worried about the seriousness of the affair and spoke to the girl's father, who was outraged. What made a common ship's officer think he could pay court to his daughter? He marched straight onboard the ship and demanded that the captain forbid any further contact between the two lovers. Returning home, the father informed his daughter that she was never to see the young man again.

The captain did not take kindly to the father's demands, especially since the officer in question was his favorite nephew. Perhaps he aided the young couple. At any rate, the two lovers found a way to meet. When all those within were asleep, the girl would put a light in her upstairs window, and the young officer

Heriot-Tarbox House, Georgetown

GEORGETOWN 37

would know that all was safe. The two would then meet in the garden for a few brief but tender stolen moments.

The young woman would wed no other man and continued to live in her parents' house. Whenever the officer's ship was in port, the couple held their romantic trysts. Then, without explanation, the officer's visits suddenly ceased.

The heartbroken girl continued to place a lamp in her window every night. After a time the light came to be a symbol of the love that she could never forget, yet was doomed never to be. Eventually she became a recluse and was rarely seen outside of the house. Following her parents' death, the servants and the dogs were her only companions.

As the Civil War drew its dark wings about Georgetown, stealthy blockade runners would use the light in the window of the Cannon Street house for navigation. The saddened but loyal woman still faithfully placed the lamp in the window every night. Most thought she was doing what she could to aid

Winyah Indigo Society Hall

the Southern cause. Only a few knew the real reason for this strange practice.

It was not long after the war that neighbors, alerted by the barking dogs, discovered the poor woman's body in the house. She had apparently died of a heart attack. Some might say that it was a broken heart.

In the years that followed, many families lived in the old house. Strange noises were heard from time to time, and a light was often seen shining from the upstairs window. One resident even saw the form of a beautiful girl walking down the front steps into the garden. Others told of seeing a ghostly visage surrounded by barking dogs. The house was finally abandoned for many years and acquired a sinister reputation.

In the 1930s, the present owners restored the house to its former glory, and it became one of the great showplaces of the Georgetown historical district. Its whitewashed walls and bright windows now look proudly over the harbor, recalling the grandeur of lost days. But there are many who will tell you that the sad ghost still maintains her lonely vigil each night from the upstairs window.

Lest you think this story too fanciful, the present owner herself told this writer that there was indeed a ghost in the attic. While the spirit has never appeared to her, she has seen the lights on the second floor many times. Even on a warm summer morning, this tale seemed to bring a bit of a chill to the air.

Georgetown History In 1526, the Spanish visionary Lucas Vasquez de Ayllon attempted to found a settlement in the Georgetown area. Little is known of this early attempt at colonization save the fact that it was a total failure. Some historians claim that only 150 of the original 500 colonists survived. Nevertheless, this effort, however futile, was one of the first European colonies founded in the New World.

Georgetown was first laid out in 1729 by William Swinton at the request of newly appointed royal governor Robert Johnson. Johnson, one of South Carolina's most able and popular colonial governors, sought to ease the hardships of the settlers living north of Santee River, whose legal business had to be prefaced by a long and exhausting trip to Charleston, and whose exports had to be shipped over tortuous land routes to the capital city. Finally, in 1732, the new town was declared a port of entry and the first royal customs officer took up residence.

Under British rule Georgetown quickly became a prosperous port. England placed bounties on the production of naval stores and indigo, both readily produced in the lands about the port. Many ships sailed from the Georgetown waterfront for the mother country with valuable cargoes of lumber and dye.

Shipbuilding began in Georgetown by 1738. As the wealth of the Georgetown merchants increased with expanding trade, it became profitable for them to acquire their own ships rather than share profits with a shipping agent.

In 1735 the citizens of the Winyah area petitioned the colonial assembly to "set forth the necessity of laying buoys and erecting beacons or landmarks, and maintaining pilot boats to attend the bar of the harbor of

Georgetown." Clearly the town was well on its way to becoming a bustling port.

As the clouds of war spread across the colonies, voices in Georgetown cried for American rights. Georgetown planters made substantial contributions to aid Boston when its harbor was closed after the Tea Party. In December of 1774, Georgetown had its own "tea party." When local patriots discovered that a ship in the harbor had a cargo of taxed tea in her hold, they demanded that the ship's master dump his cargo overboard. He soon complied with the less-than-gentle demands of the patriots. While it did not have the far-reaching implications of the more famous Boston incident, the Georgetown Tea Party certainly demonstrated the resolve of the local citizenry.

For the first four years of the Revolution, Georgetown was little touched by the war, although they were visited by one of the war's great heroes, the Marquis de Lafayette. In

A street in Georgetown

1777 the marquis made landfall at nearby North Island and traveled through Georgetown on his way to Charleston.

Georgetown was occupied by the British in July of 1780. It was not long before Francis Marion, the famed "Swamp Fox" of history and legend, began to strike at the English forces from the dark recesses of the Pee Dee swamps. Marion is credited with being the father of guerrilla warfare. He and his band of irregulars repeatedly struck the vastly superior British forces gathered around Georgetown and then melted away into the seemingly impenetrable wilderness.

In January of the same year Marion joined forces with Lighthorse Harry Lee and briefly overran the town. Lacking sufficient artillery, Marion was forced to withdraw, but in 1781 he drove the British from Georgetown once and for all. The liberation of the port was followed by a disastrous fire, set by an English raiding party, which consumed more than forty-two houses.

In the latter stages of the Revolution, Georgetown was most important to the American cause. With Charleston still in British hands, the port served as an invaluable supply depot.

Following the war the area rice culture began its rapid rise. Free from the constraints of the British trading system and the requirements of war, the Georgetown rice planters began to carve a great empire from the muddy recesses of the tidal swamps. By 1840 the Georgetown area was said to produce 45% of all the rice grown in America. Fabulous fortunes were won, and the opulence of the rice culture became a standard for others to envy.

Surprisingly, Georgetown did not benefit as much from the rise of the rice culture as might have been expected. Many rice planters sent their goods directly to Charleston for transshipment to other markets. The prestige of the capital port, with its long transcontinental shipping tradition, persuaded many planters to bypass Georgetown's shipping facilities. Georgetown was never able to compete effectively with its southern rival.

Additional problems were caused by the shallow Winyah Bay inlet bar. It carried only some ten to twelve feet of water, a bit shallow for oceangoing ships of that era. This problem led to various schemes to build an artificial inlet across North Island and a canal connecting the bay with Santee River. All of these projects ended in failure. Georgetown had to wait until the 1880s, when the Mosquito Creek Canal successfully joined the bay to Santee River.

Georgetown was largely spared the worst pains of battle during the Civil War. The town was not occupied until February of 1865, and little damage was done to the town's historic buildings.

The end of the war saw the beginning of the end for the rice culture. Georgetown suffered through the years of reconstruction as did most other Southern cities. Times were hard until the twentieth century, but the town's economy began to improve when the ICW was opened in the 1930s. There followed the stabilization of the Winyah Bay inlet channel and the location of modern port facilities on Sampit River.

Today Georgetown is a small but busy port that retains, for the most part, its charm and historic character. An active chamber of commerce and local historical society work diligently to maintain the mementos of the port's days of glory. Every visitor is indebted to their efforts. Those desiring to learn more of Georgetown's history should acquire Ronald E. Birdwell's excellent booklet, '. . . *That We Should Have a Port* . . . .' It gives a very readable account of Georgetown's maritime history from 1732 to 1865. The book is available at the Georgetown Rice Museum.

Rice Culture History Rice was grown in South Carolina as early as the 1690s, but it was not until McKewn Johnstone perfected the tidal flow method of rice cultivation in 1758 that "Carolina Gold" became king of Georgetown county. In his fascinating booklet, *No Heir to Take Its Place,* Dennis Lawson comments, "From the earliest settlement at the beginning of the eighteenth century until the first decade of the 1900s rice was synonymous with Georgetown County . . . The history of Georgetown until the modern era is the history of its rice culture . . . it is likely that no other area of the United States has ever been as dependent for as long a period of time on this one crop . . . . "

Following the invention of the tidal flow irrigation system, rice planting settled down to a regular pattern in the Georgetown area. First, swampy areas were cleared, then diked by building banks along the rivers. Then the fields were subdivided by smaller earthen banks so their flooding could be individually controlled. Floodgates or trunks were installed in the large banks. These most important devices controlled the time and level of the field's flooding. Highly skilled slaves known as trunkminders were solely responsible for the maintenance of the floodgates. Bank mending was another unending chore.

By flooding the fields on a regular basis, the fertility of the soil was continually renewed. This practice was in sharp contrast to that of the cotton plantations, which habitually exhausted their fields. The rice plantations retained their fertility until the end of the rice culture.

The clearing of the fields, construction and maintenance of the banks, and cultivation of the crop was a very labor-intensive task calling for hundreds of workers, almost exclusively black slaves. As I stood on the banks of an old rice field one summer afternoon, with the sun hot on the back of my neck and flies buzzing around my head, I could not help reflecting on the backbreaking toil of the many slaves who once worked there. Without their labor, there would have been no affluent lifestyles for the rice master. When considering the romance of the rice culture, one should remember just what sacrifices were required to maintain such a way of life.

Because the cultivation of rice was so labor-intensive, the large landowner with heavy capital reserves was better suited for success than the smaller farmer. By 1850 the great wealth of the rice culture had become concentrated in the hands of a few large planters, such as "King" Joshua John Ward, the greatest planter on the Waccamaw. In 1850 he produced almost 4,000,000 pounds of rice on six plantations with more than 1000 slaves. The Black and Pee Dee rivers also had extensive rice fields.

The Civil War spelled the doom of the rice culture. Without cheap slave labor, profits declined every year. Rice planting began in the gulf states following the war. The firmer soil of the gulf region was suitable for mechanized cultivation, while South Carolina's swampy earth would not support the use of modern farm machinery. Several great hurricanes struck the coast from 1894 to 1906, severely damaging the rice crops. Finally, in the early 1900s, rice culivation was abandoned almost entirely, marking the end of an age for the Georgetown area.

The reader will appreciate that it has been possible to present only the barest outlines of the rice culture in these pages. To learn more, plan a visit to the Rice Museum located along the Georgetown Waterfront. It is easily recognized by its tall clock tower. Here you can learn the full story of the fabulous rice culture. Dennis T. Lawson's booklet, *No Heir to Take Its Place,* is also highly recommended. As you come to understand the flavor of that era, you may agree with Mr. Lawson that the bygone rice culture "truly left 'no heir to take its place.'"

Georgetown Navigation

Once through the Highway 17 highrise bridge on Waccamaw River, consider running a compass course past flashing daybeacon #94. As you will notice in a quick study of chart 11534, there is very shallow water on both sides of the waterway channel.

The entrance to Sampit River and the principal Georgetown Waterfront is found to the west of flashing daybeacon #30. The stream is deep and easily navigable. To enter, strike a course to pass between flashing daybeacons #29 and #32. Follow the northern loop of the channel and watch to starboard. The first of Georgetown's facilities will soon come abeam to the northeast.

Just upstream of the westernmost marina are the Georgetown Municipal Docks, also to starboard. Passing boaters are welcome to moor here temporarily, but no overnight dockage is allowed.

Transient boaters sometimes choose to anchor along the waterfront. Protection is adequate for all but the heaviest of weather. There is enough swinging room for almost any craft under 50 feet. Georgetown's attractions are just a quick dinghy trip away. Select a spot far enough from the docks to avoid waterfront traffic and set the hook.

Sampit River As shown on chart 11534, the Georgetown Waterfront channel swings around to the south and forms a loop that carries the boater back to the bay. The western portion of the loop is used by large ships and tugs, as are the upper reaches of Sampit River. Large barges are often moored on the loop's northern shore at the docks of a large scrap metal facility. Do not anchor here. This portion of the channel must be kept clear for large-ship traffic.

If you cruise through the western portion of the loop, you will note a strange buoy configuration. Unlighted nun buoy #46 sits to the west of flashing daybeacon #40. Both aids are red, and the visiting cruiser could easily be confused. For best depths, set your course to pass #46 to its "western" side. Depths between the two aids fall off to some 8 feet.

The main body of Sampit River breaks off to the southwest from the Georgetown loop. The upper reaches of the stream are very commercial, with large ships often docked along the northern shores. Also located in this area is a paper mill, part of the unfortunate price of Georgetown's present prosperity. When the wind blows from the wrong quarter, the smell of progress is not so sweet.

Soon the river leads under a fixed highrise bridge. Although this structure carries only 34 feet of vertical clearance, a new bridge with far greater clearance is now under construction. When the old span is finally removed, tall sailcraft will be able to make the acquaintance of the lower Sampit River.

Good depths of 15 to 30 feet are held for at least 1.3 nautical miles past the bridge. Further upstream, as shown on chart 11532, depths become unreliable. Most of the shoreline on the stream's lower reaches is undeveloped. The area is well protected and can serve as an overnight anchorage for almost any vessel able to clear the fixed bridge. There are no facilities on this section of the river. One word of warning: If the wind should be blowing from the northeast, the paper mill can make for a smelly evening.

To reach Georgetown Landing Marina, begin cruising north on the wide Pee Dee River entrance channel at flashing daybeacon #30. While not charted, the channel is currently marked as far north as the marina with privately maintained nun and can buoys. Pass between these aids. Shallow depths are found to the east and west, so don't be too casual about navigation in this area. Be sure to enter the marina from its eastern side, which faces the main body of the river. The entrance is lighted with red and green beacons.

Pee Dee River

The Pee Dee River, sometimes known as the Great Pee Dee, is a somewhat disappointing body of water for cruising purposes. To enter the river from Winyah Bay, you must be able to clear a fixed bridge with only 20 feet of vertical clearance. Some 4.5 nautical miles north of the stream's juncture with Black River, the Pee Dee enters a delta region, where depths become too inconsistent for most cruising craft. As noted in the last chapter, the upper Pee Dee is accessible from Waccamaw River via Thoroughfare Creek, but this area, too, has its navigational problems.

The lower Pee Dee River maintains minimum 7-foot depths from Winyah Bay to the delta region. While the stream is unmarked and there are a few shoal areas to be avoided, navigation on this part of the river is fairly straightforward and does not present any real problem.

Despite its limited reaches, the lower Pee Dee does offer good cruising ground in a pleasant atmosphere. This part of the river has lovely, undeveloped banks and offers anchorage possibilities just south of the delta. Much of the shoreline is composed of abandoned rice fields. Watch carefully as you cruise along; you can still see several old floodgates along the eastern shore.

While only a few reminders of the era remain, these shores were once very much a part of the rice culture. If you have the time and can clear the bridge, you might consider a cruise of the Pee Dee.

Jericho Creek

Jericho Creek is a large stream that splits off from the Pee Dee and leads northeast into Waccamaw River. The creek maintains minimum depths of 8 feet and affords good overnight anchorage. Protection is excellent, even for heavy weather. The southern reaches of the stream have enough swing room for craft as large as 45 feet. The entire shoreline is undeveloped and composed mostly of abandoned rice fields. There are no facilities available on the creek. Jericho Creek has a true feeling of isolation. Consider dropping the hook here for an evening of peace and security.

Nightingale Hall

Some 1.2 nautical miles to the north of the Pee Dee-Jericho Creek intersection, the Nightingale Hall Plantation house is readily visible on the western shore. This plantation was one of the many holdings of the illustrious Alston family. Following the Civil War the Alston properties were broken up and Nightingale Hall was sold.

Nightingale Hall Plantation on Pee Dee River

Pee Dee River Navigation

After passing under the Highway 17 fixed bridge, watch carefully to the east and west for the remnants of an old low-level span. Pass between the two groups of old pilings. Once through, stick to the mid-width. Keep a sharp watch for crab pots on this section of the stream.

Black River splits off from the Pee Dee's western shore some 2.2 nautical miles north of the Highway 17 bridge. This stream will be covered in the next section. Avoid the point of land separating the two rivers. Shoal water extends southward from the point.

Continue to cruise on the mid-width. North of the intersection the stream provides enough shelter for overnight anchorage. Another 2.6 miles will bring the boater to the southern entrance of Jericho Creek. Good anchorage is available on this stream as well. Good depths of 8 feet or more are held all the way to the Waccamaw.

The westerly branch of the Pee Dee begins to enter the delta region. The stream remains navigable for some 1.5 nautical miles. North of this point depths become inconsistent. Just south of the shallow water area, the Nightingale Hall Plantation house is visible on the western shore.

Black River

Black River is, quite simply, one of the most beautiful streams in northeastern South Carolina. The Black's shores are a study in pleasing contrasts. Abandoned rice fields alternate with heavily wooded banks and even a few sandy shores. Most of the shoreline is undeveloped, though here and there a few houses overlook the water. Even in an area where beautiful shorelines are the rule, Black River's banks can bring a sigh of contentment from the most indifferent cruiser.

Although the stream is unmarked, good depths open out from shore to shore. Unfortunately, you must be able to negotiate the 20-foot clearance of the fixed bridge discussed in the Pee Dee River section before visiting this remarkable stream. Otherwise, Black River navigation is a simple and undemanding task.

Take a moment to look at your wake and you will quickly discover how the river derived its name. Colored by vast cypress swamps to the north, the waters of Black River are a dark brownish hue. This natural phenomenon somehow adds to the feeling of adventure one experiences while exploring this beautiful body of water.

The entire river is well sheltered and presents a wealth of anchorages. There is plenty of swing room for large craft. The stream's upper reaches are fit for heavy weather, while the lower sections are fine for light to moderate airs. Simply select a spot that strikes your fancy and set the hook for a memorable night. There are no formal facilities in the area.

Rotting docks and old pilings dot the banks, evidence of the brisk rice and indigo trade that once flowed along this lovely stream. Before the rise of the rice culture, the finest indigo in South Carolina was said to be grown along the Black River. The river winds through the lands of several historic rice plantations, though only one house is visible.

Over and above all these attributes, there is an indefinable quality of isolation and adventure that seems to permeate Black River's cruising grounds. Boaters who enjoy the feeling that every turn of the wheel takes them farther away from the ordinary will find Black River to be just what they are looking for.

Windsor Plantation

Windsor Plantation is found on the west bank of Black River, approximately 1 nautical mile from the Pee Dee intersection. Although the present house was built in 1937 to replace the original structure, the plantation itself dates from 1762. During the latter stages of the Civil War, Federal troops tried to burn the homeplace but were stopped by the daring resolve of eighty-year-old Miss Hannah Trapier, then owner of the property. This story should lay to rest some of the traditional notions concerning the shy and retiring character of Southern belles.

Windsor Plantation on Black River

GEORGETOWN 47

Black River Navigation

Simply follow the river's mid-width as you travel upstream. After cruising for several miles, you will spy a small island that bisects the stream. For best depths pass the small land mass to its southern side.

Some 7.8 nautical miles upstream from the Pee Dee intersection, a low bridge blocks further passage on the Black for all but the smallest craft. The span was once a swinging structure, but it appears to have been out of operation for many years. A new highrise bridge is currently under construction. When the new span has replaced the older bridge, it will be possible to explore Black River at greater length.

As you approach the bridge, look to the northern shore. There you will see a large clapboard ferry house, which was used until the ferry was replaced by a bridge in the 1930s. The building is now part of a private estate.

Old ferry house on Black River

Winyah Bay

Winyah Bay is the largest body of water on the South Carolina coast north of Charleston. It stretches some 16 miles from the Atlantic to the confluence of the Waccamaw and Pee Dee rivers. The inlet is less than 1 mile in width, but the main body widens to some 4½ miles at Mud Bay. Winyah covers 25 square miles.

Much of the bay is shallow, but two well-marked channels traverse its length. One offers reliable access to the open sea, while the other leads the ICW traveler to the Minim Creek Canal.

Navigation of Winyah Bay must not be taken lightly. Unlike the waters to the north, this bay demands that the cruising boater stick to the channel or risk prop and keel damage. Study chart 11532 carefully before entering the area to familiarize yourself with the many aids to navigation.

The Winyah Bay Inlet is the first truly reliable seaward passage south of North Carolina's Cape Fear River. The channel is used on a regular basis by large cargo ships entering the Georgetown port facilities. It is well marked and reasonably easy to navigate. However, like all inlets, it can be rough when winds and tides oppose each other. If at all possible, pick a fair-weather day before running the cut.

The bay has one excellent facility but lacks any protected anchorages. It is not the sort of place one would want to spend the night swinging on the hook.

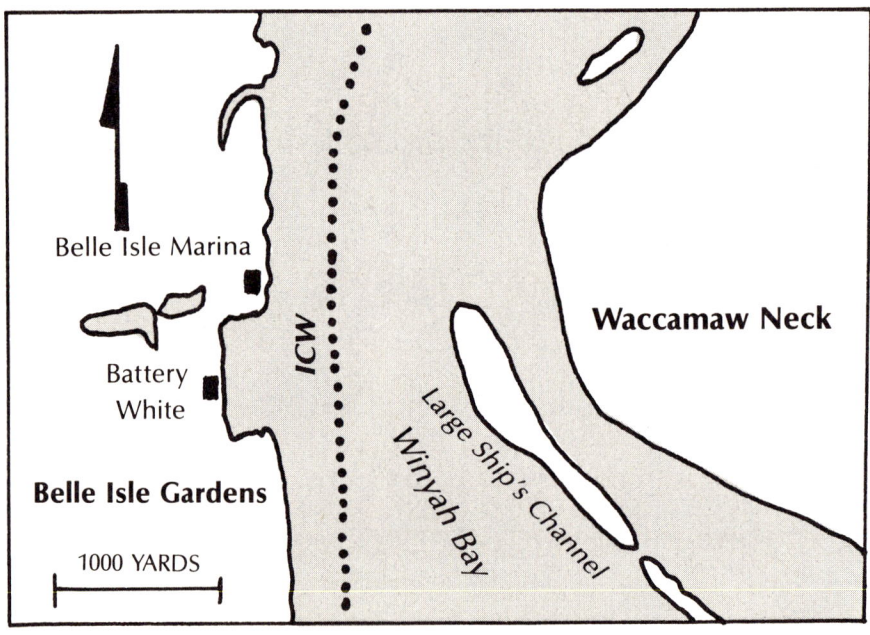

Several historical sites are located along Winyah's shoreline. A number are readily visible from the water, while one calls for an adventurous side trip.

Winyah Bay is an attractive body of water and provides pleasant cruising in fair weather. However, in stormy conditions the bay can daunt the hardiest pleasure boater. Treat Winyah with respect and you will enjoy your cruise. Take the bay too lightly and you may find yourself in need of assistance.

Belle Isle

Winyah Bay can lay claim to one of the finest marinas in South Carolina. Belle Isle Marina, found along the ICW channel on the southern banks, is an ultramodern facility that gladly accepts the transient boater. Overnight berths feature floating piers with all power and water connections. Gasoline and diesel fuel are available, and there is a well-stocked grocery and ships' store. Some repairs can also be arranged. There is a fine restaurant within walking distance though it is not currently open every night of the week. The management here is particularly friendly and often goes the extra mile for cruising boaters, particularly those in difficulty. This writer highly recommends a stop at Belle Isle for any boater who wants a warm welcome.

Belle Isle Marina is on the lands of Belle Isle Plantation. Here the brother of Francis Marion, the "Swamp Fox," lived during Revolutionary times. General Marion's plantation, Pond Bluff, was flooded by the construction of Lake Marion back in the 1930s. The war hero's grave can be seen on Belle Isle.

Belle Isle Plantation also harbors acres of beautiful gardens, which are open to the public. A visit to these serene grounds is definitely recommended for those who have seen one too many waves.

Battery White

Another historical site within walking distance is Battery White. This Civil War fortification is difficult to see from the water but is located several hundred yards south of the marina. It was constructed during the Civil War to protect Winyah Bay, but it proved ineffective.

Hobcaw Barony

One of the largest landholdings in South Carolina was once located along the eastern shores of Winyah Bay. Hobcaw Barony was a huge estate of many hundreds of acres. Over the years the property was broken up into a number of large plantations.

From 1905 to 1907 Bernard Baruch acquired most of the original holdings of the barony and rejoined the various tracts. Mr. Baruch was a great duck hunter and entertained sporting guests on a lavish scale. Franklin D. Roosevelt and Winston Churchill were two of his most famous guests.

Today the property is held under the auspices of the Belle W. Baruch Foundation. Extensive research in marine biology is carried on at the foundation by the University of South Carolina. Clemson University also uses the facilities for forestry experiments.

It is difficult to spot the main house from the channel, but adventurous skippers can take a side trip for a closer look. The route holds 6-foot depths but is unmarked and tricky.

Dover Plantation

Dover Plantation can be seen just to the west of flashing daybeacon #98. This is one of the most beautiful plantation houses visible from the water in the area. Although the house itself dates to 1810, it was moved to its present site in the 1940s from land now flooded by the Santee-Cooper watershed project. Anyone viewing this magnificent edifice will certainly agree that it was well worth saving from destruction.

Estherville Plantation

Estherville Plantation is just visible to the southwest of flashing daybeacon #100. Seasonal vegetation can interfere with the view from the water, but it is well worth a look. In 1758 Estherville was the site of the first successful experiments with tidal cultivation of rice. The house and grounds have been carefully restored by the present owners.

Georgetown Lighthouse

Rising to a height of 85 feet, the Georgetown Lighthouse watches benignly over the entrance to Winyah Bay from the western shore of North Island. Lighted in 1812 after numerous delays, the present lighthouse is actually the second to occupy this location. The first, built in 1801, was a wooden tower and was toppled by a strong gale in 1806. The light is not readily visible from the ICW channel. A voyage down the inlet channel is necessary to view this old lighthouse that speaks so eloquently of an age of the sea now long departed.

Dover Plantation, Winyah Bay

GEORGETOWN 51

Winyah Bay Navigation

Be sure to use chart 11532 for navigation of the Winyah Bay inlet channel. Chart 11534 is sufficient for the ICW route only! Pay attention to business while piloting in the bay. Watch your depth sounder! You cannot afford to be as casual with navigation here as on the deeper waters to the north.

Note that markers reverse at the intersection of the ICW and the Georgetown Harbor channel. The large ships' channel takes precedence over the waterway route, and the markers are configured as if you were putting out to sea, red to port and green to starboard. The standard waterway markings resume where the ICW channel splits off from the seaward passage below Belle Isle.

Hobcaw Barony In spite of depths shown on chart 11532, it is possible to cruise east from nun buoy #28, holding 6-foot depths, to view the main house at Hobcaw Barony. This side trip should be attempted only by adventurous skippers piloting craft less than 35 feet in length and drawing no more than 4 feet. It would be best to time your cruise to coincide with mid- or high tide.

If you choose to make the attempt, cruise south from #28 for some .6 of a nautical mile following the main channel. Then cut 90 degrees to the east and set a course parallel to the southern shore of Rabbit and Hare islands by about 75 yards to port. As you approach the mainland shore the house will be sighted just to the east.

Winyah Inlet Channel Navigation of the bay remains straightforward as far as the area between flashing daybeacon #25 and flashing buoy #26. Here the channel divides. The northerly branch leads to the inlet and the open sea. This seaward route is well marked, but take care to hold to the mid-width. Shallow water lines both sides of the channel. Follow chart 11532 carefully and keep alert.

ICW Channel From flashing daybeacon #25 the waterway splits off to the south. The marked entrance to Belle Isle Marina is found to the west of flashing buoy #24. To enter, pass between nun buoy #2 and can buoy #1 and between unlighted daybeacons #3 and #4. The entrance is then obvious.

The ICW channel is wide and deep but scantily marked. It is an excellent idea to run compass courses between aids to avoid confusion. Beware of the shoal water along the eastern side of the waterway. Have chart 11534 handy and pay attention to what you are doing.

At flashing daybeacon #2 the waterway takes a 90-degree turn to the south and enters a man-made canal. Continued navigation of the ICW route is presented in the next chapter.

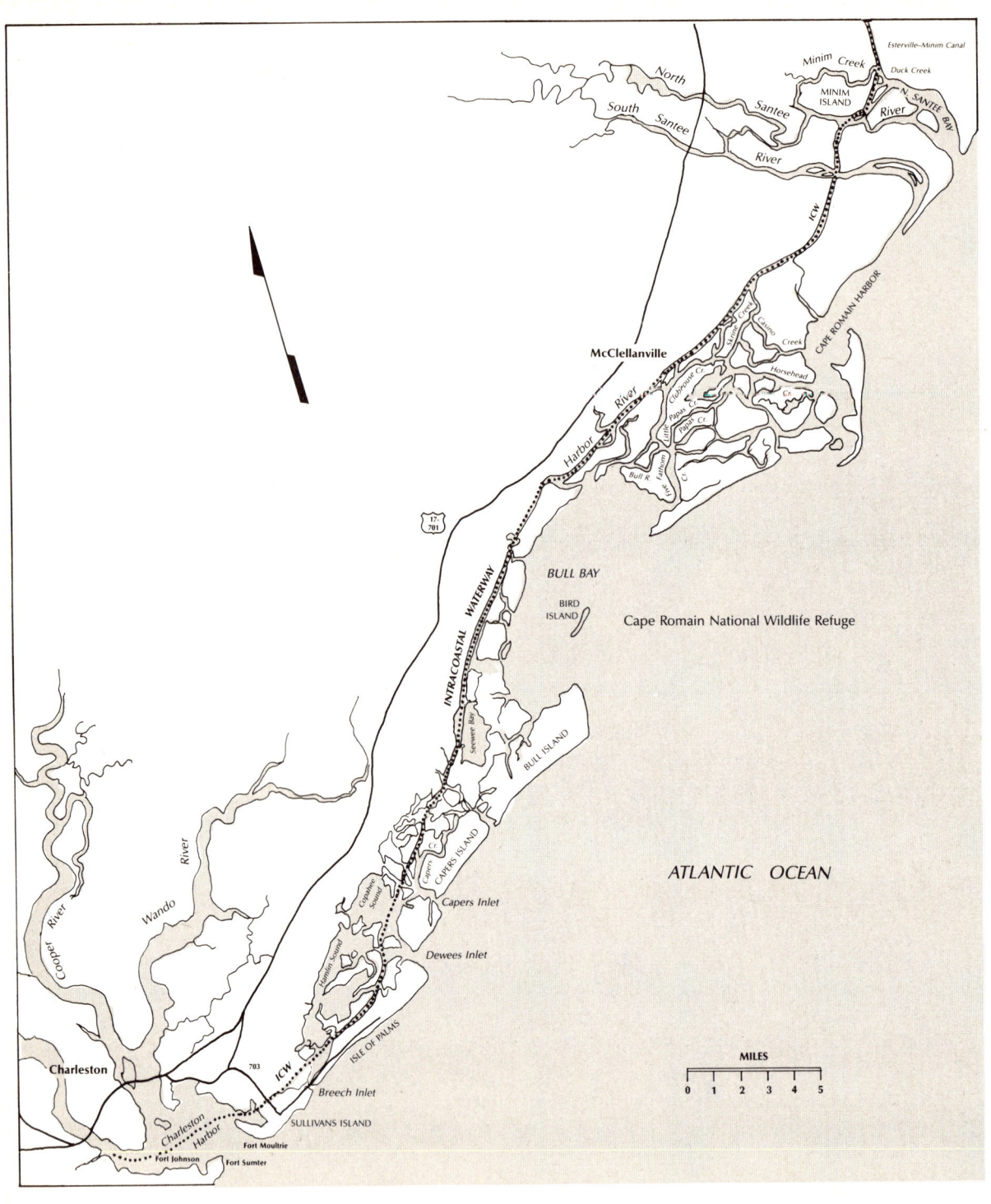

CHAPTER III

Winyah Bay to Charleston

Most boaters leaving Winyah Bay on the South Carolina ICW lean on the throttles and make a beeline for the Charleston area, never suspecting they are bypassing some unique cruising opportunities. The Santee Delta, Cape Romain Wildlife Refuge, and the small village of McClellanville offer excellent anchorages and numerous side trips on waters seldom visited by the pleasure boater.

Most of the rivers and creeks along the way are deep and reliable. However, there are some notable exceptions, particularly in the Santee and Cape Romain area.

The scenery here is very different from that along the northern rivers. Forested shorelines quickly give way to low-lying saltwater marshes. At times it seems as though the seas of grass go on forever.

Facilities are very few and far between on the northerly portion of this stretch. One friendly marina welcomes transients at the charming village of McClellanville, but otherwise the boater is on his own until reaching the Isle of Palms, many miles to the south. Numerous facilities are located along the approach to Charleston.

In contrast to the relative scarcity of marinas, good overnight anchorages abound all along the entire run. Many are seldom used, making for peaceful evenings. On the other hand, the grassy shores do not provide the protection afforded by the higher banks to the north. In really heavy weather one must be very cautious in picking a spot to drop the hook.

For the adventurous skipper who is not in a hurry, the ICW between Winyah Bay and Charleston can provide many hours of contented gunkholing. However, be warned that shallow water is found here. Take your time and watch the sounder, and some very unusual cruising experiences will be your reward.

Charts You will need several NOAA charts for successful navigation of all the waters discussed in this chapter:

11534 covers the ICW from Winyah Bay to Casino Creek.

11518 details the waterway from Casino Creek to Charleston Harbor.

11532 gives a good overview of the Santee River area.

11531 is a small scale chart covering the coastline from Winyah Bay to the Isle of Palms. This chart is required for navigation of many sidewaters off the ICW.

Minim Canal to McClellanville

The Minim Creek-Esterville Canal leads the waterway boater south from Winyah Bay to the Santee River area. Along the way the Cat Island Ferry traverses the canal on a regular basis. Another series of canals and dredged cuts allows passage through the Cape Romain area and its adjoining wildlife refuge. Finally the old fishing village of McClellanville is sighted on the western shore. Along the way many deep creeks offer anchorage and interesting side trips, but no facilities are available anywhere until reaching McClellanville.

Minim Creek

Minim Creek breaks off to the west of the ICW near the southern foot of the Minim Creek Canal just past flashing daybeacon #4.

The stream holds minimum depths of 8 feet until its intersection with Cork Creek. The eastern section of the stream affords fair overnight anchorage. There is plenty of swinging room, but the low, undeveloped grass shores do not give adequate protection for winds over 20 knots. There are no facilities on the creek.

West of the Minim-Cork Creek intersection are a few shallow water areas of 4 to 5 feet. Passage in this area is not recommended for larger cruising craft. However, small boats

Cat Island Ferry

WINYAH BAY TO CHARLESTON 55

drawing 3 feet or less can navigate through to North Santee River.

If you are the adventurous type and cruise as far as the intersection of the two creeks, look to the north and you may spy what appears to be a huge barn with a cupola on the roof. Boaters piloting from the extra height of a fly-bridge will have the best view. This structure is one of the only threshing-type rice mills left standing. The small cupola apparently housed some of the pulleys used in the mill's machinery.

Old threshing rice mill on Minim Creek

Santee River

South of flashing daybeacon #12 the waterway quickly moves towards its intersection with the Santee rivers and delta. The Santee River makes up the largest water complex in South Carolina. The great stream is formed by the juncture of the Congaree and Wateree rivers just below the state's capital city of Columbia. The river has a watershed of 15,414 square miles and drains most of the lands of northern South Carolina and western North Carolina. As it approaches the coast the

stream splits into two branches, the North and South Santee rivers. Extensive shoals guard the seaward and inland passages of the two streams. For this reason, navigation in the area can be tricky.

Santee Delta

The Santee's huge drainage has created the vast grass savannah known as the Santee Delta, shown on chart 11532 as the Santee Swamp. The delta spans the South Carolina coast from the southern foot of Cat Island to Cape Romain. At times the area's immensity is almost overwhelming. This writer was reminded of his travels in the Florida Everglades. Here, as there, the grass seems to go on and on, sometimes to the edge of the horizon. Boaters without charts and adequate navigational knowledge could become confused on the delta's sidewaters. However, if you pay attention to what you are doing, the Santee Delta's wild, untamed marshes can be the setting for a great cruising adventure.

North Santee Bay and Duck Creek

The entrance to North Santee Bay is encountered to the east of unlighted daybeacon #5. An alternate deepwater entrance can be made via Duck Creek to the northeast of flashing daybeacon #7. The vast majority of North Santee Bay is quite shallow, with 2 to 4 feet of water being the norm. However, both en-

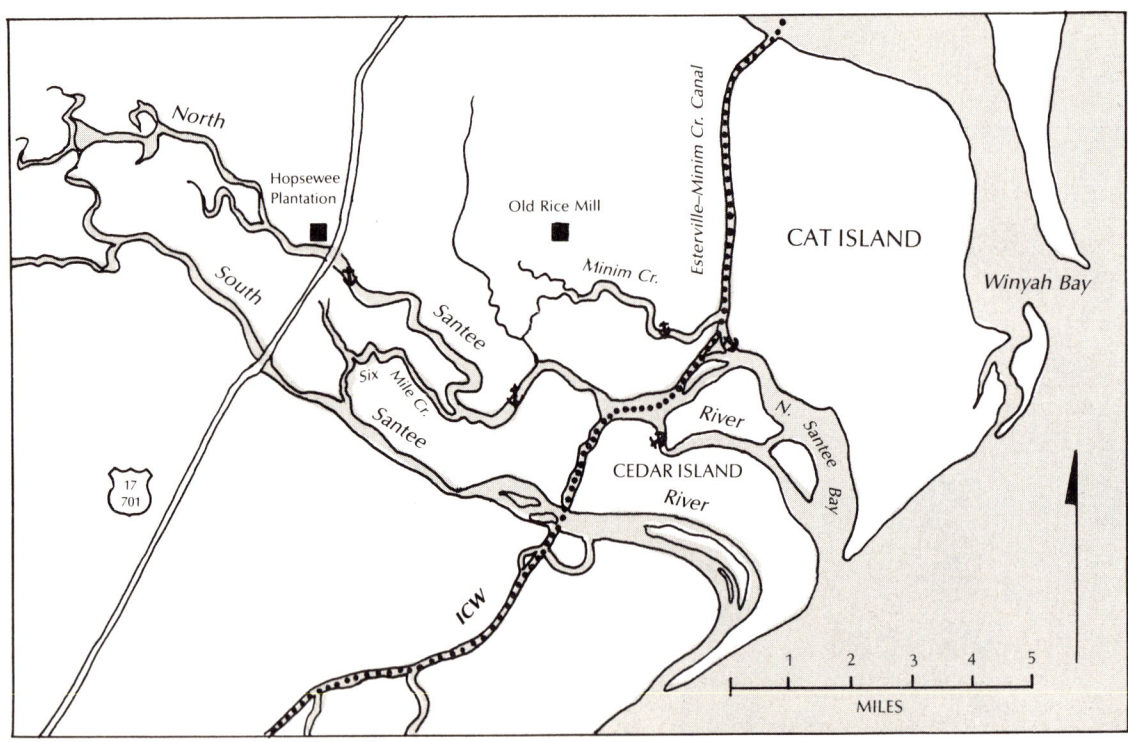

trances hold minimum depths of 9 feet. It is possible to navigate a circle around the small island separating the principal entrance from Duck Creek, thereby reentering the waterway to either the north or south. Do not cruise further to the east or attempt to enter Big Duck Creek, as depths soon decline.

The entranceway area could serve as an overnight anchorage in light airs. There is plenty of swinging room. However, strong or even moderate winds could create a very healthy chop in the area. The grass shoreline gives minimal protection in heavy blows. There are no facilities on the bay.

North Santee River

The seaward passage of North Santee River enters the waterway to the east of flashing daybeacon #15. The stream soon leads to shoal water. However, the western portion of the entrance holds 6-foot minimum entrance depths, ranging up to 20 feet for the first 1.5 nautical miles. Just when you least expect it, depths drop off to 4 feet thereafter. The deep-water portion could serve as a light air anchorage, but protection is not adequate for heavy or moderate winds.

The entrance to the mainland branch of North Santee River is found to the northwest of flashing daybeacon #18. The North Santee exhibits reliable depths of 10 to 20 feet on this arm as far as the highway span. The stream's upper reaches, seldom visited by the cruising boater, can make for a delightful side trip. Protection is adequate for anchorage in light to moderate winds once you are well upstream from the junction with the ICW. The undeveloped shoreline is at first a saltwater marsh but rises to wooded banks as one travels to the west. The Highway 17 twin fixed bridges, with a vertical clearance of 29 feet, span the river some 7 nautical miles upstream from the waterway. Further passage upstream is not possible for tall sailcraft. There are no facilities on the river.

Hopsewee Plantation

Just west of the Highway 17 span, Hopsewee Plantation is clearly visible on the northern shore. Hopsewee was the one-time home of Thomas Lynch, a fierce patriot of the Winyah district. His radical stand against England during the Revolutionary period has immortalized his name among South Carolina's great patriots. Now his plantation is open to the public and is well worth your time. Seldom will the visitor find such a beautifully preserved house of this age that is open for all to enjoy.

The old docks along the river are shoal and rotten and cannot be used. Just east of the bridge there is a launching area with a small dock that might be adequate for craft under 28 feet. Otherwise, drop the hook and break out the dinghy. Once ashore, walk north along Highway 17 until you see the plantation entrance on the left-hand side of the road.

South Santee River

The South Santee River is much shallower overall than its northern sister. Bottom configurations can change over a surprisingly short period of time. Large cruising craft would probably do well to bypass the stream entirely. Smaller boats piloted by adventurous captains may consider entering, and there is some possibility of overnight anchorage in calm conditions.

The river's seaward lane is found to the east of flashing daybeacon #22. It is possible to hold 6-foot minimum depths for some 2 nautical miles to the east, but only by following an unmarked channel. Protection is only adequate for anchorage in very light airs.

The western portion of the river is much shallower than an inspection of chart 11534 would lead one to believe. Depths of 4 to 5 feet are encountered near the western tip of Brown Island. To the east of the shoal area, minimum depths of 8 feet are held into the waterway. This arm of the river affords a bit more protection for anchorage than the seaward branch but is still too wide and ineffectively sheltered for heavy weather.

Cape Romain

Cape Romain is an absolutely fascinating area that is rarely visited by pleasure boaters. In *Glories of the Carolina Coast,* James Henry Rice, Jr., speaks of the "solitude where Cape

Hopsewee Plantation on North Santee River

WINYAH BAY TO CHARLESTON 59

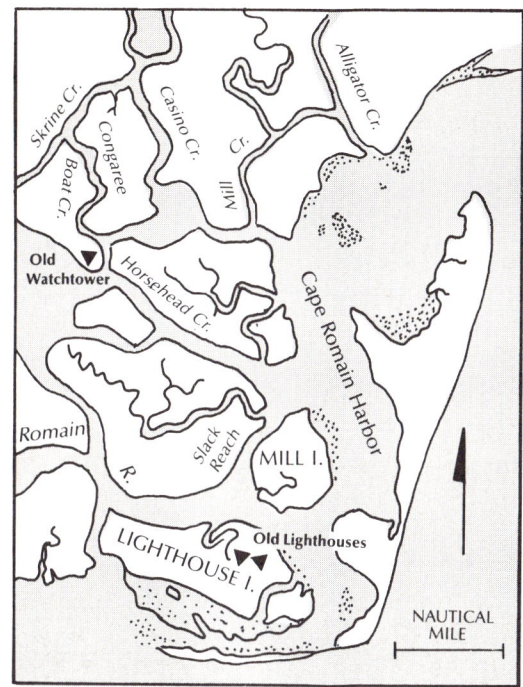

Romain Light warns mariners of the treacherous reefs, off the mouth of Santee, a region so wild that you can readily believe yourself in Asia or Africa." Mr. Rice's description is entirely accurate. Cruising the backwaters of Cape Romain, it is as if one has entered another world, very far from modern hustle and bustle. The grass savannahs seem to stretch on forever. Your only companions are likely to be the many different birds that populate the marshes. Stop your engine for a moment. The silence is eerie; then suddenly it is broken by the call of a lonely gull or pelican. If you crave the adventure that is so sadly lacking is our modern, well-planned world, Cape Romain is just what you seek.

The entire Cape Romain area is part of a huge wildlife refuge stretching from Alligator Creek, just south of unlighted daybeacon #26, to Price Creek. The refuge encompasses some 60,000 acres and at least 20 miles of shoreline. More than 250 species of birds have been identified as living within the confines of the refuge. The cape is truly a bonanza for nature lovers.

While the lighthouse Mr. Rice refers to in his book is now dark and empty, it remains as a mute monument to a far-removed age of the sea. For many a year the old lighthouse warned mariners of the vast Cape Romain shoals. Today it is a rarely used daymark.

Cape Romain National Wildlife Refuge

60 CRUISING GUIDE TO COASTAL SOUTH CAROLINA

Adventurous boaters can, in fact, see two lighthouses on the cape. The shorter structure, lacking any crown, dates from 1827, while the other light was first used in 1866. The newer tower continued to operate until 1947. With some effort, you might catch a glimpse of the taller lighthouse from the waterway, but a closer inspection calls for a long trip through the twisting streams of the cape.

Cape Romain encompasses the largest area of shallow water on the South Carolina coast. While there are deep creeks flowing into the interior from the ICW, successful navigation in the cape area calls for extreme caution. Be sure to read the Cape Romain navigation section presented later in this chapter before attempting entry.

Casino Creek

Casino Creek serves as the principal entrance to the Cape Romain area. Depths at the intersection of the creek and the ICW run between 5 and 6 feet, deepening to some 8 to 12 feet of water as one cruises downstream. The stream provides access to the other navigable Cape Romain water bodies, including Skrine, Congaree Boat, and Horsehead

Old watch tower at Cape Romain

creeks. Anchorage in any of these bodies of water is a practical consideration in all but heavy weather. However, you should not attempt entry unless your craft is less than 38 feet in length and draws no more than 4 feet.

McClellanville

The old fishing village of McClellanville sits perched on the northern shores of Jeremy Creek to the west of flashing daybeacon #35. The town is the site of the first facilities available to the cruising boater south of Winyah Bay. Jeremy Creek is consistently deep and provides reliable access to the waterfront.

McClellanville is a very pleasant stop for anyone who enjoys getting away from it all. Among a host of sleepy, charming coastal villages, McClellanville struck this writer as one of the most easygoing of the lot. Progress has made only a few small inroads here. To be sure, the village has electricity and modern transportation, but a leisurely walk along the quiet lanes reveals that little else has changed in a very long time. Beautiful old white homes line the streets, which are overhung by huge oaks trailing long beards of gray moss. Here and there an old-style drainage ditch still fronts onto the neighborhood yards. This

Old home at McClellanville

writer and his mate spent an enjoyable hour sitting on the waterfront watching two fishermen mend their nets. Besides the quiet banter of the men at work, the only sound was the sighing of the wind.

Once a year, the village's atmosphere of peace and quiet is traded for the friendly crowds that attend the Blessing of the Fleet. This traditional ceremony, held on the second Saturday in May, has evolved into a seafood extravaganza. Seafood of all types, both familiar and exotic, is prepared by a host of local cooks for all to enjoy. For one day the resident population of some 300 souls is swollen by 10,000 visitors, many of whom return year after year for the happy event.

Leland Marine Services sits proudly on the shores of Jeremy Creek and offers full services to the transient boater. Overnight berths with all power and water connections as well as gasoline and diesel fuel are available. Many waterway craft stop here for the night, and you may well be joined by several fellow boaters. The management is very friendly and most anxious to meet all the needs of passing cruisers. This marina, while not as large as some, can be recommended without reservation.

McClellanville can also boast of one restaurant, The Crab Pot. While not within walking distance, the management will be glad to send a car for boaters in the evening (call 803-887-3156). The menu is usually posted on the door of the Leland Marina office.

McClellanville has a certain charm that is hard to identify, but its secret certainly seems to lie in peace and relaxation. If you are in the area at the end of a long cruising day, I highly recommend that you stay for the night and give the village's magic a chance to soothe away your cares. Don't be in such a hurry to reach the "Holy City" of Charleston that you pass McClellanville without a thought.

McClellanville History The present-day visitor to McClellanville would probably be surprised to learn that the town has an illustrious past, beginning in 1822 when a devastating hurricane destroyed several summer homes on nearby Cedar Island. These homes belonged to wealthy planters, a list of whose names reads like a *Who's Who* of post-Revolutionary South Carolina, including the Palmer, Pinckney, Lucas, and Doar families. Understandably, the planters immediately sought a safer haven for the hot summer months. They purchased land on the northern shore of Jeremy Creek from the McClellan family, and the town was born.

Following the Civil War, summer visits by the affluent planters ended. The community that had grown up around the retreat turned to commercial fishing for its livelihood. During prohibition, rum-running was a popular occupation. As the years passed, McClellanville remained a small fishing village, and it survives pretty much intact to this very day.

Five Fathom Creek

Five Fathom Creek is entered from the ICW via a marked channel through Town Creek just south of flashing daybeacon #35. The stream provides fairly reliable access to the open sea and is the only marked inlet available to the cruising boater between Winyah

WINYAH BAY TO CHARLESTON

Bay and Charleston. Entrance depths run around 8 feet, deepening to some 15 feet of water on the creek's interior. The creek's outlet to the sea, while marked, is changeable and depths are uncertain. Check at Leland Marina on the McClellanville Waterfront before attempting the cut.

Five Fathom Creek also provides access to several other deep streams, including Bull River, Little Papas, and Papas creeks. All these water bodies offer anchorage possibilities, but only in light to moderate breezes. The grassy, undeveloped banks give only minimal protection. There are no facilities on any of the streams.

ICW to McClellanville Navigation

Navigation on this section of the waterway is rather simple and fairly straightforward. Simply hold to the mid-width and be on guard against any side-setting currents, particularly near the North and South Santee rivers. Several of the sidewaters call for greater caution and careful navigation. The boater must be particularly alert for shoals in the Cape Romain area. Otherwise, keep a weather eye on the sounder and your cruise should be a delight.

Cat Island Ferry Some .7 of a nautical mile south of the Minim Creek-Estherville Canal entrance, the Cat Island Ferry crosses the waterway on a regular basis. Signs displaying flashing red lights warn boaters approaching from the north and south to slow down. "No Wake" is strictly enforced for several hundred yards on both sides of the ferry route. Slow down and proceed at idle speed until past the sign at the opposite end from your approach.

Leland Marine Services, McClellanville

Minim Creek To enter Minim Creek, cruise west into the main body of the stream from flashing daybeacon #4. There is plenty of swing room as far as Sand Creek, a small sidewater on Minim's southern shore. Pick any likely spot and drop the hook, but remember that protection is not adequate for heavy weather.

Don't attempt to cruise past the Cork Creek intersection unless you draw less than 3 feet. To the west of the junction, some 4-foot depths are encountered. Small craft with shallow draft can continue following the stream until it intersects North Santee River.

The old rice threshing mill described earlier can be seen to the north as one approaches the intersection of Minim-Cork creeks.

On the ICW Swift tidal currents are often encountered in the Santee section of the ICW. Sailcraft and trawlers should be particularly alert for side-setting currents as the waterway cuts across North Santee River south of flashing daybeacon #15. Another area of concern is the passage across the South Santee at flashing daybeacon #22. Keep a careful watch to your stern so you can quickly note any leeway slippage.

North Santee Bay The boater has a choice of two routes to enter the navigable section of North Santee Bay. Both the principal entrance east of unlighted daybeacon #5 and Duck Creek at flashing daybeacon #7 hold minimum 9-foot depths as far as the eastern tip of the small island separating the two channels. Don't attempt to cruise further to the east on the bay, as depths soon drop off to 3 feet or less.

North Santee River To enter the seaward branch of North Santee River, favor the eastern shore a bit until reaching the stream's first sharp turn to the east. Swing back to the mid-width here. Minimum depths of 6 feet continue for some 1.75 nautical miles east of the entrance.

Successful navigation of the mainland entrance of the North Santee is a simple matter. Just follow the mid-width of the stream as it cuts to the west. Use chart 11532 for navigation of the river's upper reaches.

Soon after leaving the ICW channel you will see several uncharted U-shaped dump buoys on the river's southern shore. Keep clear of the area.

Continue on the stream's mid-width. Good depths are held at least as far as the fixed, twin-span highway bridge, which crosses the North Santee some 7 nautical miles west of the river's intersection with the waterway. The higher, wooded banks on the stream's western section afford better protection for overnight anchorage than the lower, grassy shores to the east. In light airs feel free to drop the hook almost anywhere, but in a heavy blow it would be better to cruise upstream for several miles before selecting a spot.

South Santee River Those boaters who choose to cruise the mostly shallow seaward branch of South Santee River should enter on the stream's mid-width. As seen on chart 11534, best depths can be held by favoring the southern shore after proceeding downstream for a hundred yards or so. Shallow water is encountered past the western tip of grassy Grace Island, which bisects the river.

Depths shown on the current edition of chart 11534 for the mainland branch of the South Santee are not accurate. Past the western tip of Brown Island, 4-foot readings are soon encountered. Confine your cruising to the area east of this point.

As one can see from a study of chart 11534, best depths are maintained by heavily favoring the northern shore when entering. The most sheltered spot for anchorage is found as the mid-width of Brown Island comes abeam to the south.

Cape Romain As stated earlier, the Cape Romain area is one of the shallowest stretches on the South Carolina coast north of Charleston. Do not attempt to enter unless your craft is less than 38 feet in length and draws 4 feet or less. Chart 11518 covers the entrance, but you must use chart 11531 for the interior portion of the cape.

For best depths, enter Casino Creek via the mid-width of the small creek to the *north* of flashing daybeacon #29. Depths in this cut run from 6 to 12 feet for the most part, but some 5-foot readings will be encountered as the creek curves to the southwest. Casino Creek's principal entrance, to the south of #29, carries only 4 to 5 feet of water at its intersection with the waterway. Once into the main body of the creek, however, depths improve, running from 8 to 15 feet of water.

To obtain a good view of the lighthouses described earlier, carefully cruise downstream on Casino Creek until the stream intersects Cape Romain Harbor. Do not proceed any further! Depths quickly fall off past the intersection of the creek and the harbor. Look to the south and you will have a good view of the lights on Lighthouse Island.

One can catch an even better view of the old sentinels while cruising on Congaree Boat and Horsehead creeks. Additionally, the adventurous captain who takes this fascinating side trip will likely encounter many interesting birds as well as an abandoned lookout tower. However, this cruise is not recommended for boats over 30 feet.

If you choose to make the attempt, abandon Casino Creek at its juncture with Congaree Boat Creek. Cruise west on the smaller stream until coming abeam of a small cut to the south, which leads past the old lookout tower. Make a wide turn into this stream, holding strictly to the mid-width. Minimum depths of 8 feet are found in the middle of the creek, but the shores and the points are shoal. Make another wide turn to port to enter Horsehead Creek. You can cruise to the southeast for 100 yards or so in 8-foot minimum depths, but shoal water is encountered soon thereafter.

Skrine Creek, which breaks off to the west from the upper reaches of Casino Creek, holds good depths of 8 feet or more until it intersects with Congaree Boat Creek. This stream affords more fine bird watching and offers anchorage possibilities.

McClellanville If you choose to enter Jeremy Creek and visit the charming village of McClellanville, turn 90 degrees to the north at flashing daybeacon #35 and cruise into the stream's mid-width. Depths are adequate for large craft well upstream. Several seafood docks will soon come abeam to starboard. Here it is sometimes possible to purchase seafood that has been caught the same day. Further along, the docks of Leland Marine Services come into view, also to starboard.

Five Fathom Creek The entrance to Five Fathom Creek is located across the ICW from Jeremy Creek. The creek's upper

Georgetown Shrimp Company, McClellanville

reaches are quite deep and well marked. Cruising craft of almost any size can navigate the stream's northerly section with confidence. As stated earlier, the seaward passage is changeable, and local knowledge is desirable, though not absolutely necessary, before using the inlet. Chart 11518 covers the stream's upper section, but you will need 11531 to cover the inlet navigation.

Most boaters will probably want to enter the creek by way of the marked stream at flashing daybeacon #35. This small channel soon leads to the main body of the creek. Northbound cruisers on the ICW may choose to enter the area by using Matthews Creek north of flashing daybeacon #38. This small creek holds minimum depths of 7 feet into Five Fathom Creek.

The unmarked extreme upper reaches of Five Fathom Creek, east of flashing daybeacon #20, hold minimum depths of 8 feet for some distance upstream. This area would make a good anchorage in light to moderate airs, but again, the grassy banks do not give enough protection for heavy weather.

There is one area of very shallow water to the east of unlighted daybeacon #17. Pass #17 to its southerly side and be careful not to let leeway ease you to the north.

Between unlighted daybeacons #16 and #14, Bull River breaks off from Five Fathom Creek to the west. This stream holds minimum depths of 10 feet until it empties into shallow Bulls Bay. Anchorage would be possible in light airs.

East of unlighted daybeacon #14, Papas and Little Papas creeks enter Five Fathom. Both streams have minimum depths of 6 feet for some distance upstream but are too small to afford sufficient swing room for craft over 30 feet.

At unlighted daybeacon #10 the channel begins to enter its seaward passage by passing around Sandy Point. Beyond flashing daybeacon #7, depths become more uncertain until past the last seaward aid, unlighted can buoy #1. Study chart 11531 carefully before attempting the inlet! Take heed of any local knowledge you might be lucky enough to obtain, and watch the sounder. While certainly not as reliable as the Winyah or Charleston inlet channels, the Five Fathom cut is used on a fairly regular basis by pleasure craft and should not present any great difficulty.

McClellanville to Charleston Harbor

South of McClellanville the ICW follows the upper reaches of Harbor River for several miles. The waterway then enters a long, dredged cut that carries the boater through the shallow waters of Bulls and Sewee bays. As the ICW begins its approach to the Isle of

Palms, the route continues to track through extensive saltwater marsh, sometimes dignified with the designation of "sound." Finally, the waterway passes both the Isle of Palms and Sullivans Island to the east and enters Charleston Harbor.

The wide but shallow area of Bulls and Sewee bays, as well as Copahee and Hamlin sounds to the south, can allow enough fetch for a sharp chop when winds are above 15 knots. Small craft should be alert for these conditions before venturing out on this section of the waterway.

While the vast majority of the so-called bays and sounds between McClellanville and Charleston harbor are quite shallow, the waterway is pierced at regular intervals by deepwater creeks that can serve as overnight

McClellanville Harbor

anchorages. Without exception, however, these streams have low, grassy shores that give inadequate protection in high winds.

Several streams just north of the Isle of Palms lead seaward to shallow inlets. All are unmarked and unreliable. One currently boasts a barely navigable passage out to sea between two walls of breakers, but this cut is not for the faint of heart.

From McClellanville the cruising boater must follow the waterway south for some 25 nautical miles before coming upon any facilities. This is a fairly lonely stretch, so make sure your tanks are topped off before leaving McClellanville behind. On the Isle of Palms, one of the finest marinas in the state welcomes transient boaters, and additional facilities are available at Breach Inlet.

Sullivans Island guards the eastern flank of the ICW's entrance into Charleston Harbor. Here old Fort Moultrie is a constant reminder of the great battle that helped give South Carolina her state flag.

While certainly not as attractive as some stretches of the waterway, the run from McClellanville to Charleston Harbor does have its moments. Some anchorages are available, and good facilities are to be found on the southern portion of the run. All in all, the cruising boater can enjoy this passage while he anticipates the glories of Charleston.

Awendaw Creek

Awendaw Creek makes off to the south from flashing daybeacon #48. The stream holds minimum depths of 8 feet until it intersects the shallow waters of Bulls Bay. The stream can serve as a light air anchorage, but protection is not sufficient for winds over 15 knots.

Graham Creek

Graham Creek, to the south of unlighted daybeacon #64, is one of the best overnight anchorage possibilities in the area for craft under 50 feet. The southern bank of the creek is much higher than the norm for this section and gives good protection in southwesterly breezes. Minimum depths of 8 feet are held well into the stream's interior. The shoreline is undeveloped, though some construction seems to be in progress just west of the entrance. There are no facilities on the creek.

Price Creek

Price Creek is a deep stream to the east of flashing daybeacon #86. The creek eventually leads to a small, unmarked inlet. At the time of this writer's research, an 8-foot channel was available out to sea. It was necessary to pick one's way between two lines of breakers, but the cut was passable. However, due to the changeable nature of all inlet areas, this channel should not be attempted without specific local knowledge.

The northerly portion of the creek maintains minimum depths of 8 feet and can serve as an anchorage in light to moderate winds. Similarly, Bull Narrows Creek, which cuts off to the east from the main body, gives relatively good protection and has sufficient swing room for craft under 35 feet.

Price Creek's shoreline is mostly undeveloped saltwater marsh. However, the banks of the inlet are wooded, higher ground, and there is some sort of commercial fishery on the southern shore. Again, the grassy banks do not afford enough protection for high winds.

Capers Creek

Capers Creek is a large, deepwater stream that leads southeast to an impassable inlet. The creek has three branches opening onto the ICW; the southernmost is known as Toomer Creek. All maintain minimum 7-foot depths on their mid-width, as does the stream's main body. The banks are shoal, however.

The stream is too broad for anchorage consideration in all but the lightest of airs. However, the Capers Island shoreline to the northeast is quite attractive. If you are taking a leisurely cruise, follow the creek as far as the inlet. This area is seldom visited by pleasure boaters and is a good opportunity for serious gunkholing.

Whiteside Creek

Whiteside Creek is yet another deep stream that can serve as a light to moderate air anchorage for craft under 50 feet. It is found on the waterway's western shore north of flashing daybeacon #96. Minimum depths are around 10 feet, but there is one shoal area to avoid on the creek's interior. The shores are undeveloped and no facilities are available.

Toomer Creek

The mainland branch of Toomer Creek north of flashing daybeacon #99 holds minimum depths of 8 feet until it splits as it moves inland. Protection is adequate for anchorage in winds of less than 20 knots. There may not be enough swing room for craft over 45 feet. The shoreline is undeveloped saltwater marsh and there are no facilities on the creek.

Dewees Creek

The eastern branch of Dewees Creek, to the south of unlighted daybeacon #109, leads to another impassable seaward cut. While the main body of the stream holds minimum depths of 10 feet, deepening to 45 feet of water in a few spots, the inlet is surrounded by very shoal water as it passes out into the ocean.

The westerly reaches of the creek are bounded by saltwater marsh, but the interior section borders Dewees Island to the north and the Isle of Palms to the south. Dewees Island has higher, well-wooded, attractive shores with some residential development.

The main body of Dewees Creek is too open for effective overnight anchorage. However, the stream has an unnamed branch skirting the eastern edge of Big Hill Marsh that does afford good protection in all but heavy weather. Depths run between 10 and 25 feet until abeam of the northern tip of Big Hill Marsh. There is plenty of swing room for larger craft. This stream is one of the best anchorages available to the cruising boater on this run. Do not attempt to reenter the waterway from this branch, however, as depths decline upstream.

As shown on chart 11518, the landward stretch of Dewees Creek looks like a three-fingered hand. The northerly finger is unnamed, but the southerly branch is called

WINYAH BAY TO CHARLESTON 71

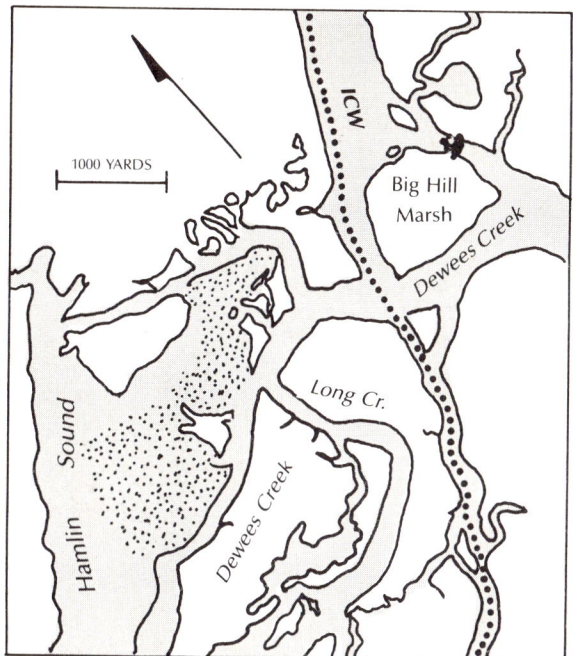

Long Creek. This area is much larger than a casual inspection of 11518 would lead one to believe. Protection is minimal between the marshy shores. All three streams lead inland to shallow Hamlin Sound and Gray Bay. Do not attempt to cruise into these waters. Shoals are quickly encountered, as this writer's bent prop can readily attest.

The opening of each of the three fingers holds 8-foot minimum depths. However, there is very little to see, and protection is sufficient only for light air anchorage. All in all, this section should probably be bypassed except by those hardy souls who want to see it all.

Wild Dunes Yacht Harbor
Just south of flashing daybeacon #116, one of the newest and most modern facilities available to the cruising boater north of Charleston is found along the waterway's eastern shore. Wild Dunes Yacht Harbor (formerly Isle of Palms Marina) welcomes the transient boater and provides overnight berths on floating docks with all power and water connections. Gasoline, diesel fuel, and a nicely stocked, 24-hour grocery and ships' store are all readily available. The marina has a mechanic on call and can usually handle any engine, generator, or electrical difficulty you might have. An excellent on-site restaurant serves the freshest of seafood. As if that were not enough, transients receive golf, tennis, and dining privileges at nearby Wild Dunes Beach and Racquet club.

It is not a good idea to attempt entry of Charleston Harbor at night without local knowledge, so if you are in the Isle of Palms-Sullivans Island area at the end of the cruising day, it would be a good idea to dock at this unusually well-appointed facility and wait for the light of morning before approaching Charleston.

Isle of Palms History The Isle of Palms was known as Long Island until modern times. The island was rarely visited until a sort of carnival resort was developed on the strand in 1898. Visitors would ride the trolley from Charleston and enjoy the seashore, the hotel, and the amusement rides at the carnival. It was not until the 1940s that a private developer purchased the land and residential development began. A bridge was built connecting the beach with Sullivans Island in 1945, and the resort's development has continued unabated ever since.

Hamlin Creek

South of unlighted daybeacon #117, Hamlin Creek leads west between Little Goat Island and the Isle of Palms Waterfront to Breach Inlet. Many private docks border the southern shore, but there are no facilities for the transient boater along the creek. The stream is well protected and is one of the best anchorage possibilities for craft under 50 feet, particularly in heavy weather, on this section of the ICW. Minimum depths are 9 feet until just north of the inlet, where the water becomes shallow. About the only difficulty associated with anchoring here is the considerable small-craft traffic the creek sometimes supports. Pick a spot far enough away from the island docks to avoid passing craft and drop the hook for a night of security.

Swinton Creek

West of flashing daybeacon #118 Swinton Creek makes into the northern shore of the ICW. The stream holds 8 to 15 feet of water well downstream. It exhibits typical grassy, undeveloped shores that give only enough protection for anchorage in light to moderate winds. There is probably not enough swing room for craft over 35 feet. No facilities are to be found on the creek.

Inlet Creek

Inlet Creek, north of unlighted daybeacon #119, holds minimum depths of 10 feet for quite a distance downstream. The shoreline consists of undeveloped, grassy marsh. There are no facilities on the stream. As is usual in this area, protection is only sufficient for light to moderate air anchorage.

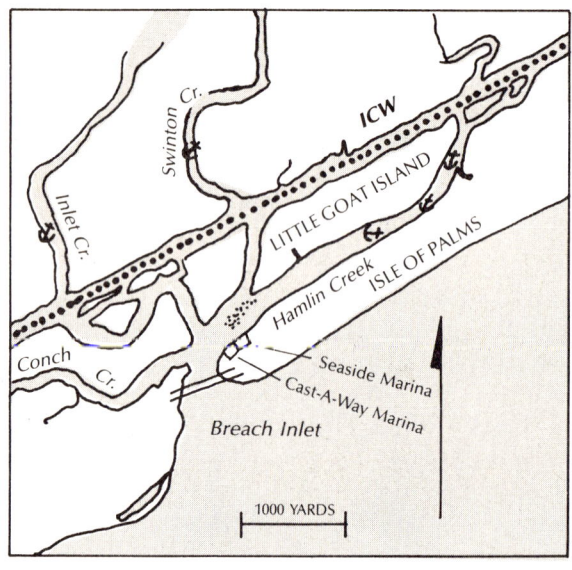

Breach Inlet

Breach Inlet is a small, shallow seaward cut that separates the Isle of Palms from Sullivans Island. The channel is spanned by a low-level fixed bridge between the two islands, rendering the cut useless to larger pleasure craft even if it were not so shallow.

Two marinas are to be found just to the east of the bridge on the Isle of Palms. Cast-A-Way Marina is a relatively small facility offering limited dockage space for transients. Gasoline and diesel fuel as well as all power and water connections are available. Approach depths are around 6 feet.

Seaside Marina, just east of the above facility, does not offer any services for transients, but there is an on-site sandwich shop. Boaters who dock at Cast-A-Way Marina may want to visit this restaurant for the tempting varieties of submarine and cold cut sandwiches offered there.

WINYAH BAY TO CHARLESTON

Breach Inlet can be approached by four separate channels from the waterway. All but one are deep and reliable. Make sure to read the Breach Inlet navigation section later in this chapter, however, before attempting entry.

Conch Creek

The mainland branch of Conch Creek, just north of unlighted daybeacon #121, can serve as a light to moderate air anchorage for craft under 35 feet. Minimum depths run around 7 feet. The grassy shores are undeveloped.

Tomers Cove

Tomers Cove Marina is found on the waterway's northern shore just west of the Sullivans Island swing bridge. At the time of this writing, this facility was closed for extensive renovation into a large marina-condominium project. Reportedly, the marina will reopen in 1985. At that time, transients will be offered overnight berths on floating docks with all power and water connections and 6- to 10-foot dockside depths. Gasoline and diesel fuel will be available, and there will be a restaurant on the premises.

Sullivans Island

A small cut leads south from flashing daybeacon #125 to a National Park Service dock on the northern shore of Sullivans Island. Passing boaters are welcome to moor here while visiting the Fort Moultrie historic monument, a short walk away. Unless you are in a hurry, don't fail to stop. The old fort makes for a fascinating visit.

The small stream also affords a good view of the Sullivans Island Lighthouse. The black and white rectangular tower, 163 feet tall, is readily visible to the southeast. Designed to withstand even the gales of a hurricane, it exhibits, according to the South Carolina Sea Grant Consortium, "the brightest light . . . in the Western Hemisphere."

Wild Dunes Yacht Harbor

Sullivans Island History Sullivans Island was named for Captain Florentia O'Sullivan, a member of the original Charles Towne colonization party. As early as 1706, the strategic military value of the island was recognized, and a makeshift fort was built on the island's eastern tip. During the Revolutionary War, Colonel William Moultrie supervised the construction of Fort Moultrie on the same point. The heroic story of Colonel Moultrie and his men will be related later in this chapter.

Following the Revolution, Sullivans Island was used as a quarantine station for imported slaves. By 1800 Charlestonians began building summer homes on the island to escape the oppressive heat of the city. By 1817 more than a thousand seasonal residents flocked to the island's four hotels and two hundred resort homes. In 1854 a severe hurricane nearly leveled all development, but the loyal vacationers began rebuilding immediately thereafter, and Sullivans Island has remained a popular resort to the present day.

Story of Fort Moultrie It was June of 1776, and news had already been received in Charles Towne of a massive fleet, commanded by Sir Peter Parker, voyaging south from New York with the express intention of making the city a base for British operations in the South. On board was Sir Henry Clinton, with an army of several thousand seasoned veterans. The English were confident that their powerful force could easily defeat any defensive measures the patriots threw in their way.

Meanwhile, Charlestonian patriots were feverishly preparing the city's defenses. Warehouses bordering the waterfront were torn down to clear a path for cannon fire. Continental companies drilled daily. Citizens with military experience predicted that the battle would very likely hinge upon the fight for the outer harbor. If the Americans could stop the British there, the British superiority in shipping and infantry could not be brought into play.

On the southern tip of Sullivans Island, Colonel William Moultrie was supervising the construction of a new fort. Palmetto logs were cut on Capers Island to the north and quickly brought south by horse-drawn cart. The fort's double walls were built of thick Palmetto planks, reinforced by a layer of sand in between. Moultrie's men worked night and day, expecting to sight the enemy on the horizon at any minute.

There were those who did not believe in Moultrie's plan. Some said that the combined cannon of the British fleet would obliterate the small fort in the first broadside. It was only a waste of lives and resources to continue with such folly. Why not draw back and muster their defense at the lower tip of the peninsula? Well, if Moultrie was stubborn enough to try the fool scheme, he could go ahead, but he wouldn't be allowed to squander the city's whole powder supply.

Moultrie turned a deaf ear to his critics and urged his men on to even greater speed. By the time Sir Peter Parker sighted the Charles Towne Bar, the patriots had accomplished the miraculous. Stout walls faced the enemy on three sides, and a host of cannons were mounted on their platforms. The rear quarter of the fort, however, still lay open to attack.

The British generals laid their plans carefully. While the great fleet pounded the fort in a bold frontal assault, Sir Henry Clinton would land his army on undefended Long Island to the north. From there he would cross shallow Breach Inlet, thrusting aside the small force of patriots stationed there, and sweep against the fort from the rear. Parker and Clinton probably boasted that Charles Towne would be in their hands within a week.

On the morning of June 16, a strong contingent from the British fleet rolled out their massive cannon and stood in towards the impudent patriots blocking their way. No challenge was yet heard from the fort's cannon. Unknown to the British, the defenders were saving their scant powder supply until the fleet was at point-blank range.

Suddenly, the waters of Charles Towne Harbor exploded with British fire and smoke. Over 300 guns smote the walls of Fort Moultrie in a single cannonade. Confident ship masters waited for the smoke to clear and reveal the shattered walls.

What astonishment must have shown on the face of every sailor, from the lowliest tar to the fleet admiral, when they saw that the fort's spongy palmetto logs had simply soaked up the British cannonballs with no apparent damage!

Then it was Moultrie's turn. The patriots' cannon spoke. When the smoke cleared this time, the fort's defenders cheered as they surveyed the broken spars and shattered decks of the once-great force in front of them.

The battle continued throughout the day. At one point Moultrie's powder ran so low that only a few cannon were in action. A new supply was rushed out from the city and the battle was again joined in earnest. The English tried to maneuver several ships around to the fort's unprotected rear, but the vessels ran aground and were riddled with shot. The fort's proud crescent-moon flag was shot away, only to be retrieved by a Sergeant Jasper. This soldier's brave effort is forever immortalized by a statue on the Charleston South Battery.

Meanwhile, Clinton's 2,200 troops had successfully landed on Long Island, only to discover that Breach Inlet was far too deep for the men to ford. The determined band of patriots guarding the inlet's southern banks kept the enemy at bay with grapeshot and rifle fire. Eventually it was necessary to reembark the troops to the fleet offshore.

By the time the sun set on that amazing day, the British naval force that had attacked the fort was in tatters. Sir Peter even had the ignoble fate of being wounded in the buttocks by flying splinters. Within the walls, Moultrie's men stared out to sea with powder-blackened faces. They could hardly believe it. The British forces were limping away, glad to leave the fury of Fort Moultrie behind. The defenders had faced the might, the very cream, of the British navy and had bested that confident force in a pitched battle. Their victory was to remain one of the soundest English defeats of the entire war.

Following the end of the Revolution, the South Carolina legislature adopted the symbol of the palmetto tree as a part of the state flag. Along with the crescent moon symbolizing liberty, it has since waved proudly over the "Palmetto State," forever a memorial to those brave men who fought against such overwhelming odds on that hot June day in 1776.

McClellanville to Charleston Harbor
Navigation

Running this stretch of the ICW is a simple matter of sticking to the marked channel. While tidal currents can run swiftly, particularly in the vicinity of inlets, they are not usually as severe as those found in the Santee area. Sailcraft and trawlers should nevertheless be on the lookout for excessive leeway. Also, be on guard for some official "No Wake" signs posted near several private dockage areas on this run.

Most sidewaters can be entered simply by sticking to their mid-width. Streams that call for more caution are noted below. Be careful not to cruise too far upstream on any of the area sidewaters. Almost without exception they eventually lead to shallow water, which could result in a most unpleasant grounding far from the waterway channel.

Awendaw Creek Be sure to use the stream's primary entrance to the south of flashing daybeacon #48 if you choose to explore Awendaw Creek. The two small creeks that make off from the waterway at unlighted daybeacon #49 and eventually lead into the main stream are both shoal and should not be used by cruising craft. Don't attempt to cruise very far to the southeast, as depths rise sharply in Bulls Bay.

Graham Creek Depths begin to drop off in Graham Creek as the stream takes a sharp turn to the east. Discontinue your exploration of the creek before reaching the bend.

Price Creek Good depths are held on the mid-width of Price Creek as far as the large power lines that cross the inlet. Here depths become inconsistent, and you should not continue without local knowledge.

Capers Creek All three entrances into Capers Creek have some shoaling problems. Slow down and watch the sounder until you are on the stream's main body. The northernmost branch is probably the best of the three despite depths shown on chart 11518. On-site research revealed 8-foot minimum depths on the northern cut's mid-width.

The central channel also holds plenty of water on its mid-width, but the western shore is shoal. Favor the eastern bank just a bit when entering.

Make sure to avoid the point of land separating the central and northern entrance cuts. This point has built out well into the creek. Shoal water with depths of less than 4 feet is encountered for a considerable distance south of the intersection.

The southern channel, known as Toomer Creek, is the smallest of the three but carries 6-foot depths at this time. Hold carefully to the mid-width until reaching the main body.

Cruising beyond the eastern and western

WINYAH BAY TO CHARLESTON

points of land that guard the inlet's flanks is strictly not recommended. Depths rise quickly and massive breakers are soon encountered.

Dewees Creek   The main body of Dewees Creek does not present any navigational problems. However, do not attempt to enter the stream by way of the northern cut at unlighted daybeacon #105 or the southern arm near flashing daybeacon #111. Both channels are too shallow and unreliable for the cruising boater.

If you choose to enter the northern arm from the creek's interior to anchor, avoid the point that separates the two branches.

Again, as with the two inlets to the north, depths begin to drop off rapidly as the stream approaches the ocean. Do not cruise further downstream than the power line crossing.

Enter the landward branch of Dewees Creek with caution. While good depths are held well upstream, all three branches of the creek eventually lead to very shallow water. Do not attempt to explore the dump area, marked on chart 11518, found on the lower reaches of Long Creek. Waters are much too shoal for cruising craft.

Hamlin Creek   Don't attempt to approach Breach Inlet from Hamlin Creek. While most of this creek borders the principal area waterfront and is quite deep, the extreme southerly tier of the stream is shoal, with some 4-foot depths in evidence.

Breach Inlet   There are five possible entrances to the Breach Inlet area. One, Hamlin Creek, was discussed above. Of the other four, all but one are basically reliable.

To successfully navigate the northerly branch, you must heavily favor the northern shore once through the marsh grass. Continue holding to that shore until reaching the deeper water of the inlet to the west.

The central channel, just west of unlighted daybeacon #119, is the most navigable of the three. Simply follow the midwidth until you begin to approach the Breach Inlet Bridge. You will spy the two marinas mentioned earlier on the southeastern shore. Don't cut in towards the facilities too quickly. There is shoal water, as marked on chart 11518, to the east. Continue on the main channel until you are about 25 yards from the bridge. Then cut 90 degrees to port and enter the marina.

The westernmost cut, known as Conch Creek, can also be used to reach the main channel. The stream has two mouths opening onto the ICW. However, the lower of the two, just east of the Sullivans Island Bridge, has only 4 feet of water near its entrance and is quite narrow. The branch near unlighted daybeacon #121 is far more reliable.

On the ICW   South of unlighted daybeacon #121 the waterway quickly begins its approach to the Sullivans Island swing bridge. The span has a closed vertical clearance of 31 feet. Craft that cannot clear this height must contend with restrictive opening times. The bridge will not open at all on Monday through Friday from 7 A.M.

to 9 A.M. and from 4 P.M. to 6 P.M. On Saturdays, Sundays, and legal holidays the span opens only on the hour and half hour from 2 P.M. to 6 P.M. At all other times it opens on demand.

Immediately after passing under the bridge you will observe Tomer's Cove Marina on the northern shore. This facility should be open by the summer of 1985.

Sullivans Island Channel The small channel leading to the Fort Moultrie National Park Service dock is found just to the south of flashing daybeacon #125. Hold to the mid-width and watch to starboard. The dock will soon come abeam.

Entrance to Charleston Harbor As you approach the entrance to Charleston Harbor, you will pass nun buoy #126 to the north of the waterway channel. This aid marks the ruins of an old bridge that once connected Mount Pleasant and Sullivans Island. Be on guard for this hazard at night.

After passing flashing daybeacon #127, the wide expanse of Charleston Harbor will open out dead ahead. Continued navigation of the ICW and the Charleston area is presented in the next chapter.

Charleston Battery

WINYAH BAY TO CHARLESTON 79

Avenue of Oaks, Boone Hall Plantation near Charleston

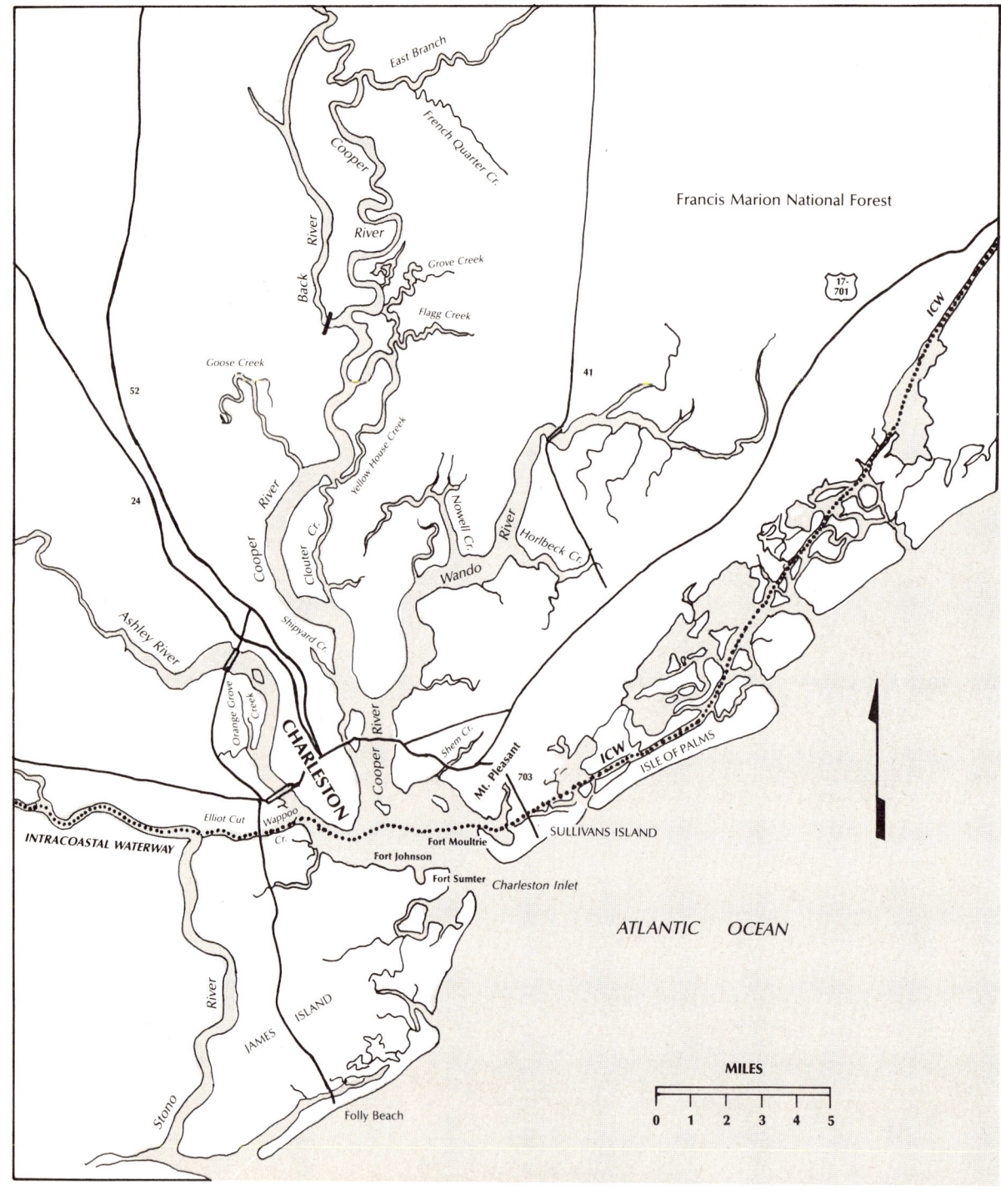

CHAPTER IV

Charleston

As you round the point from Sullivans Island, you will see the spires of Charleston to the north. Shimmering in the summer haze, the city often looks as if it has been plucked from the pages of an old novel. You can almost feel the romantic promise of exciting Old World opportunities. The cruising visitor need not fear disappointment. The reality of Charleston is even more fascinating than its promise.

Charleston is clearly "the" stop on the South Carolina ICW. Boaters who fail to make the acquaintance of Charleston will miss what is, quite simply, one of the most beautiful and exciting cities *in the world*. The city stands ready to greet you with a mind-boggling array of attractions. Beautiful old mansions that look as if they have stepped out of another era, countless fine restaurants, and a multitude of interesting shops and businesses are only a part of the town's attractions. There are movies to see that reveal much of the Charlestonian character, and native craftsmen and artists to be watched as they go about their traditional tasks. It would take months to appreciate all of the city's attractions fully, but fortunately, many can be enjoyed in the space of a few days.

In the following pages we will explore the often vague, sometimes fleeting, but always exciting qualities that make Charleston a city apart from all the rest. You may confidently use this information as a base of reference for your visit. However, various publications recommended in the following sections can arm you with additional knowledge of the city. The fortunate cruising visitor who makes Charleston a port of call would do well to acquire all the information that he can before embarking on his journey through this timeless city.

Charts You will need several charts for complete coverage of the Charleston area:
11518 follows the waterway across Charleston Harbor and into Wappoo Creek.
11523 covers the Charleston Inlet and outer harbor.
11524 is the principal Charleston Harbor Chart, covering the lower sections of the Cooper, Wando, and Ashley rivers. This is the single most important chart in the Charleston area.
11527 provides navigational information for upper Cooper River including the "Tee."
11526 details the upper Wando River. Unless you gain access through the usually closed highway bridge, this chart will not be needed.

Charleston

Native Charlestonians will tell you that the Ashley, Cooper, and Wando rivers flow down their respective channels to form first Charleston harbor and then the Atlantic Ocean. While this may be somewhat at variance with accepted geographic theory, it clearly shows what a high regard this city has for its waters. Indeed, until very recent times, Charleston's waterways were its highways of commerce.

Today, two full-service marinas serve the Charleston area. Both are located on the Ashley River and both gladly accept transients. The Charleston historical district is within walking distance, but it is a fairly long hike. In order to see as much of the city as possible within a fairly short period of time, it may be necessary to arrange for an auto rental. Call any of the major dealers at the Charleston Airport for further information or to arrange for dockside delivery. Taxis are another possibility for transportation. This writer was impressed by the unusually prompt and courteous service of Charleston cabbies.

The George M. Lockwood Municipal Marina is located on the eastern bank of the Ashley near can buoy #5. The facility is enclosed by a large concrete breakwater. The southerly portion of the harbor comprises the marina, while the Charleston Yacht Club occupies the northerly section.

The marina welcomes transients, though the nightly traffic during the spring and fall is sometimes too much for the facility to handle. This can lead to considerable "rafting-up" in order to accommodate everyone. Slips feature all power and water connections, and both gasoline and diesel fuel can be purchased. Low tide dockside depths are a commendable 20 feet, so even long-legged craft should not have any problem. Some mechanical repairs can be arranged, and there is an on-site restaurant and small grocery store. A boat lift within the walls of the marina facilitates below-the-waterline repairs. A nearby, well-stocked ships' store and a marine electronics dealer add to the marina's offerings.

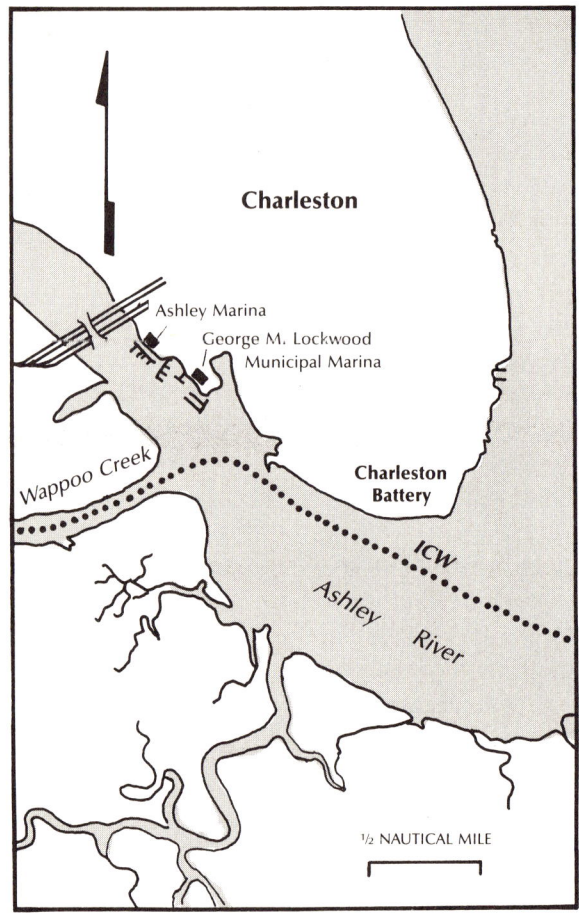

The Ashley's tidal range will astound the non-resident boater. Take care when mooring to fixed pilings and piers. While the municipal marina has some floating piers, most are of conventional design.

As might be expected, the marina's staff is very accommodating to passing cruisers and strives to do all in its power to make overnight guests as comfortable as possible. This writer has talked to many satisfied boaters who have stopped here for a night, a few days, or even a week. However, because the facility is so popular, it would be an excellent idea to make reservations ahead of time.

Ashley Marina is located just to the north of the municipal facility. This ultramodern marina offers numerous transient berths on floating docks. The floating piers are a considerable advantage on the Ashley, with its substantial tidal range. All power and water connections are readily available, as is diesel fuel. The marina can usually handle almost any mechanical repair problem. A host of restaurants, grocery stores, and other shoreside businesses are within walking distance, though rather a long walk. The marina can also help you with car rental.

Ashley Marina is quickly becoming one of the most popular stops on the South Carolina ICW. The facility's management is eager to greet the transient boater. Couple this warm welcome with the marina's impressive facilities, and Ashley Marina can be highly recommended.

For those who have seen one wave too many and want to escape for a while, Charleston offers a wide assortment of inns and hotels. Some of the finest are located in historic homes. The fortunate visitor who stays at one of these romantic establishments for a night or two cannot help moving closer to an understanding of the city.

The Heart of Charleston

"Charleston isn't a city. Charleston is a way of life." I reflected on the truth of this singular statement by tour guide Kenney Mallard as my mate and I enjoyed the Charleston Battery by horse-drawn carriage one cool spring after-

St. Philip's Episcopal Church

noon. Long rows of lovely mansions slipped dreamily by, followed by a breathtaking view of the harbor. As the cool sea breeze hit my face, I thought, "The more one knows Charleston, the more one comes to understand what a unique city it really is." Indeed, without an understanding of that very special character that makes Charleston what it is, you cannot fully enjoy your visit as you should.

Charleston has had many titles since it first began as a struggling colony on the banks of

Town Creek in 1670. These designations are at least a partial key to understanding the city's character. Charleston has often been called a living museum. While America's past has been recreated in such places as Williamsburg, Virginia, and Sturbridge Village, Massachusetts, these centers are monuments to our heritage. In Charleston, local citizens live and work every day in the city's historic homes and buildings. You might say they are actually living in the framework of the past, not just remembering times that are now far removed. This unique condition seems to impart a very special quality to Charleston. It is almost as though the past were somehow a closer and more tangible entity.

Charleston is also called the Holy City. This title refers to the many steeples that dot the skyline. Certainly Charleston has always been a very religious community, usually in the very best sense. The roots of religious tolerance stretch far back into the colonial era.

It takes far more than titles, however, to understand the very special community that is Charleston. In his book *Charleston in the Age of the Pinckneys*, George C. Rogers, Jr., lays bare the soul of the city in a clear, concise, and very readable manner. While, to be sure, there are many other works that detail more of Charleston's history, there is perhaps no other that offers such penetrating insight into the background of the city's unique character.

Mr. Rogers divides the social history of Charleston into two eras. The first he terms the "Open City." This period lasted from colonial days until the 1800s. During this time Charleston acted as a giant sponge, soaking up education, culture, and science from all over the world. The port's vast waterborne commerce made contact with other American and European cultures an everyday occurrence. Charlestonians picked from the very best of these influences and founded a social order that was admired throughout the western world. Education flourished and intellectual societies were established. There was no rigid social order. Men of ability were often admitted to the highest echelons of society, even if they were not of noble birth. It was an exciting time to live and work in Charleston. Men and women strove for betterment and often achieved their goals. Who among us does not have at least a little envy for those fortunate enough to have lived in those golden days?

The second era, which Mr. Rogers terms the "Closed City," began in the early 1800s. It was during this period that large sums of money began to be concentrated into the hands of wealthy, slave-owning planters. A rigid planter aristocracy soon developed, and the Charlestonian way of life began to change. No longer was it open to the influences of the outside world. The planters believed they had found the perfect existence. The lower classes were there to toil, and the aristocracy was there to reap the benefits. This way of life was to be jealously guarded and the traditions of the past were to be preserved at all cost. Those who argued for change were the enemy. It was this attitude, coupled with economic friction, that led to the Civil War.

Yet for all its closemindedness and social injustice, this period produced much that was glamorous and romantic. Many of the tales and beautiful homes that so enthrall us today

CHARLESTON 85

have their roots in the planter society. Indeed, you cannot understand Charleston if you do not appreciate the vague but ever-present sorrow that permeates the city, a sorrow for that gracious way of life that is lost forever.

In the final pages of his book, Mr. Rogers tells of a young woman's travels back to her native Charleston following the end of the War Between the States. This touching passage can perhaps do more than any other account to put the reader in touch with that very special, bittersweet quality that will forever be the heart of Charleston.

". . . 'Scarcely a farm house, not an elegant and hospitable plantation residence on the way, all ruin, ruin . . . I journeyed with a coffin where was laid my love and earthly hope, and came home.' What she saw was a city devastated, her home plundered of all books, private papers, pictures, her church's cemetery filled with the debris and overgrowth of four years of war and neglect. Yet many flow-

Basket lady at Boone Hall Plantation

ers bloomed amid the ruins. And so she sighed: 'I could not help thinking yesterday, as I saw the flowers look up and smile when the superincumbent weight and decay and ruin were removed, that they set us a good example politically. But then, flowers have no memory.'"

Charleston History In 1663, all of what was to become North and South Carolina was granted by King Charles II to eight "Lords Proprietors." These eight men were friends of the king who had helped him regain power following the death of Oliver Cromwell. Though in later times the colony was to come under royal authority, the early years, for good or ill, were presided over by the Proprietors.

In 1669, three ships set sail from England to found a colony in the new land of Carolina. The expedition made landfall at Port Royal Sound, but on the advice of the Cacique of Kiawah, the expedition removed to the banks of the Ashley River to the north. Here on the shores of Town Creek they founded Charles Towne, named by the colonists in honor of their king.

Around 1680 the small settlement was removed to Oyster Point, located on the neck of

Interior of French Huguenot Church

land separating the Ashley and Cooper rivers. The site was deemed to be (and still is) ideally situated for waterborne commerce. Plans were carefully laid out for streets and lots before the move took place, making Charles Towne the first planned community in America.

In 1680 the young colony got a boost with the arrival of a number of French Huguenots or Protestants. Fleeing religious persecution in their homeland, these first immigrants presaged many others who would brave the wave-tossed Atlantic to take advantage of South Carolina's religious tolerance. Eventually the colony was to be influenced by Dutch and German immigrants as well, though the French influence was certainly the strongest of the lot. This melting-pot atmosphere is often credited for Charleston's resiliency and worldliness.

A strong Spanish-French fleet threatened the small colony in 1698, but the intruders were soundly defeated, both by land and by sea. This event is typical of the courage and bravado that Charlestonians have always exemplified in times of military threat.

By 1730 Charles Towne had become an important, bustling port. Tragically, in 1740, the town was the victim of a great fire that burned many of the city's houses. Over the course of its history, Charleston has suffered many major fires, several violent hurricanes, and even a strong earthquake. As George C. Rogers so aptly comments, "It is a wonder that Charleston still looks like an eighteenth-century city."

As the Revolution approached, Charles Towne took a decidedly patriot point of view. The news of the battles of Lexington and Concord was greeted by a parade of South Carolina militia as well as a resolve by the assembly to raise three regiments and prepare the colony for war. Charlestonians did not have long to wait. In the battle already described, the British were soundly repulsed at Fort Moultrie. The English returned, however, in 1780, and after a brief siege captured the city. The fall of Charleston was to rank along with the loss of New York as the worst American defeat of the war.

The main English army was defeated by Washington at Yorktown in 1781, but it was not until December of 1782 that Charleston was evacuated by the British, thus effectively bringing the war to an end.

Following the close of the war, the Charles Towne council changed the name of the city to Charleston. It seems that the local citizens no longer relished the idea of their fair town bearing the name of an English sovereign.

The years between the Revolution and the Civil War were mostly prosperous. Both the developing rice culture to the north and the rise of Sea Island cotton to the south aided Charleston's economy. Vast quantities of goods left the city's wharves bound for European and Northern ports. Rich planters built many residences in the city. It was quite fashionable to have a "city house" in addition to one's plantation lodgings. During this period many of the small creeks and ponds on the Charleston peninsula were filled in to make room for further development. Several modern-day streets are located atop the one-time passage of these small streams.

South Carolina continued to be highly agricultural as did most of the southern states.

When the economic interests of the agrarian South conflicted with those of the industrialized North, confrontation became inevitable. In a fight with the federal government over tariff laws, South Carolina's great statesman, John C. Calhoun, argued for the doctrine of nullification, an affirmation of a state's right to reject federal laws with which they could not agree.

Finally, of course, this war of words turned into a military conflict, which began within sight of Charleston. The story of Fort Sumter will be told later in this chapter; for now it is sufficient to note that the Civil War's first major conflict occurred between state forces at Fort Johnston on James Island and federal troops occupying Fort Sumter.

Though Beaufort, to the south, fell to Northern forces early in the war, it was not until February of 1865 that Union troops occupied Charleston, and then only after the Confederate army evacuated the city. South Carolina Confederates fought valiantly throughout the war, time and again denying the passages to Charleston to vastly superior Union forces.

Though Charleston suffered some damage from bombardment, it was not grievously decimated by the war as were many other South Carolina cities. There has been much speculation about why Sherman, the usually cold-blooded Union commander, did not put the torch to Charleston as he had to other proud cities. We know that he had visited Charleston before the war and admired the community. Some claim that he spared the city simply because he liked it, while others have argued that he had promised friends in the North that he would preserve the town. Another theory claims that he did not act because the war was nearly over. Whatever the reason, Charleston survived the war better than any other major city in South Carolina.

The years following the Civil War were hard ones for Charleston. It was not until World War II that Charleston began to prosper again. This long depression has proven to be a hidden boon for the city. While other communities were busy tearing down their historic buildings and widening their streets, Charleston was forced by lack of capital to make do with what it had. In the 1950s and 1960s Charlestonians awoke to the unique opportunity afforded by a city that still retained its historic character. Renovation projects began on a wide scale, and they continue to this day. While some areas are still not fully renovated, vast sections of the historical district have been restored to their former glory. How fortunate we are that times were too hard in Charleston for "modern improvements" following the War Between the States.

Many visitors to Charleston will want to read more detailed accounts of the city's fascinating history. Inspiring tales and colorful figures season the story of Charleston like grains of salt. Several very readable accounts of the city's heritage are readily available. This writer's personal favorite is *A Short History of Charleston* by Robert Rosen.

As you tour Charleston, pause often in your travels to reflect on the history of this great city. There are few places in America that can lay claim to such a treasure trove of tradition and heritage as can Charleston. Listen carefully and perhaps you can still hear faint music from the old Dock Street Theater, or the powerful voice of John Calhoun arguing forcibly for his state's rights. For those who seek with a knowledgeable interest, Charleston never fails in her reward.

Charleston Attractions

Charleston boasts a wide array of attractions waiting to fascinate the cruising visitor. Some of this writer's favorites will be reviewed in the following pages. For a complete listing of the city's many sights, however, you will need to purchase one of the many fine Charleston guide books. My favorite is *The Great Charleston Catalogue,* published by Lentz Enterprises. This excellent publication helps the visitor sort out the city's bewildering selection of tourist attractions.

First-time visitors should begin their tour at the Charleston Visitors Center, located at 85 Calhoun Street. Here you will see a remarkable multi-screen slide show. The presentation not only helps to put you in touch with the spirit of Charleston, but also serves as an excellent introduction to the city's sights and attractions. The center is too far away from the area marinas for walking. You will need a rental car or taxi for a visit.

The Old Market is definitely one of Charleston's premier attractions. It is enclosed by North and South Market streets and, to the west and east, Meeting and East Bay streets. You will often hear the area referred to as the "old slave market," which is a misnomer, as slaves were never sold here. The land was given to the city by the Pinckney family with the stipulation that it must always be used as a marketplace. In earlier days the market was employed as a giant farmer's fair. Over the years it has evolved into a huge craft show, though fresh vegetables can still be bought in season.

The visitor who strolls through the market on any day, but particularly on Saturdays, will find a wide array of handcrafts ranging from traditional dolls to baskets. These baskets are woven from native sweet grass by the black women of the city. Their art has been passed

Sidewalk art show, Charleston

down through the generations, reaching far back into the slave era.

A large collection of gift shops and restaurants are found around the market. Here you can dine at some of the city's finest eateries or select from many gifts and handicrafts. The market is certainly one of the best spots for shopping and dining in the city.

Several horse-drawn carriage lines depart regularly from the Old Market for tours of the city's historical district. This writer highly recommends these interesting excursions. The witty and knowledgeable tour guides will give you a thorough, often humorous insight into Charleston's past.

St. Philip's Episcopal Church is the oldest congregation in the city. The present church stands near the intersection of Church Street and Queen Street. The first building on this site was occupied sometime between 1710 and 1724. This structure burned and was replaced by the present building in 1835. The tall, gray stone steeple is a striking sight at night, when it is lit with a series of soft lights. The old sentinel seems to be a warm friend overlooking the city.

St. Philip's cemetery is bisected by Church Street. According to tradition, only native-born Charlestonians can be buried in the section adjacent to the church. Those born elsewhere, no matter how famous, are interred across the street. John C. Calhoun, perhaps South Carolina's greatest statesman, was laid to rest at St. Philip's in 1850. Though he was universally beloved in Charleston, Calhoun had been born in Columbia. Thus he was buried in the western portion of the cemetery.

As the Civil War entered its last dark days, patriotic citizens feared the desecration of Calhoun's grave by Union troops. One night they stealthily moved his coffin to an unmarked grave next to the church. Some years later, Calhoun's remains were returned to their original resting place, where his gravestone may still be seen today. One of our tour guides commented that not only was John Calhoun the state's greatest political figure in life, he was one of the most traveled in death.

St. Michael's Church is located at the corner of Broad and Meeting streets. It was built on the original site of St. Philip's in 1751, when for some reason now lost in the mists of the past, the congregation split into two church bodies. St. Michael's is a beautiful white building with a tall, stately spire and mellow bells that toll the time of day.

Before the Civil War Charleston was constantly plagued by fires. The inefficient means used to fight the frequent blazes greatly contributed to the problem. Until well after the war there were a dozen or more private fire fighting companies in the city. If you wished to be protected, it was necessary to purchase a badge from one of the companies and affix it to your building or home. During the night a constant watch was kept for fires from the steeple of St. Michael's. If flames were sighted, the alarm was given, and *all* the companies turned out. They were guided to the blaze by swinging lanterns from the steeple. When they at last arrived, the company whose badge was in evidence fought the fire while everyone else went home.

Located at 21 East Battery Street, the Edmondston-Alston House is one of the few homes in the city open to the public. This proud structure is perhaps the best example of an affluent planter's Charlestonian home. Dating from 1835, it was acquired soon after it was built by one of the illustrious Alstons, a family of wealthy Waccamaw rice planters.

Guided tours of this striking house are conducted throughout the day by the Historic Charleston Foundation. Be sure to visit the second floor balcony and take in the magnificent view of the harbor. Those lucky enough to catch a sea breeze there will begin to appreciate what a wonderful experience it was (and still is) to live on the Charleston Battery.

The extreme southern tip of the Charleston peninsula is known as the High Battery. In Charleston's early years the point was a little-used saltwater marsh. Beginning in 1737, the first in a series of forts and batteries was constructed on the point. These military fortifications were to be built and rebuilt throughout

Carriage tour passing in front of Edmondston-Alston House

A Portion of Historic Charleston

1. Visitor Information Center
2. The Old Market
3. St. Philip's Episcopal Church
4. St. Michael's Church
5. The Nathaniel Russell house
6. Calhoun Mansion
7. Heyward-Washington House (1730)
8. Edmondston-Alston House
9. White Point Gardens
10. The Battery Carriage House
11. Two Meeting Street Inn

the city's successive conflicts until the end of the Civil War. The area's name is derived from the one-time presence of these batteries.

In 1820 a stone seawall was completed along the point's shoreline. The new wall replaced several earlier brick structures, which had been decimated by a series of strong hurricanes. Extensive repairs were necessary following a severe storm in 1893, but otherwise the wall has lasted to the present day.

In 1837 a park, now known as White Point Gardens, was established between South Battery Street and the point. It was from this vantage point that many Charlestonians flocked in 1861 to watch the fateful battle for Fort Sumter. Since that time the park has never again been put to military use. It is now the site of numerous war memorials.

After the Battery was walled, some of the state's most affluent citizens began building large mansions just north of the park. This location was highly prized for the cooling sea breezes that blew across the harbor. Over the years some of the most beautiful homes in the city have been built here. Most have been in the same family for many generations and are in excellent condition. Stroll along South Battery Street at your leisure and admire these graceful, luxurious old homes.

The park itself contains an old bandstand, where open-air concerts are still held from time to time. There is an excellent view of the harbor from the shade of the grounds, and you will find many historical memorials to ponder. Truly, the visitor who has not seen the High Battery and White Point Gardens has not really seen Charleston.

One of the best ways to see the Charleston historical district is by foot, even if you have been lucky enough to obtain a rental car. I advise first taking one of the carriage tours described earlier to get your bearings. Once you are oriented, however, feel free to strike out on your own. There are many, many possible walking tours. This writer's favorite route is detailed below.

Begin your tour at the intersection of Church Street and the Old Market. Walk south on Church. You will soon encounter St. Phillip's Church and its interesting cemetery. Continue along Church as far as Broad Street. In Charleston's earlier years many lawyers, doctors, and other professionals kept their offices on Broad.

Turn right on Broad and walk to Meeting Street. Here you can stop to admire the cool serenity of St. Michael's Church. Then turn left on Meeting and continue in this direction for several blocks. The Nathaniel Russell House and the Calhoun Mansion, both open to the public, are found along this section of Meeting Street.

Retrace your steps towards St. Michael's and turn right on Tradd Street. This street was named for the first male child born in the Charles Towne colony and is lined by some of the oldest surviving homes in the city.

Turn left where Tradd intersects Church Street. Here you can visit the Heyward-Washington House. Built in 1730, the old edifice was the home of Thomas Heyward, a signer of the Declaration of Independence. George Washington was entertained here during his tour of the Southern states following the Revolution.

Note the twin circular entrance staircases in

this house. They are known as "welcoming-arms stairs." Tradition claims that the genteel ladies of the Old South would ascend one side while their gentlemen companions climbed the other. This way, the ladies' ankles would not show.

Go back to Tradd Street and continue east to East Bay Street. Turn right and you will soon approach the Battery. The Edmonston-Alston house is found to the right of the street. Pause in your tour for a few moments to stroll along the parapet of the Battery seawall. There is usually an excellent view of the harbor and Castle Pinckney. On a clear day you can also see Fort Sumter.

Continue your tour by turning right up South Battery Street. Here you can see many of the magnificent mansions mentioned earlier. There are also two inns along this street. Both The Battery Carriage House and Two Meeting Street Inn are housed in historic homes and afford an unforgettable experience for those fortunate enough to lodge there for a night or two.

Turn right on Meeting Street and retrace your steps to the Old Market. Now you have seen some of Charleston's history and you are just in time for a cold drink at one of the market's many restaurants.

View from balcony of Edmondston-Alston House

Charleston Restaurants

Charleston boasts a multitude of fine restaurants with a wide array of cuisine. Everything from the most sophisticated continental offerings to fresh fried and broiled seafood is readily available. It would take weeks to sample all of Charleston's gastronomical delights. *The Great Charleston Catalogue,* mentioned earlier, gives excellent dining advice, as do most of the other fine Charleston guide books.

There is only time to mention a few of this writer's favorite establishments, and you should feel encouraged to experiment. Charleston is one of those magical places where a turn around a dark corner can lead the visitor to an obscure little eatery just waiting for someone to discover its charms.

82 Queen Street is a restaurant named for its address. If one were to attempt (a foolhardy gesture) to compile a list of Charleston's "best" eateries, this unique dining spot would certainly be somewhere near the top of the list. Veal, chicken, beef, and the freshest of seafood are all prepared in inimitable fashion by the master chefs of 82 Queen.

Another secret of the establishment's popularity is its lovely decor. The restaurant is actually laid out in a series of glass-enclosed buildings overlooking a central garden. In nice weather the outdoor tables are at a premium.

To say the least, 82 Queen is a very popular spot for both locals and tourists. Reservations are almost mandatory. For weekend meals it is often necessary to call several days in advance to secure your desired seating time.

For those with a taste for duck prepared in the marvelous Low Country fashion, the Cotton Exchange, bordering on the Old Market, is sure to please. Excellent beef, chicken, veal, and seafood dishes are also offered. In addition, the Cotton Exchange features one of the finest selections of French wines this writer has ever enjoyed. Service is deft and pleasant here, making one feel more like royalty than just a simple tourist. For those who prefer a before-dinner drink and appetizer, a first-rate raw bar is joined directly to the restaurant. The Cotton Exchange exudes the atmosphere of a restaurant that does everything in its power to please. They succeed most admirably. The secret has long been out, so make your reservations early.

After a while, cruising travelers may just want a break from the fresh seafood regimen. No matter how fresh or tasty the fish, the palate can begin to crave a change of pace. If this description fits, Garibaldi's, across the Old Market from the Cotton Exchange, is for you. I have been privileged to partake of some of the finest Italian cuisine available in America, but I have never found any better than the succulent offerings of Garibaldi's. The Veal Parmigiana is particularly noteworthy. Make your reservations well ahead of time and groom your palate for a real treat.

Cafe 99 is located just up South Market Street from Garibaldi's and is housed in a remodeled warehouse. In a region noted for its fried seafood, Cafe 99 is one of the few eateries to specialize in broiled catch of the day. There were those who scoffed at the future of a restaurant offering only broiled dishes deep in the southern-fried heartland. The critics have long since been silenced, except perhaps in their enthusiastic praise. I was delighted by fresh brook trout stuffed with apple-flavored crabmeat, while my mate was equally taken with grouper baked in paper.

Cafe 99 usually offers live entertainment and exacts a cover charge after 9 P.M. Call ahead for dinner reservations, though the crowds are not usually quite as thick here as in the aforementioned eateries.

During our second carriage tour of Charleston, one of our guides made the unusual observation that Charleston chefs were surely bound for heaven. When queried about this bold claim, the tour guide responded that once the Almighty got a taste of Charleston cooking, nothing else would do. After enjoying a number of the city's restaurants, you may not find this statement very difficult to believe.

Charleston Harbor

Charleston Harbor often reminds this writer of author Mike Greenwald's description of the Mediterranean—it is like "the girl with green eyes. There is often a surprise behind her smile." Indeed, on a day of light breezes, if the current is contrary, the harbor can still bear a wicked chop. On the other hand, the sightseeing opportunities are many and varied. Charleston Harbor boasts several historic sites of great interest. It is a true thrill to see Fort Sumter and the aircraft carrier *Yorktown* from the water. The cruising boater has the opportunity to view these monuments from a perspective that is denied to the landlubber.

Be sure to study chart 11524 carefully *before* attempting entry of the harbor, and have the map close at hand while cruising. The harbor is crisscrossed by a bewildering maze of buoys and other aids marking a variety of channels. These varied markers and channels can be very confusing to boaters not familiar with the harbor. Nighttime passage is particularly wrought with peril.

To make matters worse, Charleston Harbor has extensive shoal areas. While all of these are well marked, you must be readily able to interpret the buoys if you are to stay off the bottom. To say the least, the cruising boater must take navigation seriously in this area or a very unpleasant grounding could be the result.

There are very few facilities for the pleasure boater on the harbor itself. Shem Creek, found in the extreme northeasterly corner of the water body, does offer a few services. Otherwise you are on your own while cruising Charleston Harbor.

Similarly, there are no opportunities for protected anchorage in Charleston Harbor. If you choose not to proceed on to the area marinas, select an anchorage to the north and enter the harbor the next morning.

Unlike the off-the-beaten-path spots discussed earlier, Charleston Harbor hosts many pleasure boaters, who take advantage of its cruising opportunities in great numbers. You are likely to find yourself among several fellow boaters on your cruise. Join them in a most pleasurable experience.

Charleston Inlet

The Charleston Inlet is the most reliable seaward cut on the entire South Carolina coast. It is deep and very well marked. The channel has served the port of Charleston reliably since its earliest years. Today many large freighters, tankers, and naval craft use the inlet on a regular basis. If you plan to put to sea anywhere along this section of the coastline, Charleston Inlet is your best bet.

Shem Creek

Shem Creek is located in the extreme northeasterly corner of Charleston Harbor. It is a lovely stream with many interesting sights and several dining opportunities. One marina on the creek offers limited services to cruising boaters.

The Mount Pleasant Channel, which leads from the ICW to the mouth of Shem Creek, holds minimum depths of 9 feet. Careful navigation must be practiced in this cut. On the creek itself, depths are more than adequate for all cruising craft. Upstream passage is eventually blocked by a low-level fixed bridge.

Once on the stream's interior you will be delighted with the many picturesque shrimp trawlers docked along the banks. The largest number of commercial fishermen in the area make their homes on Shem Creek. Have your camera ready for some shots with true Low Country flavor.

About halfway between the creek's mouth and the bridge, Darby Marine Supply will come abeam on the starboard shore. Darby offers extensive mechanical and below-the-waterline repairs, but no overnight dockage except for those craft undergoing service.

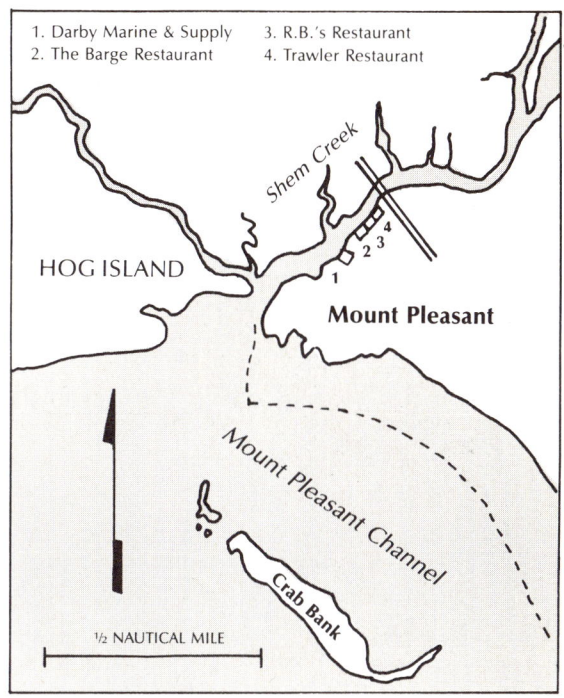

Both gasoline and diesel fuel are available.

Just upstream from Darby, three seafood restaurants will come abeam, one after another, on the starboard shore. The first two have outdoor decks overlooking the creek, and the middle establishment, RB's, offers dockage for its patrons. While the restaurant's piers are not extensive, there should be room for two 30-footers to squeeze in together.

RB's has a widespread reputation for serving the finest in fresh seafood. It is a warm, informal, and convivial establishment with a nautical bar where you can wait for your table on crowded evenings. Consider the crab spread for an appetizer. This writer also recommends the jumbo deep-fried shrimp stuffed with crabmeat as an entrée. All in all, a visit to RB's is sure to be remembered as a gastronomical delight.

Just to the south of RB's, the Barge Restaurant also offers fresh fried and steamed seafood, as does the Trawler to the north. Both eateries enjoy a good reputation, but neither has the convenience of waterside dockage.

While many tourists have come to know and love the Shem Creek restaurants, the stream seems to be consistently overlooked by visiting cruisers. This writer highly recommends that the reader take advantage of this tasty body of water.

Mount Pleasant

As you are following the channel to Shem Creek, you will see many beautiful homes on the eastern shore. These lovely showplaces are part of the old community of Mount Pleasant. Originally the village consisted of five separate communities that were established in the 1700s. Two were built around ferries that provided passage across Shem Creek, while another sprang up around a water-powered rice and lumbermill. Following the Revolution all these separate settlements were combined into the single community of Mount Pleasant.

Dining dockside at RB's Restaurant, Shem Creek

Fort Moultrie

Our previous chapter told the story of the courageous battle at Fort Moultrie during the opening months of the Revolution. There is an excellent view of that old fort from Charleston Harbor. The fortification was much altered during the Civil War, and today's visitor will gaze on masonry walls rather than the palmetto logs that stood so bravely against British fire. You will catch sight of the walls just east of nun buoy #2 on the western banks of Sullivans Island. It is possible to cruise to within some 50 yards of shore and still hold 7-foot depths. Feel your way in carefully.

Fort Sumter

To the west of flashing buoy #25, Fort Sumter, one of the great historical sites of Charleston Harbor, is readily visible.

In 1829 the federal government began to stabilize the shoal west of Fort Moultrie. Here they constructed Fort Sumter, which was named after Revolutionary general Thomas Sumter. In 1860, although the work was not yet complete, the small Union garrison of less than a hundred men at Fort Moultrie was transferred to Fort Sumter by command of Major Robert Anderson. Feeling that conflict with Southern forces was inevitable, he believed the newer fort was more defensible.

As the garrison left Fort Moultrie, they spiked the cannons. The state's governor, Andrew Pickens, considered this a hostile act. State troops were mobilized, and shoreside batteries bearing upon Sumter were quickly constructed. Following a failed conference in Washington, D. C., General Beauregard,

Fort Sumter, Charleston Harbor

commanding the South Carolina forces, called upon Anderson to surrender. He refused, and a thirty-hour assault on Sumter began on April 12, 1861. Eventually, Anderson was forced to surrender, and the first major battle of the Civil War was over.

Fort Sumter was quickly manned by the Confederates. From 1863 to 1865 the fort was under almost constant Union bombardment. Yet as late as 1863, a Union amphibious assault was beaten off with heavy Northern losses. The South Carolina Sea Grant Consortium notes that the fierce resistance of Fort Sumter became a "symbol of courage for the South." The fort was finally abandoned in 1865, when Federal troops occupied the area from the rear.

Today the cruising visitor can easily view this monument, which has been carefully preserved as a memorial to the brave men who fought so long against such overwhelming odds. While the inner fortifications have been carefully restored, the outer walls are mostly original. Cruise to flashing buoy #25 and work your way slowly to the west. Be on guard against the shallow water to the north and south.

There is a small floating dock on the north-

Home at Mount Pleasant

CHARLESTON 101

eastern corner of the fort where pleasure craft are welcome to tie. Tour boats also leave Charleston Municipal Marina on a regular basis. They are well worth your time.

Fort Johnson

Prior to the construction of Fort Sumter, Fort Johnson, located on the northern shore of James Island, was a strategically important site in the defense of Charleston Harbor. Today a group of modern buildings marks the spot, about 1 nautical mile west of flashing buoy #26, where the fort once stood.

Fortifications were first constructed here during Queen Anne's War. A brick powder magazine, which still survives, was built in 1766. In 1775 South Carolina patriot forces seized the fort and feverishly began to prepare its defenses for the assault that eventually fell on Fort Moultrie.

The fort was refurbished during the War of 1812 but was decimated by a severe hurricane in 1813. In 1861, batteries at Fort Johnson joined in the attack on Sumter. The fort was finally abandoned in 1865, when federal troops occupied Charleston and the harbor.

It is a strange twist of fate that an area which has seen so much hostility is today being put

Fort Johnson, Charleston Harbor

to such important peaceful uses. Housed in the buildings that today occupy the site are many agencies engaged in maritime and marine research studies. Included in the Fort Johnson offices and laboratories are the College of Charleston, the National Marine Fisheries Service, the U. S. Fish and Wildlife Service, the South Carolina Wildlife and Marine Resources Department, the Medical University of South Carolina, and this writer's good friends at the South Carolina Sea Grant Consortium. There is no provision for dockage at the center for pleasure craft. However, if you can obtain the use of a rental car, a visit would be well worth your while.

Morris Island Lighthouse

Look to the southeast from Fort Johnson and you will spy the Morris Island Lighthouse. The island has been used to light the harbor entrance since 1673. In 1767, a 102-foot brick tower, one of the first in the country, was built near the present site. This light was severely damaged by the fierce fighting that took place on Morris Island around Fort Wagner during the Civil War. It was replaced in 1876 by the

Marshlands Plantation, Charleston Harbor

present tower. With the construction of the Sullivans Island Lighthouse in 1962, the Morris Island light fell into disuse. Since that time it has been used as a daymark.

Marshlands Plantation

Marshlands Plantation can be seen through the trees just west of the Fort Johnson complex. Built in 1810 by John Ball, this elegant house was originally located on the shores of Cooper River. Because that land was eventually acquired by the United States Navy, the old home was moved by barge to its present location in 1961.

Castle Pinckney

Castle Pinckney is located on the southern tip of Shutes Folly Island near unlighted daybeacon #36. This small fort served as an inner defense for Charleston Harbor, but as far as this writer has been able to determine, it never fired a shot in anger. Built in 1798, it was renovated in 1800 and again in 1808.

The small fortification was named in honor of Charles Cotesworth Pinckney, one of South Carolina's greatest statesmen, following the Revolution.

After the seizure of Fort Sumter, the Union troops taken prisoner were transferred to Castle Pinckney, where they were imprisoned until the end of the war. High tides forced the miserable prisoners to stand in water up to their waists.

Surprisingly, Shutes Folly Island was planted in orange trees during the early 1700s. Over the years, erosion has taken a heavy toll on the small island, and there is no evidence left of the once-luscious orchards.

Patriots Point

East of flashing buoy #10, Patriots Point boasts the "Largest Maritime Museum in the World." The huge exhibit includes the aircraft carrier *Yorktown* and the USS *Savannah*, the world's first nuclear-powered merchant ship. Several other naval vessels are also exhibited,

Castle Pinckney, Charleston Harbor

including the *Clamagore,* one of the last oil-powered submarines to serve in the United States Navy. Surprisingly, there is also an eighteen-hole golf course as part of the complex, and there are plans to build a marina for pleasure craft.

Currently, it is best to view the exhibit from the main channel of Hog Island Reach. While chart 11524 shows an unmarked channel leading in to the ships, it is too treacherous for visiting cruisers.

The *Yorktown* is the most visible of the ships. It sits broadside to the channel. The large white ship docked perpendicular to the river is the *Savannah.* You will need a rental car or a taxi for a tour of the facility by land. If you have the time, this is an attraction that should not be missed.

Charleston Harbor Navigation

Successful navigation of Charleston Harbor for nonresident boaters is a far more exacting process than one might expect. To be sure, there are many deep, well-marked channels that are used on a regular basis by large commercial and naval craft. However, the multiplicity of channels and markers can readily lead to confusion.

Shrimp trawlers on Shem Creek

CHARLESTON

Charleston Harbor is also cursed with many shoals that can bring the unwary boater to grief.

This writer has talked with a professional captain who entered Charleston Harbor at night from Sullivans Island and became immediately confused by the many lights. Even though he slowed to idle speed, a hard grounding was the eventual result of his consternation.

Nighttime entry into Charleston Harbor is strictly not recommended for nonresident boaters. Even in daylight, have chart 11524 at hand and keep a wary eye on the sounder. If you take your time and actively practice good navigation, a cruise of Charleston Harbor can be one of the most pleasurable experiences offered by South Carolina waters. Failure to take the proper precautions, however, can result in a dangerous grounding.

Entry From Sullivans Island All boaters entering Charleston from the ICW at Sullivans Island should pass flashing daybeacon #127 to its northerly side and flashing daybeacon #130 to its southern quarter. At #130 the Mount Pleasant Channel splits off to the north and leads to Shem Creek.

Mount Pleasant Channel The Mount Pleasant Channel is wide and well marked but is flanked by shoal water on both sides. To enter the cut, continue past flashing daybeacon #130 for some 100 yards, then swing 90 degrees to the north and point to pass between unlighted daybeacons #1 and #2. Continue on to the north by passing between unlighted daybeacons #3 and #4. From here to flashing daybeacon #8 all aids should be passed by some 25 yards to their westerly sides.

At #10 the channel begins to bend to the west. Pass unlighted daybeacons #10, #12, and #14 to their southerly sides. Set a course to come abeam of flashing daybeacon #16 to its southerly side. Continue on course for some 10 to 15 yards and then turn 90 degrees to starboard to enter the main body of the creek.

Into the Harbor From flashing daybeacon #130, boaters wishing to follow the ICW or enter the Cooper or Ashley River should set a compass course to the mid-width of the Rebellion Reach Channel south of flashing buoys #1 and #2. Be careful to avoid the shallows to the north around Crab Bank.

At Rebellion Reach the boater has several choices. A swing to the north will lead to the wide Cooper and Wando rivers. A turn to the south carries the boater to Ashley River, the Charleston Marinas, and the ICW route. The Charleston Inlet beckons to the southeast.

Entrance to Cooper River To cruise north into the Cooper River, follow the well-marked Rebellion, Folly, Shutes, and Horse Reach channels. Be careful to avoid the considerable area of shoal water that surrounds Shutes Folly Island to the west.

Charleston Inlet To enter the reliable Charleston Inlet, turn southeast from Rebellion Reach and follow the well-marked Mount Pleasant and Fort Sumter ranges to the open sea. Be on guard against the twin jetties flanking the inlet to the north and south past the tips of Sullivans and Morris islands.

There is a shortcut channel that breaks off to the south at unlighted can buoy #19. The cut runs through a break in the southern jetty marked by unlighted can buoy #1 and unlighted nun buoy #2. The channel skirts several shallow water areas and borders some breakers. This passage is not recommended for boaters without local knowledge.

Ashley River and ICW To enter the Ashley River and follow the ICW route, set course from Rebellion Reach to pass the unnumbered flashing buoy to the east of Castle Pinckney on its southerly side. Turn west up the South Channel cut. Along the way you will pass Fort Johnson and Marshlands Plantation south of your course.

Strike a course to bring you abeam of the red and black junction buoy southeast of the Charleston Battery to its southern side. Be on guard against the considerable area of shoal water that extends south from the Battery. Do not approach the seawall! A very unpleasant grounding will probably result from such a foolhardy maneuver.

Continue upstream on the Ashley via the well-marked river channel. Both Charleston marinas will come abeam on the eastern shore beyond unlighted nun buoy #4.

The waterway cuts south from Ashley River at unlighted nun buoy #2 and follows Wappoo Creek. Continued navigation of the ICW is presented in the next chapter.

Cooper River

The Cooper River offers Charleston's greatest variety of cruising opportunities. Everything from modern naval shipyards to historical buildings and industrial complexes is waiting to greet the Cooper River cruiser. The river also borders acres of abandoned rice fields along its upper reaches and affords another glimpse at the remnants of that old culture. If you have only enough time to cruise one of Charleston's rivers, the Cooper should be your choice.

For the most part, the Cooper is a navigational delight. The river is well marked as far inland as Bushy Park. Upstream, there are a few shoal areas to avoid, but careful attention to chart 11527 should see you through. The stream divides into two branches about a mile above the Dean Hall industrial site. This area, known as "the Tee," can lead the adventurous boater to some obscure, unspoiled cruising finds. Many abandoned rice fields border the channel in this section, but it is far easier to

CHARLESTON 107

pick out the correct passage than a cursory examination of chart 11527 would lead one to believe.

The Cooper's shoreline offers widely varied sightseeing. Completely undeveloped areas alternate with navy shipyards, Polaris submarine bases, and large industrial sites. Cruising the Cooper will never be a dull experience.

Good anchorage can be found on the upper Cooper, but there is almost no opportunity for an overnight stay until you are well upstream from the twin bridges. Surprisingly, there is not a single marina catering to the cruising boater anywhere on the river's length. Town Creek Boatyard is found on the lower Cooper's western shores, but the facility does not offer any dockage. However, the yard does provide below-the-waterline repairs. Arrangements for service at Town Creek Boatyard can usually be made through the Ashley Marina in Charleston.

All in all, Cooper River is an enchanting, readily navigable stream that is consistently overlooked by cruising boaters. This writer highly recommends that you make it a point to explore this fascinating body of water before pushing on to the south.

Cooper River History Settled early in the history of colonial South Carolina, the Cooper became the second richest rice growing region in the state before the Civil War. Only in the Georgetown area to the north was the growing of "Carolina Gold" a greater concern. Sadly, there is little evidence left today of this fabled way of life. Only a few plantations survived the turmoil of the war years, and none of these is visible from the water.

Freighter passing under Cooper River Bridge

Nevertheless, a cruise on the river, particularly on the Tee, is like journeying back into another era. It does not require too much imagination to see the old tidal flats heavy with rice heads, echoing with the sad singing of the slaves at their sweaty work. The Cooper River is part and parcel of the proud South Carolina Low Country tradition, and its place should not be forgotten.

Charleston Shipyard

As you cruise up the western entrance to Cooper River on Town Creek Reach, you will pass one of Charleston's major port facilities on the western shore. Here large freighters can usually be observed loading or unloading their cargo. Watch your wake and you are welcome to take a close inspection.

Shipyard Creek

Shipyard Creek is a deep stream found on the Cooper's western shore near flashing buoy #48. The creek is home to several large wharves and commercial repair facilities. There is no room for anchorage by pleasure craft, but a slow cruise of the stream is highly recommended. The many large commercial ships usually docked there make for a most interesting visit.

Clouter Creek

Clouter Creek is a long, unremarkable stream on the river's eastern shore. It snakes its way north for some 3 nautical miles and then rejoins the Cooper. The southerly entrance is found near unlighted buoy #50 and carries minimum depths of 6 feet in its unmarked channel. The creek's lower reaches border extensive saltwater marsh and are suitable for anchorage by craft over 35 feet in length. The cut is navigable all the way to its northern junction with Cooper River for craft that can stand some 5-foot readings. Most of the route is deeper, but there are a few shoal spots. A large naval barge facility is located on the starboard shore just before the stream rejoins the river. This section of the creek is too narrow for anchorage by all but small craft. The northerly intersection with the river carries 6-foot depths, but again you must follow an unmarked channel.

Clouter Creek should probably be avoided by larger pleasure craft. Its unmarked entrances and shoals can be hazardous. The creek's shoreline is far from attractive, and while anchorage is possible in the lower reaches, more desirable spots are found upstream.

Naval Base

Extensive naval wharves are located along the Cooper's western shores just above Clouter Creek. Here the visiting cruiser can see many naval craft of all types, ranging from destroyers to Polaris submarines. The docks extend intermittently up the river for several miles. Often one can catch sight of a ship leaving or returning to port, always an interesting operation to watch. Boaters have even seen submarines surfacing in the area. Be sure to take advantage of this unique opportunity to see our naval forces at such close quarters.

The land on which the naval base now sits was once a part of Belmont Plantation, owned by the illustrious Charles Cotesworth Pinckney, chief justice of the state. Justice Pinckney's wife, Eliza Lucas, carried on extensive experimentation with the culture of silk. While her efforts never produced enough of the prized material to be commercially successful, she did manage to weave cloth for two silk dresses, which are now on display in the Charleston Museum.

North Charleston Port Terminal

The North Charleston Port Terminal is found on the Cooper's western shore near flashing daybeacon #58. The wharves are overshadowed by a massive concrete building that is apparently used for grain or phosphate storage. It makes a very impressive sight for the boater cruising up the river.

Goose Creek

Goose Creek is a surprising stream that breaks off from the western banks of Cooper River near flashing buoy #62. For the first 100 yards or so the creek is lined with a less-than-eye-pleasing collection of old army barges and tugs. However, further upstream, past extensive saltwater marsh, the creek runs past some beautiful homes and a golf course. There is swing room for craft under 30 feet and fair protection for overnight anchorage. The entrance and main body maintain 7-foot depths well downstream, though there is one shoal area to avoid.

Yellow House Creek

Yellow House Creek, also known as Slack Reach, enters Cooper River on its eastern shore near flashing buoy #66. The creek holds minimum 8- to 10-foot entrance depths, but there are some unmarked shoals to avoid. Once into the main body, waters deepen to 10- and 20-foot readings and continue well upstream. Large dolphins line the creek for a considerable distance. While no commercial

Naval wharves, Cooper River

craft were moored here during this writer's research, it would seem that somebody certainly put the piles there for some purpose.

The stream's westerly section is wide enough for anchorage by craft less than 36 feet in length. However, the creek's considerable depth calls for a great deal of anchor scope. The shores are mostly undeveloped saltwater marsh, though the port banks are a bit higher and do provide some protection in a southerly blow. There are no facilities on the creek.

While not suitable for heavy weather, Yellow House Creek does offer one of the best anchorage opportunities on the lower Cooper River. If you draw less than 5 feet, don't hesitate to enter, but be sure to read the Yellow House Creek navigation section presented later in this chapter.

Flagg Creek

Flagg Creek makes off from the Cooper's eastern shore across from flashing daybeacon #75. Minimum entrance depths run around 8 feet, but there is one shoal area to avoid. The banks are undeveloped marsh and provide only minimal shelter. There are no facilities on the stream.

Flagg Creek's lower reaches near the river are wide enough to serve as anchorage for craft under 40 feet in length. However, as noted, protection is not adequate for heavy weather.

If you choose to enter, be *sure* to read the Flagg Creek navigation section presented later in this chapter. Depths shown on chart 11527 for the creek's upper reaches are inaccurate and could lure the boater into a most unpleasant grounding.

Back River

Back River once opened onto the Cooper's western shore near unlighted daybeacon #88. In the 1930s the stream was dammed in order to provide a ready source of fresh water for the industrial complexes at Cote Bas and Dean Hall. Today, a wide, deep cove cuts in towards the dam. The small bay's shoreline is mostly undeveloped, though it is a bit higher than the norm in this area. This sidewater holds minimum depths of 9 feet and provides adequate shelter for light to moderate air anchorage.

If you need supplies, there is a small grocery and tackle shop just south of the dam. Ice and snacks can also be purchased here. To visit, anchor within about 50 yards of shore and break out the dinghy.

Grove Creek

Grove Creek is a small stream that enters Cooper River north of unlighted daybeacon #89. It eventually leads to Grove Plantation,

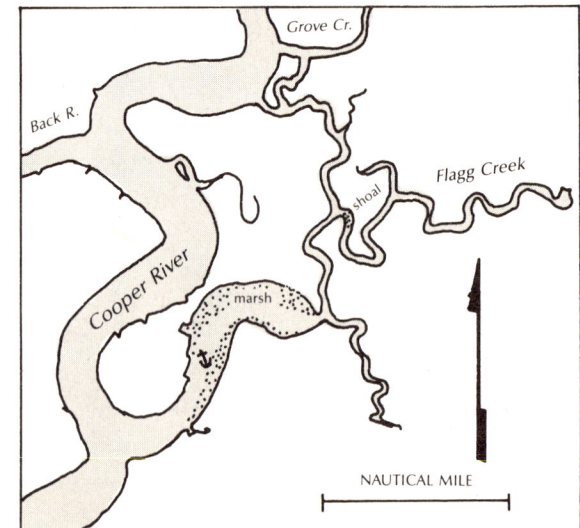

CHARLESTON

but no historic buildings are visible from the water. Most of the shores are undeveloped marsh. Minimum depths are 8 feet, and craft under 30 feet in length could anchor in the area near the intersection with the river. Protection is not adequate for heavy weather. There are no facilities on the creek.

Moreland Plantation

Moreland Plantation was once located along the eastern banks of Cooper River in the sharp loop that cuts to the west below Cote Bas. Today the only traces of the plantation are the many bricks and pilings lining the shore.

Cote Bas

A large industrial complex is readily visible as the Cooper takes a sharp bend to the west. The exceptionally large building, which can be seen for many miles, is some sort of manufacturing facility run by General Dynamics.

Dean Hall

Old Dean Hall Plantation is located along Cooper River's western shore near flashing daybeacon #C. From the water, the plantation is hidden from view by several industrial buildings. It is nevertheless one of the Cooper's greatest attractions. In the early 1900s Dean Hall's owner, Benjamin R. Kittredge, donated a large portion of his property to the city of Charleston. Here Mr. Kittredge improved upon the magnificent cypress trees growing naturally in the impounded fresh water by planting many flowering shrubs. He named his creation Cypress Gardens, and it soon became one of the great showplaces in coastal South Carolina. Unfortunately, there is no access to the gardens by water. You will need to rent a car in the city to visit Mr. Kittredge's magnificent achievement.

East Cooper River

As noted earlier, Cooper River splits into eastern and western arms at the Tee. The eastern branch provides wonderful cruising ground, anchorage opportunities, and at least one historic site. This area is seldom frequented by larger pleasure craft, and those hardy cruisers who venture this far will be rewarded by the special excitement that comes from exploring where few have gone before. The twin branches are much frequented by fishing skiffs, however. This writer observed dozens of hopeful anglers during his research. One might infer from the numbers and the devotion of its fans that the area produces a plentiful catch of bass and bream.

Minimum depths on the river's mid-width are around 8 feet. However, you must be careful not to mistake the large, abandoned rice fields bordering the stream for the main channel. Because the stream is relatively narrow and there is the possibility of becoming entangled in the old flats, neither of the upper Cooper's branches is recommended for craft over 40 feet or those drawing more than 5½ feet.

While there are no facilities on this arm of the river, the entire area provides enough shelter for all but heavy weather anchorage. Simply select a likely spot, drop the hook, and settle down for a restful evening.

Most of the river's shoreline is undeveloped, though you will sight a house from time to time. The banks consist of tidal flats for the most part, but in other spots the shores rise to heavily timbered woods. Select the wooded areas for best protection when anchoring.

At one point a Girl Scout camp borders the northern bank. It is built on land once owned by Edward Rutledge, a signer of the Declaration of Independence.

French Quarter Creek

East Cooper River boasts only one sidewater of significant proportions. French Quarter Creek makes into the river about halfway between the Tee and Pompion Hill Chapel. It is named for several French Huguenot families who once lived along the creek.

While the stream is too small for anchorage by all but small craft, adventurous skippers with craft of 28 feet or less can follow the stream for a considerable distance holding 6-foot minimum depths. The trip will give you a chance to observe several old rice fields at close quarters. Again, you must be careful to differentiate the flats from the channel.

Pompion Hill Chapel

Perhaps the East Cooper's greatest attraction is historic Pompion Hill Chapel, which sits on the southern banks near the river's eastern cruising limits for pleasure craft. The small church was built as a "chapel of ease" in 1765, according to the South Carolina Sea Grant Consortium. Locally the chapel is known as "Punkin Hill."

There is a magnificent view of the stately but humble old chapel from the East Cooper. Don't try to land, as the shore is littered with old pilings placed there to slow erosion. If you make it this far, you will be treading waters that have known almost nothing but small fishing skiffs for the last hundred years.

Abandoned rice fields, East Cooper River

CHARLESTON 113

Pompion Hill Chapel, East Cooper River

West Cooper River

The western branch of Cooper River runs far inland to Lake Moultrie. This great lake was created in 1942 by the huge Santee-Cooper Project, which has since generated many a kilowatt. Much of the water that used to flow into Santee River was diverted through this arm of the Cooper by the several dams constructed during the project.

Unfortunately for larger pleasure craft, passage on the western branch is soon barred by a railroad bridge. While this span supposedly opens on demand, its hours of operation are somewhat erratic. It is a good idea to discontinue your cruise at the bridge anyway. Minimum depths of 8 feet are held as far as the span, but depths become uncertain thereafter.

Near the beginning of the West Cooper's second sharp turn to the west you will spy a ruined building on the eastern shore. This ruin is all that is now visible of Rice Hope Plantation, once the abode of Royal Governor Nathaniel Johnson. The old building was apparently used as a warehouse for goods bound to Charleston.

The upper reaches of Back River enter the West Cooper on its western banks at its second sharp turn to the east. While the entrance and the canal that follows hold 6-foot minimum depths, passage is soon blocked by two low-level fixed bridges with only 6 feet of vertical clearance.

Just short of the railroad span, the old town of Childsbury watches over the West Cooper River from the northern banks. This community was founded by James Childs in 1707 and was once the site of horse races held between gentlemen planters.

Quite frankly, the West Cooper is not as appealing as the eastern branch, but it does share that same isolated, unexplored quality. So if you are one of those skippers who has to see it all, don't hesitate to cruise as far as the bridge.

Cooper River Navigation

There are two routes by which the pleasure boater may enter Cooper River. Both are wide, well-marked channels used regularly by large commercial and naval craft. The most direct passage follows Town Creek Reach between the eastern banks of

114 CRUISING GUIDE TO COASTAL SOUTH CAROLINA

the Charleston Peninsula and Drum Island. After paralleling the Charleston shore for about 1 nautical mile the channel passes the lower Charleston port facility wharves to the west. The reach then flows quickly under the twin highrise spans of the Highway 17 bridge.

As you cruise upstream from the highway bridge, watch to port for flashing buoy #7. This aid marks a long pier that once served as a coal exporting facility. Today the old piles are abandoned and dilapidated.

The second entrance follows Hog Island Reach north from Charleston Harbor. The channel passes between Hog and Drum islands. Along the way, Patriots Point will be passed to the east. The route then cuts sharply to the west and follows Drum Island Reach past the northern tip of Drum Island, rejoining the main Cooper River channel near flashing daybeacon #46A.

From this point the Cooper remains well marked and easy to follow for many miles upstream. Simply stick to the channel and have charts 11524 and 11527 ready at hand to resolve any questions that might arise.

Shipyard Creek To enter Shipyard Creek, continue cruising on the main Cooper River channel until the stream's mid-width comes abeam to the west. Only then should you turn into the creek. While Shipyard Creek has a broad entrance channel, there is

Nuclear submarine and tender, Cooper River

some shallow water to the north and south, easily avoided by the above-outlined maneuver.

Clouter Creek If you choose to enter Clouter Creek, favor the eastern banks at the stream's mouth, but don't approach this shoreline too closely either. Feel your way in with a watchful eye on the sounder. Be very careful to avoid the considerable area of shoal water, clearly shown on chart 11524, that extends out into Cooper River to the west of the creek's entrance.

The stream's lower reaches provide the most swing room for overnight anchorage. If you do choose to proceed further upstream, stick to the mid-width and remember to expect some 5-foot depths at low tide. Be particularly alert for trouble if you attempt to reenter the Cooper from the stream's northern mouth.

Yellow House Creek Shoals guard the eastern and western flanks of the entrance to Yellow House Creek. If you decide to enter, proceed at idle speed. Strike a course to enter the stream's mid-width and keep a wary eye on the sounder until well into the creek's interior.

Once inside the main body, depths improve for a good distance upstream. You will soon spy the dolphins described earlier lining the port side of the stream's mid-width. For best swinging room do not proceed too far upstream before dropping the hook.

Goose Creek Favor the port side of the creek when entering from the Cooper. For the first several hundred yards or so the stream is lined by old barges, ships, and tugs. The creek then takes a sharp turn to starboard. Favor the port shore as you round this turn. There is some shoal water on the opposite banks. Continue cruising down the creek and watch to port. Soon you will catch sight of several large white homes overlooking the stream from high ground. You can anchor in this area with enough protection for all but heavy weather if there is sufficient swinging room for your craft.

Flagg Creek Chart 11527 accurately shows one area of shoal water on the mid-width of the otherwise deep entrance to Flagg Creek. To avoid this hazard, favor the southern shore when entering. Once on the creek's interior, depths improve remarkably. Discontinue your cruise on the creek well before reaching its fork. In spite of depth readings shown on chart 11527, very shoal water of 2 to 3 feet is encountered on this section of the creek.

Back River The arm of Back River that is accessible from this section of Cooper River is wide, deep, and easily navigable. Simply enter anywhere near the mid-width and drop your hook at a likely spot. Good depths continue almost to the banks.

Grove Creek Grove Creek's entrance is relatively small but quite deep. Strike a course to enter on the stream's mid-width and you should not have any difficulty.

Remember to avoid the arm of the creek

that turns off to the south just east of the entrance. Depths are too uncertain in this branch for larger cruising craft.

On the Cooper The Cooper's last official aid to navigation is unlighted daybeacon #89. While there are several unmarked shoal areas to avoid further upstream, they can be easily bypassed. Take your time, have chart 11527 ready at hand, and watch the sounder, and you should not have any undue difficulty. Some of the river's best scenery is found in this area, so don't hesitate to continue if your craft draws 5 feet or less.

The first significant shoals are found on the river's northern shore as the stream cuts sharply to the west not far upstream from

Lower Charleston Port Terminal with Cooper Bridge in foreground

#89. Favor the southern shore to avoid this trap.

Another area of very shallow water is found on the Cooper's mid-width in a sharp loop to the west, north of the industrial facilities at Cote Bas. Heavily favor the western shore as you pass through.

From here to the Tee, no further shallows are encountered. Stick to the mid-width and enjoy the sights.

East Cooper River As stated earlier, it is much easier to follow the deep channel on the two branches of the upper Cooper River than a casual inspection of chart 11527 would lead one to believe. The small islands that separate the channel from the tidal flats are more readily identifiable than you might expect. Again, as is true with all unfamiliar, isolated waters, you should proceed slowly while maintaining a careful watch on the sounder. If you do become confused, slow to idle speed, study the chart, and select the correct passage.

To enter the Cooper's eastern branch, cut sharply to the east just after passing through the main river's mouth into the Tee. Follow the southern shore around the sharp point, which leads first to the east and then almost due south, by favoring the starboard banks. From here to Pompion Chapel, stick to the channel's mid-width and you should meet with no difficulty. Depths begin to drop off past the old church. Discontinue your cruising at this point.

If you choose to anchor, just select any likely spot and drop the hook. Have the fishing rod ready at hand. Rumor has it that the fishing on the upper Cooper's two branches can be spectacular.

French Quarter Creek East Cooper River's only significant sidewater is French Quarter Creek. While the stream holds minimum 6-foot depths on its mid-width, it is too narrow for any craft over 28 feet in length. If you do choose to enter, be careful to avoid the tidal flats lining much of the stream's banks.

West Cooper River To enter West Cooper River, turn 90 degrees to port just after entering the Tee. Stick to the mid-width and don't be fooled by the many tidal flats flanking both sides of the river. The channel is free of shoals as far as the railroad bridge.

Back River reenters the Cooper on its western banks just before the stream cuts sharply eastward and heads toward the property of Rice Hope Plantation. While this entrance holds minimum depths of 7 feet, the stream is blocked some distance downstream by two low-level fixed bridges.

The railroad bridge will often open on demand, but the stream soon leaves the confines of chart 11527 and depths become uncertain. If you do choose to continue, feel your way along.

Wando River

The Wando River splits off from the Cooper at Remley Point and strikes to the northeast for some 10 nautical miles before it encounters a low-level fixed highway bridge, which can be opened only with 24 hours notice. While the Wando is quite attractive, it offers relatively few cruising and anchorage opportunities. Many boaters will probably choose to bypass this stream, but for those who have the time to cruise its blue length, some beautiful scenery will be the reward.

Large tracts of the shoreline are higher and more heavily wooded than is typical of most streams in this section of coastal South Carolina. Here and there pockets of residential and commercial development break the natural landscape, just enough for a pleasing variety.

Wando River is well marked by nun and can buoys as far as the fixed highway bridge. The channel is wide and easy to follow, though some aids are spaced so widely apart that it might be a good idea to run compass courses between buoys. Outside of the marked channel, good depths often hold well into shore, but there are several areas of shallower water. The wise cruiser will stick to the marked cut.

Just short of the highway bridge, a commercial fish house is located on the southern shore. It is often possible to tie to the docks

Port facility, Wando River

CHARLESTON

here long enough to purchase seafood caught the same day.

There are no facilities catering to the cruising boater anywhere on the Wando, and there is only one real opportunity for overnight anchorage. The Wando is certainly not the greatest cruising find in coastal South Carolina. However, for the boater who enjoys winding lazily up a river with few other pleasure craft in evidence, Wando River may be just the ticket.

Wando Port Facilities

A large containerized cargo port facility is found on the Wando northeast of flashing buoy #4. Here the passing cruiser can often watch as huge oceangoing cargo ships are loaded with containers by several large cranes. Watch your wake and you can cruise quite close to the facility for a good view.

Nowell Creek

Nowell Creek is a fairly large stream found on the Wando's northern shore near can buoy #11. Minimum depths of 7 feet are carried well upstream. While the creek's lower reaches are a bit too open for anchorage, there is one section further upstream that offers excellent protection and enough swing room for craft up to 40 feet. The marshy shores are entirely in their natural state and no facilities are available on the creek.

Navy dry-dock facility, Wando River

Horlbeck Creek

Horlbeck Creek is located on the river's eastern banks near nun buoy #16. This stream leads inland to fabulous Boone Hall Plantation and its famous mile-long avenue of live oaks. The plantation is one of the great showplaces of the South Carolina Low Country. Unfortunately, numerous unmarked shoals make entry into the creek too hazardous for large cruising craft. Furthermore, there is no dock at the plantation and it is only possible to catch a fleeting view of the house from the water. This writer recommends that you visit by rental car from Charleston.

Navy Dry-dock Facility

The passing cruiser has the opportunity to observe a large navy dry-dock facility on the Wando's southern shore near unlighted nun buoy #32. Large craft are often being serviced here by crews of technicians. The different ships make for fascinating viewing, so slow down and break out the camera.

Wando River Navigation

Successful navigation of Wando River from its intersection with the Cooper to the highway bridge is a simple matter of following the deep, well-marked channel. Gaps of almost 1 nautical mile separate some of the Wando's aids to navigation. It is therefore a very good idea to run compass courses between the various buoys.

Another unusual navigational problem on the Wando is brought about by the many pelicans that frequent the river's various buoys. In many cases their droppings have completely obscured the aid's number. Be sure to plot your progress carefully on chart 11524 in order to have an accurate position reckoning at all times.

Nowell Creek Enter Nowell Creek by striking a compass course from can buoy #11 to avoid the shoal water to the east and west of the stream's mouth. Once on the interior, stick to the mid-width.

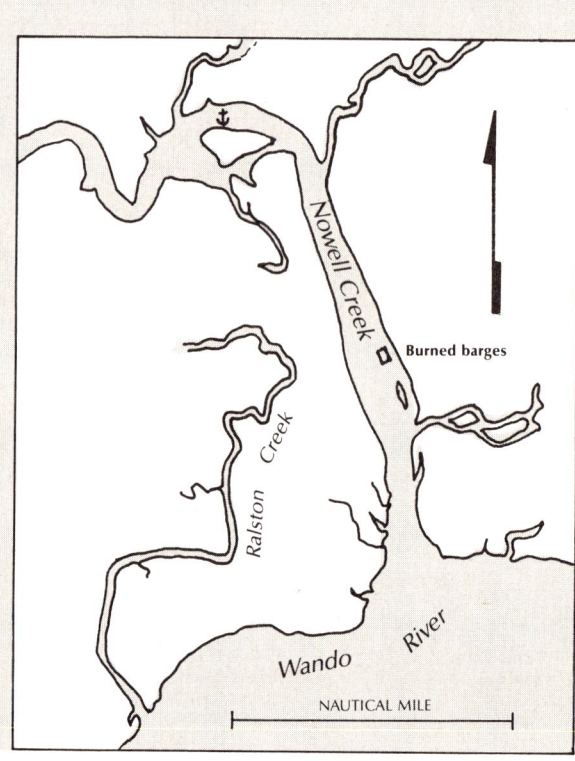

CHARLESTON 121

> After proceeding for a short distance upstream you will sight a large, partially sunken derelict on the eastern shore. The wreck is designated as a green square on chart 11524 and marked as "PA" (position approximate). Several barges, lashed together and anchored in the creek, apparently burned here some years ago.
>
> The best spot for overnight anchorage is found as the creek makes a sharp turn to the west. Drop the hook somewhere in the body of the bend and settle down for a restful night.
>
> Don't attempt to cruise farther upstream than the sharp point of marsh encountered on the northern shore as the creek cuts sharply to the north. Past this point depths become uncertain and unmarked shoals are encountered.

Ashley River

The Ashley River is Charleston's most disappointing body of water for the modern cruiser. At one time many large and lovely plantations lined the Ashley's shores. Unfortunately, most of these were destroyed during the Civil War, and the ones that survived are not accessible to larger cruising craft from the water.

While the Ashley's lower section is deep and well marked, shoal water not noted on chart 11524 is quickly encountered after passing the river's second bridge. All but two of the river's historic sites are found upstream of this point.

The eastern shoreline of the lower river is dotted here and there with commercial docks, while the western banks exhibit light residential development. This section of the Ashley is not particularly attractive. Very few of Charleston's historical sights are visible, and no plantations grace the western banks.

As mentioned earlier, both of Charleston's

Ashley Marina, Ashley River

marinas are located on the Ashley. The Charleston Municipal Marina is found east of unlighted can buoy #5, and Ashley Marina is just upstream. If you seek shelter but do not choose to berth at one of the area marinas, you must travel south for some distance on the ICW before finding a suitable area. There are no sidewaters available to the cruising boater on the navigable section of Ashley River, and consequently, no anchorages are to be found.

Most boaters will choose to visit only those sections of the Ashley followed by the ICW and adjacent to the two area marinas. Of course, there are always hardy souls who must see everything. Frankly, this writer favors the more conservative practice.

Old Town and Orange Grove Creeks

Old Town and Orange Grove creeks, found on the Ashley's western shore, were the site of the original Charles Towne settlement before

Lower Charleston Terminal, Cooper River

the town was moved to its present location around 1680. During the bicentennial celebration of 1976, the state of South Carolina constructed a very impressive commemorative park near the twin streams. Unfortunately, shoaling not noted on chart 11524 has raised the low tide depths of both creeks to 4 feet or less. Cruising boaters must visit the park by obtaining ground transportation from Charleston.

The Citadel

Just east of unlighted nun buoy #6 the passing boater can observe the campus of the Citadel. This military school was founded in 1842 as a response to fear of slave uprisings.

It was cadets from the Citadel who touched off the Civil War's first shots. Manning a cannon at Fort Johnson, they fired on the Union ship *Star of the West,* which was attempting to resupply the federal garrison at Fort Sumter. Little did they suspect that their shot was the death knell of the Old South.

Those same cadets and their fellows were to serve valiantly for the next five years in the defense of Charleston. Their contribution is part and parcel of the great Charlestonian tradition.

The campus was originally located further inland and was moved to its present site in 1922. The Citadel continues as an active, four-year military college and enjoys an excellent academic reputation. There are still many reminders of the school's storied past preserved in its archives. Few will ever attend a school with a prouder tradition.

Ashley River Navigation

Ashley River can be successfully navigated by sticking to the well-marked channel as far as the second highway bridge. The river is plagued by shoal areas outside of the marked cut, so follow the various aids and chart 11524 carefully.

Ashley River's first highway span is found to the north of unlighted can buoy #5. The bridge has a closed vertical clearance of 18 feet. The span is closed from 7 A.M. until 9 A.M. on weekdays, and from 4 P.M. until 7 P.M., seven days a week. Otherwise, the bridge opens only on the hour and half hour for pleasure craft.

Upstream of unlighted daybeacon #20 the Ashley quickly darts under its second highway bridge. Low tide depths of 4 to 5 feet are immediately encountered on the western side of the span. Discontinue your cruise at #20 unless your craft draws less than 2½ feet.

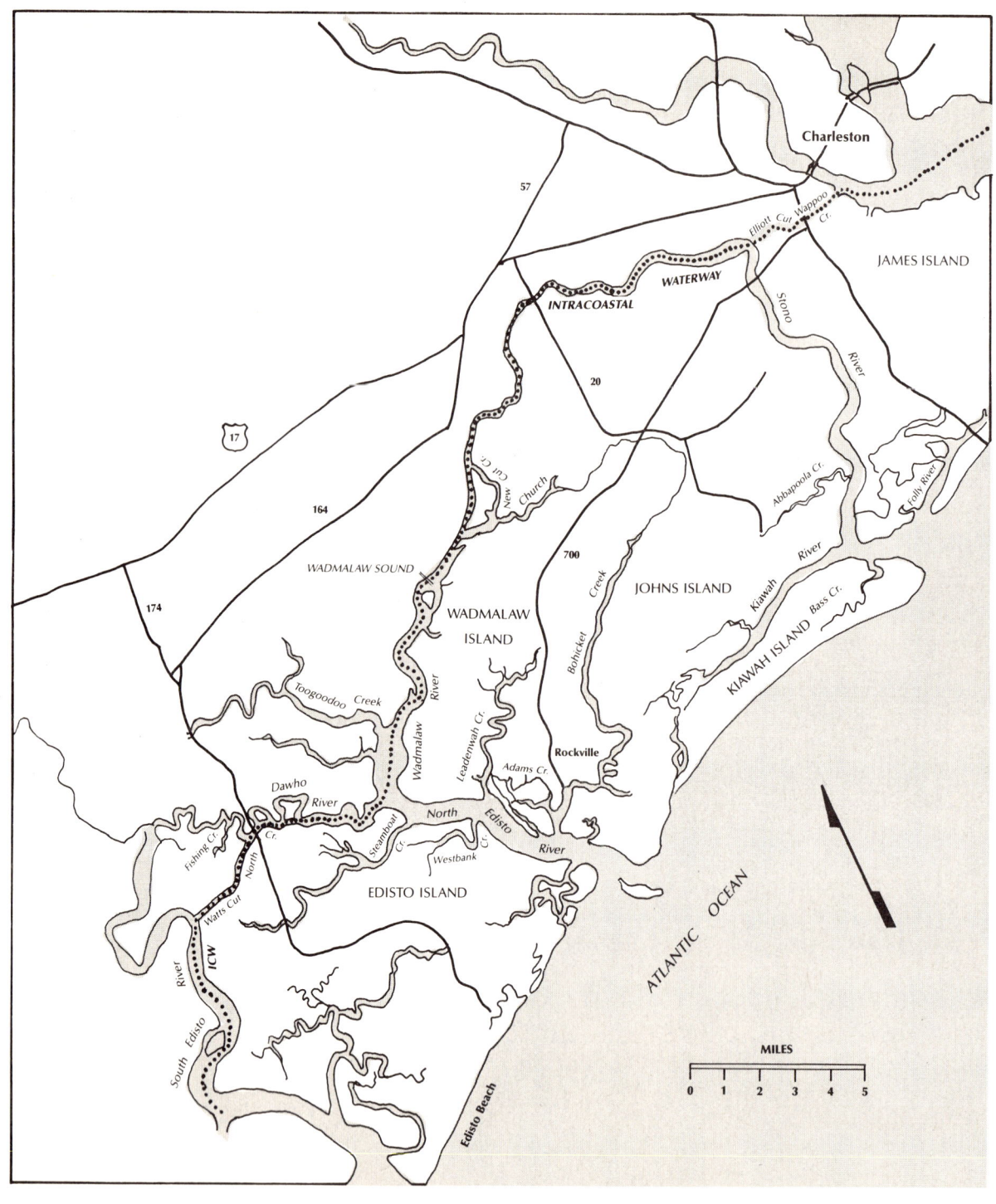

CHAPTER V

Wappoo Creek to South Edisto River

South of Charleston the state's coastline begins a radical transformation. Gone are the simple patterns of rivers and streams to the north. The boater now faces an increasingly complicated and confusing maze of creeks, rivers, and inlets, all of which flow around the plentiful Sea Islands. These small, often marshy islands are the most striking feature of the southern South Carolina coast. Separated from the mainland by multiple streams, they can provide some of the most historic and romantic cruising grounds in the state.

The main water bodies in the northern section of "Sea Island Country" are the Stono and North Edisto rivers. The smaller Wadmalaw and Dawho rivers, which run east and west, join these two principal streams and are followed by the ICW as the waterway snakes its way south.

Both the Stono and North Edisto boast excellent facilities, though long stretches of isolated waters separate the various marinas. Good overnight anchorages abound. Many of these are quite isolated and can make for adventurous evenings spent far from the most remote vestiges of civilization. Some are even within sight of historic plantation homes, which watch benignly over the waters as they have for more than a hundred and fifty years.

Shorelines vary greatly along the two rivers and connecting streams. While the saltwater marsh so much in evidence to the north is still quite prolific, there are also higher, heavily wooded banks. Large undeveloped stretches alternate with commercial and residential areas. Here and there a historic plantation is visible from the water. These old homeplaces are elegant reminders of the Sea Island culture's past majesty, and many are the settings for fascinating legends. We shall explore several of these tall tales within the body of this chapter.

Cruising the waters of the South Carolina Sea Islands is a refreshingly different cruising experience. As I performed my research, I was reminded of the rivers of Albemarle Sound in North Carolina, which were mostly bypassed by cruising boaters. In the Sea Islands, too, it is somewhat rare to spot other cruising craft far from the ICW channel. Yet it is clear that those who pass up the chance to cruise the rivers south of Charleston are missing one of the most exciting experiences offered by coastal South Carolina.

Charts You will need two charts for navigation among the Sea Islands covered in this chapter:
11518 covers the ICW through the entire area from Wappoo Creek to South Edisto River.
11522 details the lower sections of both the Stono and North Edisto rivers, as well as the upper reaches of Toogoodoo Creek.

ICW to Stono River

Wappoo Creek and Elliott Cut provide access to Stono River via the ICW. While the two streams are well marked and free of shoals, strong tidal currents regularly scour the channel. This problem seems to be particularly acute at the Stono River intersection. Sailcraft and trawlers must be especially cautious in these swift waters.

There are no facilities on the two creeks and only one anchorage opportunity. East of unlighted daybeacon #9 a deep loop of the river cuts in towards the southern shore. Here boats up to 55 feet can anchor in minimum 8-foot depths. This is a good spot to wait for morning light or a favorable tide before entering Ashley or Stono River.

The cut is spanned by one bridge with 33 feet of closed vertical clearance. Those who cannot clear this height must contend with restricted hours of operation. The span is closed Monday thru Friday between 6:30 A.M. and 9 A.M. and between 2 P.M. and 6 P.M. On Saturdays, Sundays, and holidays, the bridge opens on the half hour between 2 P.M. and 6 P.M. Be sure to plan your cruise around these opening times; otherwise, you may experience long delays.

West of the bridge, "No Wake" ordinances are strictly enforced as far as Stono River. Slow down and proceed at idle speed. The Charleston Harbor Police are known for their vigilance in this area.

The shoreline exhibits fairly heavy residential development. Here and there some truly elegant homes overlook the water, and at least one historical site is visible to the careful observer.

McLeod Plantation

Just before passing under the Wappoo Creek Bridge, look towards the southern banks and you will catch a quick glimpse of McLeod Plantation's white columns gleaming through a long avenue of oaks. The house is set back a good distance from the water, so you will have to look carefully.

This beautiful home was built in 1858 and extensively remodeled in the early 1900s. Though not visible from the water, a few slave cabins still stand near the plantation's remaining fields.

During the Civil War the plantation was used as a hospital and headquarters for Confederate forces. Later it housed a Freedman's Bureau, an agency set up after the war to aid the emancipated blacks.

Wappoo Creek History North of unlighted daybeacon #9 the shallow upper reaches of Wappoo Creek make off to the west. This seemingly insignificant body of water was the scene for one of the most important agricultural developments in the early years of South Carolina.

In the 1740s a remarkable young woman, Eliza Lucas, lived on the shores of Wappoo Creek. Her father, the governor of Antigua, moved Eliza to South Carolina with her mother, who was in failing health. Mr. Lucas was hurriedly summoned back to Antigua to deal with Spanish hostilities, leaving his young daughter in charge of the family plantation.

Apparently a woman of extraordinary drive, Eliza was not content merely to oversee the day-to-day operation of the plantation. She began to experiment with the preparation of indigo dye. She was familiar with the plant from her days in the West Indies and believed that it could prosper in South Carolina.

There followed many trials for the determined lady. Her first planting was killed by frost, and her second was eaten by worms. A successful third crop was processed incorrectly by an assistant dispatched by her father from the West Indies. Eliza persevered, and finally her father was able to send her an old slave from Antigua who could reveal the secrets of the complicated preparation process.

As a direct result of Eliza's eventual success, South Carolina's first great agricultural dynasty was born. With a generous bounty offered by the British government, indigo was grown and exported in great quantity until the Revolution. Vast fortunes were accumulated by indigo planters throughout coastal South Carolina. After the Revolution, the bounty was no more, and indigo was cultivated less and less. The final blow came as the Western world began to learn the process of preparing dyes from coal tar.

The growth of indigo is but a distant memory in South Carolina today. It is most fitting, however, to remember the courage and diligence of Eliza Lucas and to reflect on just how much can really be accomplished by a single individual who possesses the necessary drive.

Sea Island History The Sea Islands continued to shape South Carolina's economic and agricultural history when, during the early and middle 1800s, they were host to the state's last great agricultural dynasty. Planters discovered that the warm, humid climate was well suited for the growth of long-staple cotton. Much as Egyptian cotton is prized to this day for its long fiber, Sea Island cotton was very much in demand during the 1800s. The successful cultivation of this valuable commodity concentrated fantastic wealth in the hands of a few planters. There evolved among the Sea Island planters an affluent way of life that the modern mind can scarcely imagine.

Such wealth led to the construction of beautiful plantations. Many of these old estates are wreathed in a tradition of colorful folklore that the romantics among us will find hard to resist. It is apparent from reading the tales of the Sea Islands that the planters were a fiercely independent breed of men and women with fascinating characters. Their tradition lives on in the plentiful Sea Island legends.

Surprisingly, it was not the Civil War but a small insect that spelled the doom of Sea Island cotton. Following the war, cotton was again grown profitably despite the absence of cheap labor. However, the coming of the boll weevil in the late 1800s was the final act in the Sea Island tragedy. The cotton fields were decimated, and many who once hoarded great fortunes were suddenly bankrupt. Only within the last several years have scientists learned to break the life cycle of the weevil. Perhaps this new discovery will eventually bring the snowy fields of cotton back to coastal South Carolina.

Over the years, the face of the Sea Islands has changed. Here and there, descendants of former slaves have established rural communities on the sites of former plantations. Many plantation homes fell victim to the ravages of war or the passing of the years. Several of the old homes still survive, however, particularly on Edisto Island. Some of the structures stand empty, while others have been restored to their former glory. Either way, they speak eloquently of an age that will never come again.

ICW to Stono River Navigation

As already mentioned, the boater must be on guard against the strong currents that regularly plague Wappoo Creek and Elliott Cut. Sailcraft should proceed under auxiliary power and be ready for quick course corrections. All vessels should be alert for the side-setting effect of the current. Remember to watch your stern as well as your forward progress so that you may quickly note any excessive leeway.

West of unlighted daybeacon #4 the Wappoo Creek Bridge is encountered. Remember that "No Wake" is strictly enforced on the waterway west of the bridge. Slow to idle speed and spend your time observing the pleasant residential development on the shores.

The entrance to the cut's one anchorage is found to the south a little beyond the bridge. Enter on the mid-width at the eastern end. Drop the hook once you are between the marsh grass island and the mainland.

The waterway enters Stono River as it leaves the western mouth of Elliott Cut at flashing daybeacon #11. The ICW turns to the north here and follows the upper reaches of the Stono into Wadmalaw River. This discussion will now turn to the cruising opportunities of lower Stono River. Continued description and navigation of the ICW route will be presented later in this chapter.

Stono River

The Stono River is the first major body of water that the cruising boater will encounter south of Charleston. While a deep channel traverses the stream's entire length, it is dotted with numerous unmarked shoals along its lower reaches. These make successful navigation of the river an exacting process calling for great caution.

The Folly and Kiawah rivers are two major sidewaters of the Stono. Both streams join their larger sister near the Stono's inlet and offer excellent cruising opportunities.

The Stono's shoreline is generally attractive. The river is bordered along most of its length by James Island to the east and Johns Island to the west. Both land masses have figured prominently in the history of the South Carolina Low Country. A few historical sites are visible along the Stono's banks, among areas of light residential development.

The Stono's inlet is flanked by Folly Island to the north and Kiawah Island to the south. Both have been extensively developed as resorts. The inlet itself is subject to continual change and probably should not be attempted without local knowledge. Check at one of the area marinas before making the attempt.

Facilities along Stono River are excellent. Two marinas are found on the southern shore near the highway bridge, and a third facility is located on Folly River. These are the last marinas available on the ICW north of Beaufort, some 60 nautical miles away. Don't pass them by if you are in need of fuel or services.

Plans are underway to construct a fourth marina on Kiawah River. Unfortunately, there have been many delays in obtaining the necessary permits, and the management of the island has informed this writer that even when the facility is completed, transients will probably not be accepted.

Stono River presents far fewer anchorage opportunities than the streams to the south. Only a few creeks offer adequate shelter with enough swinging room for larger craft.

The Stono is certainly not the most easily navigated of the Sea Island rivers. However, it is an attractive body of water with uncrowded cruising grounds, good facilities, and several historic sites. Boaters who like to get away from the crowd should enjoy the Stono.

Buzzards Roost and Stono Marinas

Two marinas catering to the cruising boater are found on the western banks of Stono River near the Highway 17 swing bridge. Buzzards Roost is located on the northern side of the span and is one of the finest facilities in all of coastal South Carolina. Depths of 7 to 10 feet are maintained beside the floating docks. Transients are gladly accepted, and overnight berths have all power and water connections. Gasoline and diesel fuel are readily available, and some mechanical repairs can be arranged. There is also a very fine grocery and ships' store on the premises.

Cappy's Seafood Restaurant, located just behind the marina, is widely renowned for its succulent seafood. No less a celebrity than Tom Selleck has been attracted on occasion by Cappy's charms. Fried, broiled, or steamed, the seafood has the flavor that comes only from the freshest ingredients prepared with care and pride. This writer particularly recommends the combination fried shrimp and oyster platter. Cappy's also serves the largest "ten-ounce" ribeye this writer has ever seen. The chocolate mousse is a notable entry in the dessert line.

Over and above these impressive services, Buzzards Roost is managed by some of the friendliest souls you will find in this land of fine hospitality. It seems they just can't do enough for passing boaters. It is a genuine pleasure to find such a caring establishment. Certainly Buzzards Roost can be recommended without the slightest hesitation.

Stono Marina is a fairly small facility located on the southern side of the Stono Bridge. This establishment does not offer either gasoline or diesel fuel, but transients are gladly accepted for overnight dockage. The marina features all floating docks with every power and water connection. Some mechanical repairs are available. Dockside depths run between 7 and 10 feet. While not as large as some, Stono Marina is a friendly facility that the transient boater can use with confidence.

James Island History James Island comprises the eastern banks of Stono River from Elliott Cut to Folly River. The island was settled as early as the 1670s. Since that time the land mass has figured prominently in the history of the region.

Perhaps James Island's first claim to fame was its noted shipbuilding trade during the 1700s. In 1763 the *Heart of Oak* was launched from one of the island's shipyards. The proud ship weighed 180 tons and could carry more than 1000 barrels of rice in her hold.

In 1780 Sir Henry Clinton used James Island as the final staging ground for his encirclement of Charleston. He was not to be the last enemy who would attempt to use the island as a back door to the Holy City.

In June of 1862 a vastly superior Union force was defeated on James Island at the battle of Secessionville. The high command of the northern forces was so impressed with the Confederate defenses that they chose to redirect their efforts against Charleston to nearby Morris Island. Many fierce and bloody battles followed, and it was not until 1865 that Union forces finally occupied James Island.

Accounts of the courage and hardships of the defenders on James and Morris Islands are awe-inspiring. One Confederate was heard to say following the evacuation of Fort Legarre on Morris Island that he would never fear hell again because it couldn't be worse than Fort Legarre. If you would like to read more of the valiant but vain struggle for James Island, this writer highly recommends the book *James and Related Sea Islands* by James P. Hayes.

Johns Island History In 1739 an event took place on Johns Island that was to have a profound effect on the South Carolina view of slavery. Known as the Stono Slave Rebellion, the incident began at the urging of an educated slave named Cato. With the backing of the Spanish authorities in Florida, he encouraged other slaves to revolt. His plan was to head for Florida, freeing fellow slaves along the way. The mob first stormed an arms warehouse, killing two white guards stationed there. Then the ragged army began to travel south.

It was not long before they were observed by a small group of white planters, including the governor of the state. The planters rushed to nearby Willtown Presbyterian Church, where a service was in progress. In those days it was the law that everyone must go to church armed. This law was apparently a vestige of the days of Indian attacks.

The armed white congregation immediately set out in pursuit and found the rebellious slaves in a nearby field. They fired upon the mob, killing the ringleader Cato in the first volley. Several of the other leaders were hanged, and many of the remaining slaves were severely punished by their masters.

Following the Stono Rebellion, fear of black uprisings ran rife through the white population. Heavily outnumbered by the slaves, the whites believed that the blacks must be carefully controlled or other, more dangerous revolts would be the result. As a direct consequence, a new, strict, uniform Slave Code was adopted by the state of South Carolina. Among other harsh measures, the new law made it a crime to teach any slave to read or write. A series of nightly patrols throughout the countryside was instituted by the planters to hunt for fugitives and to monitor any slave gatherings. In short, the Stono Slave Rebellion led to a fear of similar uprisings that was to affect South Carolina history until the Civil War.

Battery Pringle

Though somewhat obscured by seasonal growth, Battery Pringle is visible to the careful observer on the eastern shore of the Stono. This Confederate battery was built early in the Civil War to protect Stono River from attack. Look east just as you swing back to the south from the river's first eastward jog, and you will see the earthen walls near the shoreline.

Stono Plantation

The abandoned Stono Plantation house can be seen on the eastern shore of the river about 1.1 nautical miles south of Battery Pringle. It can be recognized by its red roof and by the palmetto trees fronting onto the river.

Stono Plantation was one of the early James Island farms. In later years the property was acquired by the Hamilton family, the descendants of Paul Hamilton, Secretary of the Navy under President James Madison.

Abbapoola Creek

Abbapoola Creek is a wide stream that holds minimum 6-foot depths for some distance downstream. Swinging room is sufficient for craft up to 45 feet. The shores are saltwater marsh and would give only minimal protection in heavy weather. Consequently, the creek is recommended only for light to moderate air anchorage. There are no facilities on the stream.

Abbapoola Creek was once host to Legareville, a summer retreat for wealthy planters. As you enter the creek, watch ahead for a tin roof in the distance. Of all the original planter dwellings, this structure is the sole survivor. Unfortunately, you must enter the shallow section of the creek in order to have a good view of the house. Don't make the attempt unless your craft draws less than 3 feet.

Green Creek

Green Creek is a shallow stream that makes off from the eastern shore of Stono River. Don't attempt to enter! Depths of 4 feet or less are immediately encountered.

Kiawah River

Kiawah River is a large body of water intersecting the Stono near its inlet on the western banks. The river divides Johns, Seabrook, and Kiawah islands. While deep and easily navigable for much of its length, the Kiawah presents surprisingly few genuine cruising opportunities. It is too wide for effective anchorage, and there are no marinas in the immediate vicinity. Little can be seen of the sumptuous Kiawah Island resort to the south, and your most immediate companion for a cruise of the river is likely to be the familiar saltwater marsh grass. Some higher ground is visible on Kiawah Island to the south.

There is one exception to this rather plain

character. Large schools of porpoises often frequent the river. Sometimes, if you anchor quietly, the beautiful creatures will swim right up to your craft. Have the camera ready and you might be rewarded with the picture of a lifetime.

Kiawah Island

Kiawah Island is one of the premiere resort attractions in all of coastal South Carolina. As a splendid example of an effective compromise between developers and environmentalists, large portions of Kiawah Island have been left in their natural state, while other tracts have been developed in the most lavish style. Condominiums, hotels, sport complexes, and restaurants dot the island's central district. Many residents of coastal South Carolina have told this writer that they would rather vacation on Kiawah than anywhere else in the world.

Unfortunately, there is no water access to the resort at this time. Plans are slowly going forward for a marina on Kiawah River, but even when complete, it will most likely not

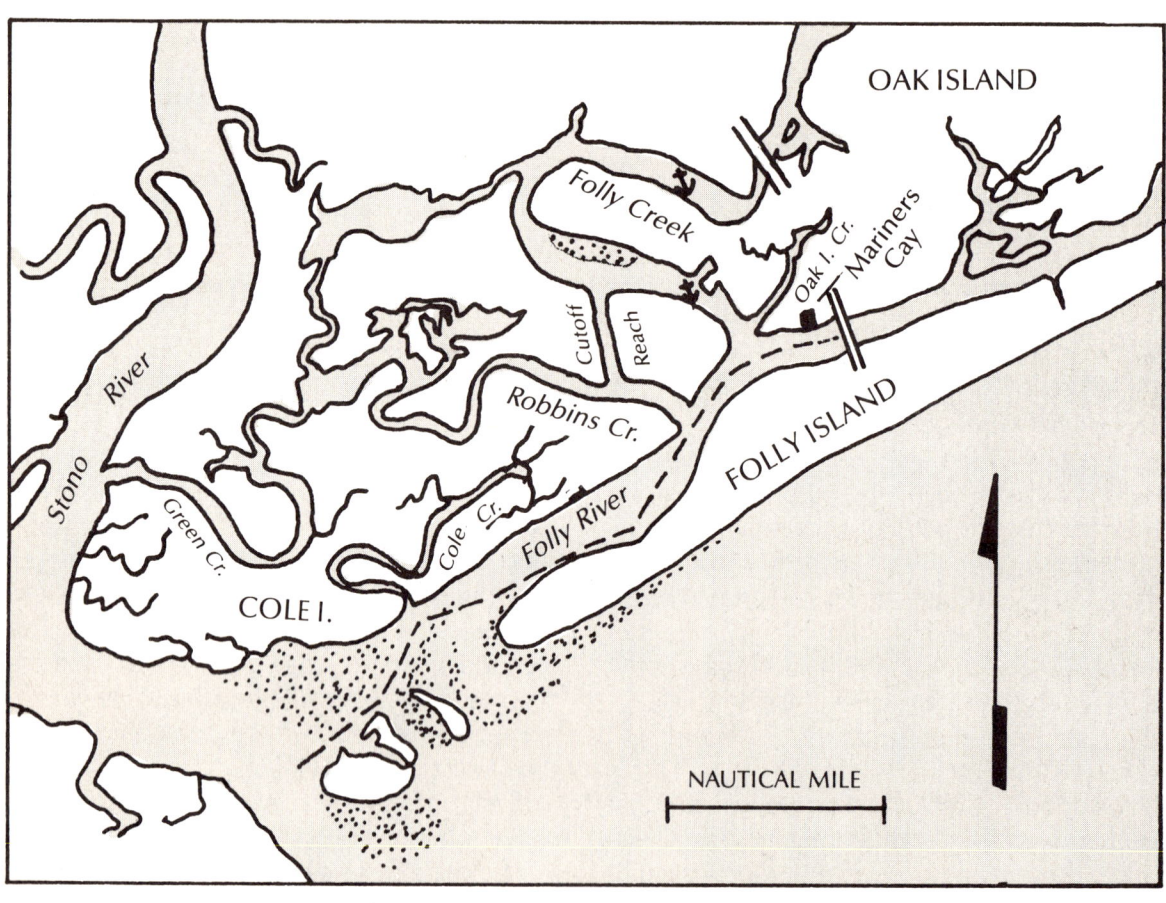

cater to transients. To visit Kiawah, make your reservations from Charleston.

Bass Creek

Bass Creek is a small stream found on the river's western banks between Kiawah and Folly Rivers. While the interior portion of the creek holds 8-foot minimum depths, the entrance is flanked by several unmarked shoals. Adventurous skippers can enter Bass Creek, but be sure to hold strictly to the mid-width and feel your way in cautiously to avoid the shoals. By all accounts you should consider entering only if you pilot a craft under 32 feet drawing 3½ feet or less.

The shoreline is mostly saltwater marsh, but the banks are a bit higher here than is the norm. They would give good protection in all but the heaviest of weather. If you do make it through the entrance, there is sufficient swinging room for boats under 32 feet to anchor. There are no facilities on the creek.

Folly River

Folly River joins the Stono on its eastern banks just short of the inlet. A well-marked channel leads inland through the stream but is eventually blocked by a fixed bridge. Caution must be exercised when running the Folly River Channel, as leeway can easily set you into the shallows.

Two marinas are found on Folly River. You may be able to buy gasoline and diesel fuel from a very small establishment on the southern shore just upstream from unlighted daybeacon #17. However, the river's principal facility is found on the northern banks just short of the fixed bridge.

Mariners Cay is a large marina-condo complex that presently reserves three slips for transients. Floating docks feature all power and water connections. Gasoline and diesel fuel are available, and there is a well-stocked grocery and ships' store on the premises. There is even a restaurant within walking distance. Future plans call for an even larger dining establishment, which is being built in conjunction with a condo expansion project. When complete, this too will be accessible by foot from the docks. Mariners Cay is a real find for cruising boaters this far off the beaten track.

Folly Creek

Folly Creek, Robbins Creek, and Cutoff Reach are sidewaters of Folly River that make into the larger stream's northern banks. All have both deep and shallow areas. Because of the shallow obstructions, the creeks are not recommended for craft over 38 feet. If you do choose to enter, make sure to read the Folly Creek navigation section presented later in this chapter.

Anchorage on the streams is possible for craft up to 38 feet, but the marshy shores would give minimal protection in heavy weather. Your best bet would probably be Folly Creek itself. There is more swing room here than on the two smaller streams.

Eventually Folly Creek is blocked by a fixed bridge. Just west of the bridge a fish house and dock are located on the creek's southern shore. Here you can usually buy seafood caught the same day.

Folly Island

Folly Island separates Folly River from the ocean. Since 1930 the island beaches have been one of the most popular weekend getaways in coastal South Carolina. Over the years, Folly Island has steadily eroded towards the mainland, but this natural regression does not seem to have injured the beach's popularity.

Stono River Navigation

As already noted, successful navigation of Stono River is an exacting process and calls for careful cruising. Numerous unmarked shoals, which frequently shift in position, can quickly lead the unwary boater to grief. Have chart 11522 near at hand, keep a wary eye on the sounder, and proceed slowly. Do not attempt to run the river at night! If you follow these simple rules and study the navigational data presented in this section, your cruise of the Stono should be a pleasant experience.

When entering Stono River from Elliott Cut, favor the eastern shore heavily to avoid the shoals extending out from the western banks, clearly shown on chart 11522. As you round the point where the river takes a turn to the south, begin cruising back to the mid-width and point towards the Stono bridge's central pass through. By this procedure you will avoid an area of shallow water on the eastern shore.

The Stono River Bridge opens on demand. Just before you reach the span, Buzzards Roost Marina will come abeam on the western shore. Once through, you will see Stono Marina, also on the western banks.

South of the bridge, hold to the mid-width for .9 nautical miles. As the Stono begins bending to the east, favor the eastern banks. Immediately after passing into the easterly bend, begin favoring the southern shore heavily. Very shallow water is located on the northern shore, as shown on chart 11522.

The river now takes a turn to the south. Favor the eastern shore for the first .7 of a nautical mile of this stretch. Then cruise back towards the mid-width.

The Stono now begins a jog to the west. Favor the southern shore as you enter the turn. As the river bends back around to the south, begin heavily favoring the western shore. As shown on the chart, there is very shallow water on the eastern shore. Watch to the west and you will soon catch sight of the entrance to Abbapoola Creek.

Abbapoola Creek Enter Abbapoola Creek on its mid-width. The historic structure spoken of earlier is visible dead ahead. Remember not to attempt a direct approach unless your craft can stand 3-foot depths.

The stream follows a series of turns and bends. The creek first turns to the south, then to the southwest, then to the north, back to the south, and finally to the west. Discontinue your cruise before reaching this last turn to the west. Depths drop off to 4 feet or less at this point.

Kiawah River When entering Kiawah River, favor the southern shore slightly. Otherwise simply stick to the mid-width. Good depths are held for several miles upstream.

As you cruise the river, watch to the south for an occasional glimpse of the homes on Kiawah Island. A small dock fronts onto the river's southern shore some 3 nautical miles from the entrance. This pier is for the use of the residents and guests of the Kiawah resort. Here you may see a few small craft moored, but there is no room for larger cruising craft.

Depths begin to fall off on Kiawah River as the stream enters an area of extensive marsh west of Bryans Creek. Discontinue your cruise before proceeding too far.

Folly River The Folly River entrance channel is well marked and holds 6-foot minimum depths. However, leeway can quickly ease you out of the channel into shoal water unless you keep a wary eye to your stern. With proper caution, you should be able to run the cut without difficulty.

Enter Folly River by passing between flashing daybeacon #9 and unlighted daybeacon #10. Point to pass unlighted daybeacon #11 to its fairly immediate southerly side and to come abeam of flashing daybeacon #12 to its fairly immediate northeasterly quarter. Bend your course a bit to the north and point to pass unlighted daybeacon #13 to its easterly side and unlighted daybeacon #12A to its westerly quarter and to come abeam of flashing daybeacon #14 to its westerly side. Continue on the same course for some 30 yards and then swing to the east, pointing to pass unlighted daybeacon #15 to its immediate southerly side.

Maintain your course. It will appear as if you are heading directly for Folly Island. Point to come abeam of unlighted daybeacon #17 by some 50 yards to its southerly side.

Continue cruising upriver by favoring the southeastern shore. Once abeam of Robbins Creek, good depths open out from shore to shore.

Robbins Creek Enter Robbins Creek on its mid-width. Good depths of 8 feet or more are maintained as far as Cutoff Reach. Past this point, shoaling not noted on chart 11522 has apparently occurred. Low tide depths of 4 to 5 feet are soon encountered.

Anchorage might be possible on the wider sections of Robbins Creek for craft under 33 feet in length. However, a better spot is found just to the north on Folly Creek.

Cutoff Reach Cutoff Reach is a small stream that provides reliable access from Robbins to Folly Creek. Minimum depths of 8 feet are held between the two creeks. The reach is too narrow for anchorage by all but small craft. However, don't hesitate to use this advantageous shortcut if you wish to reach Folly Creek from the interior of Robbins.

Folly Creek Folly Creek, as already noted, can be entered via Robbins Creek and Cutoff Reach. Its principal entrance is located on Folly River just northwest of Oak Island Creek. Favor the port shore as far as the southern mouth of Oak Island Creek when making use of the primary entrance. Once past the smaller stream, cruise back to the mid-width for the next .4 of a nautical mile. As you make your approach to the intersection with Cutoff Reach to the south, begin to favor the southern shore heavily. As clearly shown on chart 11522, there is shoal water on the northern banks.

Past this point Folly Creek begins a loop that eventually curves back to the east, then sharply to the north. Stick to the mid-width in this section. You will soon encounter a fixed bridge with only 10 feet of vertical clearance. The fish house described earlier will come abeam on the eastern shore just before you reach the span.

On Folly River Once abeam of Folly Creek to the west, you can continue cruising east on the river as far as the fixed bridge. This span also has only 10 feet of vertical clearance and effectively blocks the way for most cruising craft. Before you reach the span, Mariners Cay Marina will come abeam on the northern shore.

ICW to North Edisto River

From the mouth of Elliott Cut the ICW follows the upper reaches of the Stono River as the stream makes a long loop to the west. The route then intersects the headwaters of Wadmalaw River. The Wadmalaw leads the waterway cruiser to the intersection of Toogoodoo Creek and North Edisto River. The entire channel is well marked and poses no unusual navigational difficulties.

The upper Stono is fairly sheltered and usually boasts smooth cruising. However, Wadmalaw River is flanked by large areas of saltwater marsh for much of its length. Stiff breezes have more than enough fetch to make for a bumpy ride.

Several small creeks along the way offer good overnight anchorage for craft under 40 feet. Larger vessels will have to find anchorages farther along, on the North Edisto. There are no facilities along this stretch, so make sure your tanks are topped off before leaving the Stono's marinas behind.

The shoreline along this stretch varies from undeveloped saltwater marsh and mud flats to higher, wooded shores with light residential development. This is an attractive section of the waterway and should provide an interesting cruise.

Stono River Anchorage

Chart 11518 shows a loop north of flashing daybeacon #39 with 10- to 13-foot depths.

WAPPOO CREEK TO SOUTH EDISTO RIVER   137

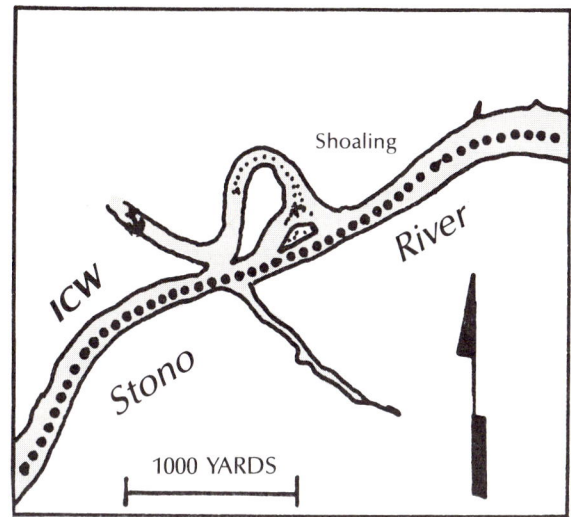

Shoaling not noted on the chart has raised entrance depths to 3 feet or less. Don't attempt to enter!

Another branch of the creek leads north from unlighted daybeacon #41. This section of the stream maintains minimum depths of 8 feet, though care must be taken when entering to avoid an unmarked shoal. Swinging room should be sufficient for anchorage by craft under 36 feet. The undeveloped marsh grass shores do not give enough protection for heavy weather but should be adequate for light to moderate airs. There are no facilities on the creek.

Further downstream, near unlighted daybeacon #52, is the general area where the Stono Slave Rebellion took place. This infamous uprising was discussed earlier in the chapter.

New Cut Creek

The mouth of New Cut Creek is found south of unlighted daybeacon #64. As chart 11518 notes, shoals guard the entrance. Don't attempt to enter. New Cut Creek can be entered from Church Creek, as discussed below.

Church Creek

Church Creek offers the best overnight anchorage on Wadmalaw River. Its entrance channel is broad and deep. The western portion of the creek's interior is wide enough to accommodate vessels of up to 40 feet. This section of the stream is well protected and should be a good spot to drop the hook in all but the heaviest of weather. Just to make your evening a bit more interesting, a beautiful old home overlooks the creek at New Cut Landing on the western banks. This venerable structure was actually built in nearby Rockville in 1842. It was moved to its present location in 1900.

Upstream, Church Creek splits. New Cut Creek leads off to the north. Continued passage on Church Creek is not recommended, and only adventurous skippers should consider cruising New Cut Creek. If you do choose to enter, make sure to read the Church Creek navigation section presented later in this chapter.

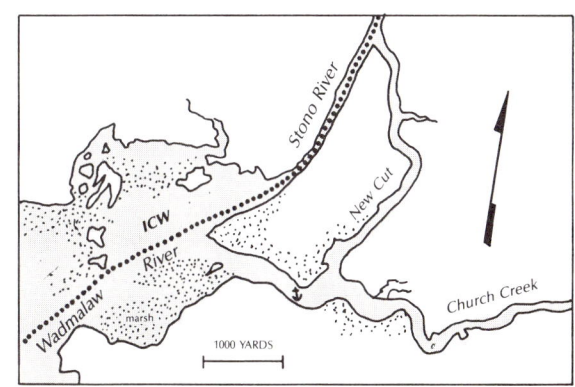

Oyster House Creek

Oyster House Creek makes into the western shore of the Wadmalaw near flashing daybeacon #90. The stream makes a good overnight anchorage for craft that can stand some 5-foot readings. The creek's entrance is guarded by shallows, but vessels under 40 feet in length that draw 3½ feet or less should not hesitate to make use of the creek, providing proper caution is exercised. If you do choose to enter, be sure to read the Oyster Creek navigation section later in this chapter.

Most of the shoreline is undeveloped marsh, but there is one beautiful home on the entrance's western point. This writer has not been able to learn the history of the stately structure, but it's a safe bet that it has guarded the creek's mouth for many a year.

Old house on Oyster Creek

ICW to North Edisto River Navigation

This section of the waterway does not present any unusual navigational difficulty, but it does require careful attention. It is well marked and generally deep. A number of ranges aid slower craft in keeping to the channel. On the negative side, several shoals flank the ICW here and there. Boaters who enjoy their cruise a bit too much and fail to take heed of the waterway markers could end up contemplating the value of coastal navigation from a sandbar or oyster bank.

Entrance from Elliott Cut When leaving Elliott Cut, point to come abeam of unlighted daybeacon #13 to its fairly immediate northerly side. Don't let leeway ease you towards the northern quarter of the river. As shown on chart 11518, a large patch of shoal water extends well out into the main body from the northern banks.

Continue on the waterway by passing unlighted daybeacon #14 to its southerly side, and point to come abeam of flashing daybeacon #15 by some 50 yards (no closer) to its northerly side. Be careful to avoid the small area of shallow water to the west of #15.

Navigation of the channel is straightforward until reaching flashing daybeacon #19. Favor the southern shore while cruising to the next upriver aid, flashing daybeacon #25.

At #25 the waterway takes a sharp turn to the north. Pass unlighted daybeacon #27 to its easterly side in order to avoid the shoal abutting the western banks. Continue to observe all markers carefully until reaching the John E. Limehouse Bridge west of flashing daybeacon #D.

The bridge opens on demand and has a closed vertical clearance of 12 feet. Past the bridge, the ICW channel narrows and can be navigated with much less difficulty.

Stono River Anchorage Remember that the small, looped creek north of flashing daybeacon #39 has now shoaled to 3- and 4-foot depths. Avoid this section of the creek altogether.

Favor the port shore if you choose to enter the navigable section of the stream north of unlighted daybeacon #41. The area with the best swinging room is found about 50 yards upstream from the mouth. Passage on the creek is eventually blocked by a low-level fixed railway bridge.

Church Creek If you choose to make use of Church Creek's excellent anchorage, continue on the waterway channel until you are some 50 yards west of flashing daybeacon #77. Then swing around to the east and point towards the mid-width of the creek's entrance.

Once on the stream's interior, continue cruising on the mid-width. Good depths are maintained as far as the intersection with the westerly reaches of New Cut Creek. One of the best spots to drop the hook is the area abeam of the attractive home visible on the southwestern banks at New Cut Landing.

Eventually the stream intersects the southern mouth of New Cut. Continued passage on Church Creek is not recommended, as depths soon become uncertain. New Cut can be cruised by adventurous captains with craft under 35 feet in length for some distance upstream. However, the creek does not have as much swing room or protection as the lower section of Church Creek. If you do choose to cruise the stream, stick to the mid-width and discontinue your passage before reaching the shoals that block the northern entrance.

Oyster House Creek Remember, do not enter Oyster House Creek unless your boat draws 3½ feet or less. For best depths, favor the port banks heavily when entering. Continue downstream until the house described earlier comes abeam to port. Consider dropping the hook here. Because depths become even more uncertain further upstream, further passage is not recommended for cruising craft.

On the ICW West of unlighted daybeacon #105 the Wadmalaw rushes to meet Toogoodoo Creek. These two streams join to form the fabled North Edisto River. This discussion will now turn to the cruising possibilities of Toogoodoo Creek, followed by those of lower North Edisto River. Continued description of the ICW will be resumed later in this chapter.

Toogoodoo Creek

Indian-named Toogoodoo Creek is such a large stream that one wonders why it is not "Toogoodoo River." Certainly smaller streams in coastal South Carolina bear the more important designation.

One well-repected guide warns against entrance of Toogoodoo by any craft. That guide claims that shoaling has raised the bottom to dangerous levels. However, during extensive on-site research, I sounded minimum depths of 7 feet. I did not find any shoals between the creek's mouth and the area where it splits into upper and lower branches, some 3 nautical miles upstream. Consequently, I recommend Toogoodoo Creek to my readers, but as always, you should proceed with caution.

Below the split, large sections of the creek's shoreline exhibit the usual marsh grass, but other portions border on higher ground. This area is quite attractive and seems to be excellent cruising ground. The stream is a bit too open here for all but light air anchorage.

Of the two branches formed at the split, the western is the better cruising opportunity. The eastern branch, known as Lower Toogoodoo Creek, is peppered with unmarked shoals that make navigation a bit too tricky for larger cruising craft. The western arm, on the other

WAPPOO CREEK TO SOUTH EDISTO RIVER 141

hand, offers good depths well upstream, excellent protection, and several sights well worth your attention.

Several hundred yards up western Toogoodoo Creek from the intersection, the marshy shores give way to higher, well-wooded banks. Several fine homes overlook the water, and a project is underway to stabilize the lower shoreline with concrete riprap. This area of the creek would make an ideal spot to drop the hook for almost any craft under 45 feet. Protection should be sufficient for heavy weather.

Further upstream, good depths continue for some distance. Eventually you will spy an old car ferry rotting on the starboard banks. Depths become uncertain past this old derelict.

Lem's Bluff Plantation

The house at Lem's Bluff Plantation is readily visible at the forks of Toogoodo Creek. Built in 1842, the home was enlarged extensively in the 1960s. Watch the starboard shore carefully as you cruise up the western branch and you can catch a quick glimpse of the older section of the house atop a high earthen bank.

Old ferry on Toogoodoo Creek

Toogoodoo Creek Navigation

Successful navigation of Toogoodoo Creek seems to be a simple study in coastal piloting. To enter, avoid the point of marsh separating Toogoodoo Creek and Wadmalaw River. Past the entrance, good depths open out almost from shore to shore.

After a run of some 1.5 nautical miles, the port shore will begin to rise. If winds are light, you might consider dropping the hook here. If you need more shelter, continue on to the creek's western arm.

Begin favoring the western banks as you approach the split. A large body of very shoal water extends out from the eastern shoreline. Curve around to port and enter western Toogoodoo Creek on its mid-width.

As you are performing this maneuver, look to the north and you will see the newer section of Lem's Bluff Plantation house. The western stream first bends to the north but soon cuts back sharply to the west and leaves the chart. Watch the starboard shore before reaching the westerly turn to catch sight of the plantation's older section.

Even though western Toogoodoo Creek soon leaves chart 11522, good depths continue far upstream. One of the best sections for anchorage is found just beyond the first sharp turn to the west. Here the northern shore is lined with tall pines and other hardwoods, which give excellent protection. Remember to stop after coming abeam of the old ferry.

North Edisto River

North Edisto River is, quite simply, one of the finest bodies of water for cruising purposes in all of coastal South Carolina. It is a beautiful stream, free from shoals and readily navigable. The shores present a pleasing contrast between marsh grass and higher, forested banks. The river boasts a number of sidewaters, several of which are well suited for overnight anchorage. The North Edisto also has good facilities. Two marinas are found on Bohicket Creek not far from the river's inlet. One is a full-service facility with an on-site restaurant and all the amenities.

Additionally, many historical sites are readily visible from the waters of the North Edisto and its creeks. Here you can pause to contemplate fine old plantation homes that once overlooked vast fields of Sea Island cotton. Many of these estates have fascinating legends attached to their history. Several of these tales will be reviewed in the body of this chapter.

About the only drawback to the North Edisto is the sharp chop sometimes spawned by strong breezes on the river's ample width. Pick a day of light to moderate airs and you should not have any difficulty.

To summarize, North Edisto River has just about every quality the cruising boater could

WAPPOO CREEK TO SOUTH EDISTO RIVER   143

ever desire. Easily navigable, attractive, and historical, this storied stream waits eagerly to greet you.

Edisto Island

Edisto Island borders the western reaches of North Edisto River for most of its length. Like most other Sea Islands, Edisto produced a thriving cotton culture before the Civil War. Unlike many others, however, most of Edisto Island's plantations survived the war. Edisto was abandoned by most of the white population before Union occupation. The beautiful homes they left behind were used to house Yankee troops and freed slaves. Edisto's families later returned and reclaimed their homeplaces. While some plantations have fallen victim to the years, many are still intact and some have been restored to their former glory.

Not only the plantation homes have survived on Edisto Island. Among a host of historical and folk accounts that this writer reviewed in preparation for this guide, Nell S. Graydon's fascinating accounts of the island planters clearly stand out as the most unforgettable of the lot. In her book *Tales of Edisto,* Ms. Graydon gives a haunting portrait of Edisto Island as it is today and as it was in days long gone. Listen as she describes her beloved island.

"Forty miles southwest of Charleston . . . within the arms of two tidal rivers, lies a fabulous Island. An aura of mystic and alluring charm hovers over the Island and its old homes. Weird gray moss shrouds with ghostly grandeur the queenly magnolias and gnarled

Old naval craft on Tom Point Creek

Octagonal House, Steamboat Creek

live oaks around the plantation houses. . . .

"In the stillness of the early evening, the faint haunting melody of a slave lullaby drifting through the twilight, the galloping of a horse passing by, the echo of a footstep, or the swish of a silken skirt can bring forth half-forgotten memories of long ago. Then, if you have been welcomed into the homes and hearts of the Island, you may hear stories of the people and the land. . . .

"Edisto changes, but somehow remains the same. Today, there is the hum of automobile tires on the highway and the bustle of holiday crowds on the beach. But the phantoms of the past persist. Amid the roar of the ocean surf . . . a wave slaps the beach with the sound of a pistol shot. The gray moss streams from live oaks like plumes from the helmets of young men dressed in the armor of the tournament. An old Island resident bows in passing with the courtesy and the calm assurance of a bygone era. Just as surely as the flood tide leaves its imprint on the shore, life marks a land."

Tom Point Creek

Tom Point Creek is a deep stream that makes into the western shore of North Edisto River north of White Point Landing. Its undeveloped, marshy shores give only minimal protection, but the creek would make a good light to moderate air anchorage. Minimum depths are around 8 feet. There are no facilities on the creek.

During research this writer was amazed to observe four large, mothballed naval craft moored on the port shore of the creek. So incongruous was this sight on this isolated creek that I spent quite some time just gazing at the old vessels in wonder. They appear to be in fairly good condition, as if someone had big plans that never came to pass for these old servants of the sea.

Steamboat Creek

The entrance to Steamboat Creek is found west of unlighted daybeacon #2 south of Dawho River. This beautiful stream leads the cruising boater to two historical sites on Edisto Island. The creek is free of shoals as far as its intersection with Russel Creek and boasts minimum depths of 8 feet.

While a bit wide for good protection, the waters of Steamboat Creek are usually tranquil unless a fresh breeze is blowing. If you do not anticipate bad weather, consider dropping the hook here for a night that will not soon be forgotten.

While most of the shore is the usual marsh grass, a stretch of higher ground will be sighted on the southern shore some 1.2 nautical miles upstream from the entrance. Here, not one, but two historical sites well worth your attention can be observed.

You will first catch sight of a small, octagonal brick building with high windows. This interesting structure was used by the island residents as they waited for the steamboats that regularly plied the waters between Edisto Island and Charleston before the Civil War. Apparently, this quaint mode of transportation also gave the creek its name.

William Seabrook Plantation

You must look carefully to the southeast behind the octagonal building to catch sight of the William Seabrook Plantation house, now known as Dodge Plantation. According to the South Carolina Sea Grant Consortium, it was built in 1810 and represents "the wealth brought to island planters by their fine long-staple cotton crops. This house set the style of houses built on the island by many other planters."

In *Tales of Edisto* Nell Graydon describes the one-time grandeur of Seabrook House. "The house is close to the water's edge, with an iron railing bordering the portico and the double front steps. Seabrook had his initials molded across the front of the ironwork. . . . Between Steamboat Creek and the house was a formal garden with a multitude of walkways bordered with boxwood. Here, on warm afternoons in the early spring and late fall, tea was served, and many a frosted glass of julep sipped."

In 1825 the William Seabrook House received one of the most honored guests it has ever known. The Marquis de Lafayette was on

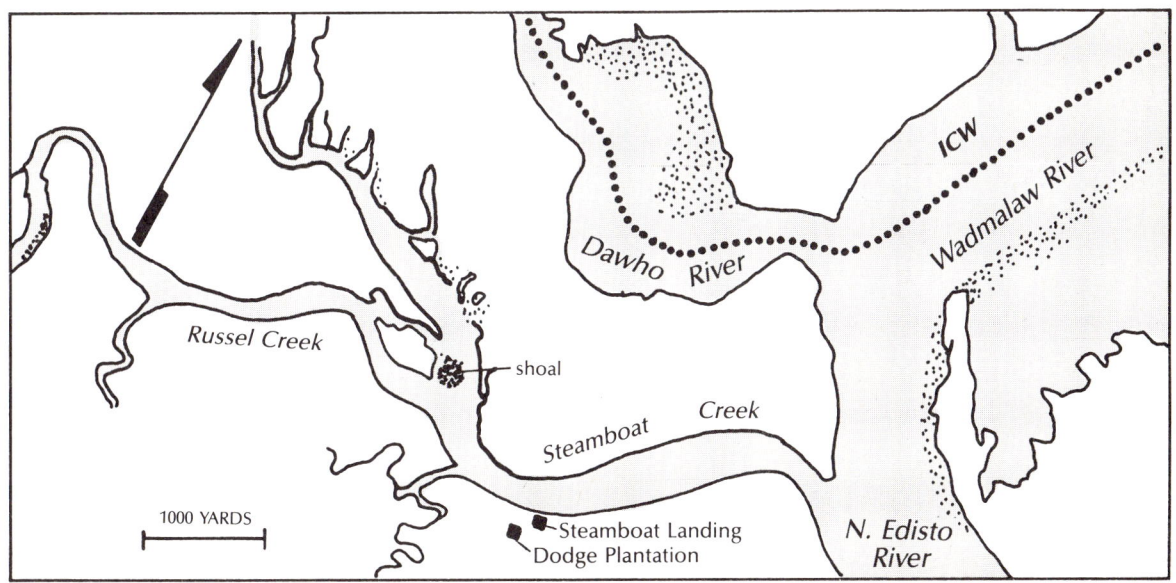

a tour of the new United States and accepted an invitation to visit the island home. The entertainment and hospitality shown to the dashing hero of the Revolution was in the best sumptuous Sea Island tradition.

While Lafayette was in residence, he was asked to name the youngest daughter of William Seabrook, who had been born just a few days before the marquis's visit. Without hesitation, Lafayette dubbed her Carolina Lafayette Seabrook. We shall meet this remarkable woman again in connection with another Edisto Island plantation.

Some years later, William Seabrook's son returned from a trip abroad and proceeded to hold forth at great length about the pomp and glitter of Paris. Eventually Mr. Seabrook, according to Nell Graydon, had enough of his young son's colorful descriptions, and "lapsing into the Gullah of the Island said, 'Yuh like 'um son, I buy 'um fur yuh.'" While, to be sure, Mr. Seabrook wasn't serious, this laughable episode shows how the Sea Island planters often became so accustomed to their own wealth that the purchase of an entire European capital did not seem too extravagant.

Westbank Creek

The mouth of Westbank Creek fronts onto the western shore of North Edisto River some 2.0 nautical miles south of the Dawho. The creek maintains 6-foot minimum depths on its mid-width and affords sufficient swing room for craft up to 36 feet to anchor. There are a few shallow water areas to avoid, but the careful cruiser should not have any difficulty.

The shores of Westbank Creek are mostly saltwater marsh and mud flats, but as the stream takes a sharp turn to the north a section of higher ground flanks the western shore. Here two splendid plantation homes watch serenely over the creek. Both were built during the height of the Sea Island cotton culture. The presence of these two landmarks makes a cruise of Westbank Creek an unforgettable experience.

Cassina Point Plantation

The beautifully restored Cassina Point Plantation house is the first of the two historic structures you will encounter on Westbank Creek. The lovely house sits back some distance from the water, but the marsh grass cannot hide the quiet grandeur of this old homeplace.

Cassina Point Plantation was the home of Carolina Lafayette Seabrook and her husband, James Hopkinson. They lived here peacefully until the end of their days, but their great house was not built without some difficulty.

Carolina Lafayette grew up in an atmosphere of unbelievable wealth in her father's house. She became a beautiful woman by all

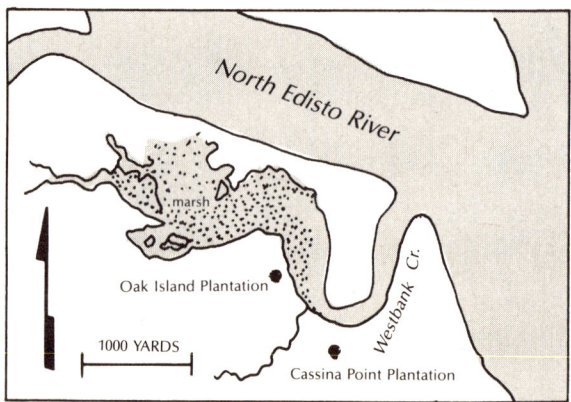

WAPPOO CREEK TO SOUTH EDISTO RIVER 147

accounts and eventually left South Carolina for a grand trip abroad to the courts of Europe. Returning to the United States, Carolina made the rounds of the party circuit in the Northeast.

In the North she met James Hopkinson, dashing grandson of the New Jersey signer of the Declaration of Independence. He became so infatuated with Carolina that he followed her home to Edisto Island. Here he quickly grew to love the island and adopted coastal South Carolina as his new home.

Carolina, however, had other ideas. She delighted in the attention commanded by her beauty and reputation in Northern society and wished to make her home in the Northeast.

When Hopkinson asked for her hand, she consented on the condition that he would agree to live in the North. The young man had already planned a grand plantation on Edisto Island and so he refused Carolina's request. So strong was the young girl's will that the lumber for Cassina Point sat on the site for three years before Carolina finally relented and the grand house was built at last.

Oak Island Plantation

Oak Island is the second plantation on Westbank Creek. It sits closer to the water than Cassina Point, and the visiting cruiser should have an excellent view of the noble structure. This plantation house, too, has

Cassina Point Plantation, Westbank Creek

been lovingly restored. It is a beautiful sight when seen from the placid waters of the creek.

Oak Island Plantation was built by the brother of Carolina Lafayette, William Seabrook, Jr. Here he lived with his wife, Martha Edings, in the greatest luxury imaginable. Shortly after the Civil War, the couple's son wrote his reminiscences of Oak Island as it was in its days of glory. Recounted by Nell Graydon in *Tales of Edisto*, this passage is almost dreamlike in its description, not only of the house and its grounds, but in the lifestyle of the Sea Island planters.

"I became so accustomed to its grandeur it ceased to impress me . . . lawns encircling the house occupied acres, outbuildings of every description, camellias of every known species, 1500 varieties of roses, an apiary and fish pond in the middle of which there was a latticed house covered with roses. A rustic bridge crossed to the Island. Walkways were covered with crushed shells. At the end of the avenue there was a park with many deer— including a white one. There was a quaint brick house where an iron chest of select wines were kept. Near the water was a dairy, a building made of crushed shells. Just be-

Oak Island Plantation, Westbank Creek

WAPPOO CREEK TO SOUTH EDISTO RIVER 149

yond the dairy was a large long boat house. Sail and row boats were kept there and above were the bath houses. In the carriage house were seven or eight vehicles. The family used to ride to Virginia Springs and carriages were kept there during their stay and sent home the first of September when the family went to New York."

Leadenwah Creek

Leadenwah Creek is located on the eastern banks of the North Edisto directly across the river from Westbank Creek. This stream has numerous unmarked shoals, making navigation quite tricky for cruising craft. There is a fairly deep channel with 6-foot minimum depths, if you can find it, and the creek does offer some anchorage possibilities. Because of its hazards, Leadenwah is recommended only for craft under 35 feet captained by adventurous skippers.

The starboard shore supports fairly extensive residential development, but the port banks are the familiar saltwater marsh. One particularly beautiful home sits prominently on the fork of the creek near its mouth. There are no facilities in the area.

Bohicket Creek

Bohicket Creek is a large stream on the eastern shores of the North Edisto near the river's inlet. This important water body is host to the area's best facilities and to numerous historical sites as well. Cruising boaters traveling on North Edisto River will certainly want to make the acquaintance of Bohicket Creek.

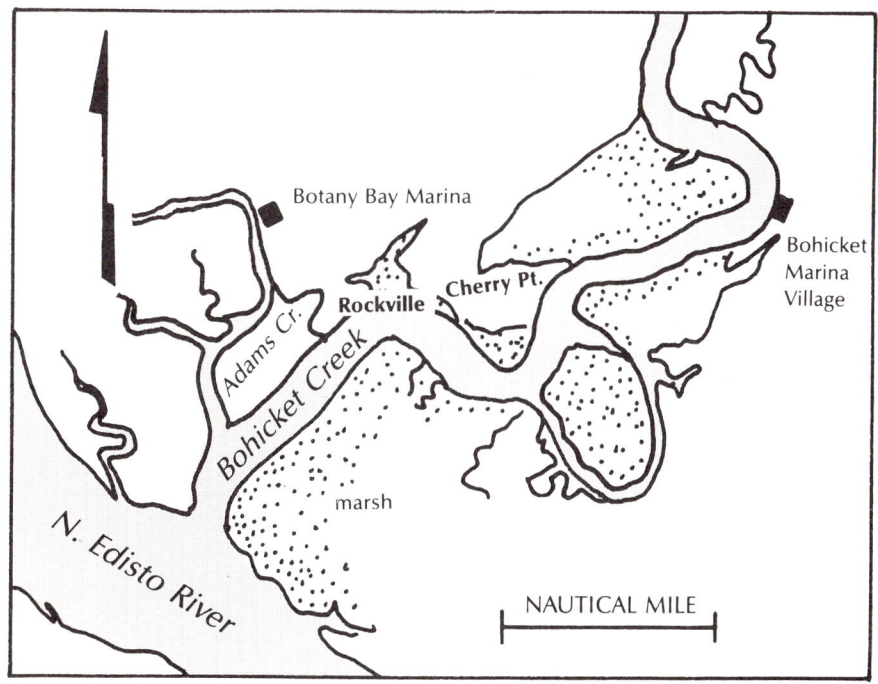

Bohicket Marina Village, one of the finest facilities of its kind in all of coastal South Carolina, is found 3 nautical miles upstream on the creek's southern banks. This ultramodern marina-condo complex gladly accepts transient boaters and boasts floating docks with all power and water connections. Gasoline and diesel fuel are readily available, as is a well-stocked ships' store. The marina offers both mechanical and below-the-waterline repairs. There is also an on-site restaurant with a far-ranging reputation for fine seafood and beef. The management is friendly and eager to greet the visiting cruiser. Bohicket Marina is about as good a spot as you will ever find to coil the lines and rest from your travels.

Lower Bohicket Creek can serve as an anchorage for craft of almost any size. However, the stream is larger than you might expect from a casual study of the charts. Protection is adequate only for light breezes. There is more shelter upstream, but there are also hazards to be avoided.

The lower creek is peppered with shoals here and there, but these hazards are marked by unlighted daybeacons as far as Bohicket Marina. Strangely enough, these aids are not marked on the current edition of chart 11522. However, navigation of the lower creek should not be a problem for the careful skipper who observes the well-placed markers.

Past the marina Bohicket Creek extends for

Rectory House, Rockville, Bohicket Creek

some 12 nautical miles to the northeast until it finally peters out in a marshy area above Hoopstick Island. While most of this route holds minimum depths of 7 feet, there are numerous unmarked shoals to be avoided. This area is not recommended for craft that draw more than 4 feet or those over 35 feet in length. If you do choose to cruise this upper portion of the Bohicket, take your time and watch the sounder.

The shoreline of Bohicket Creek offers a variety of scenery to the visiting boater. The familiar saltwater marsh is very much in evidence as you would expect. Other sections present higher, wooded shores with moderate residential development. Many of the homes on the upper reaches of the creek have long piers extending across the marsh grass to docks fronting onto the deep water. Just upstream from Bohicket Marina, a Girl Scout camp borders the port shore. Unquestionably, though, the most impressive sight on the shores of Bohicket Creek is the village of Rockville.

Rockville

Established in the 1800s as a summer watering place for the Sea Island planters, Rockville is perhaps the best preserved example of those warm weather retreats. Today Rockville, sitting serenely on the shores of Bohicket Creek, looks quietly over the waters much as it has for over 150 years. The village's simple but beautiful homes are a lovely sight from the water. More than one passing boater has paused in his travels to admire their quiet elegance.

Every summer the quiet community erupts in pageantry and enthusiasm when the annual Rockville Regatta is held on Bohicket Creek. Beginning in the 1890s, the yearly race has continued its unbroken tradition to the present day. If you happen to be in the area during the celebration, don't fail to stop by and join in the festivities.

Adams Creek

Adams Creek is an offshoot of its larger sister, the Bohicket. The smaller stream breaks off from the larger creek about .5 of a nautical mile from the North Edisto. Locally the stream is known as Breakfast Creek because large numbers of breakfast shrimp are often netted here.

Adams Creek boasts an easily followed channel with several interesting homes along the way. There is swing room for vessels under 32 feet to anchor, but you must be careful to select a spot that will avoid the commercial fishing traffic that often plies the creek. One of the best spots to drop the hook is found just past the last commercial docks as the creek takes a bend to the west.

Botany Bay Marina is found on the eastern banks of Adams Creek. This small facility specializes in all types of repair work. Both mechanical and below-the-waterline service are readily available. Gasoline and diesel fuel can be purchased. The marina does not offer overnight dockage for transients, but if you need repairs, this would be an excellent port of call.

North Edisto Inlet

The North Edisto Inlet is much wider and more stable than most South Carolina seaward cuts. It is marked by several charted aids, which usually implies the presence of a

152 CRUISING GUIDE TO COASTAL SOUTH CAROLINA

fairly stable channel. However, as is true with all inlets, it is subject to continual change and can quickly give rise to heavy seas. It would be most wise to check on current channel conditions at Bohicket Marina before running the cut. If you do make the attempt, proceed with caution and keep a wary eye on the sounder.

North Edisto River Navigation

As noted, North Edisto River is wide, deep, and generally free of shoals. The cruising boater need simply avoid the few shallow areas noted on chart 11522 for successful navigation of the river.

There are very few aids to navigation on the North Edisto. While this does not present any real difficulty as far as staying off the bottom, it does call for good observation to maintain a fix on your position. It's quite easy to cruise pleasantly down the North Edisto, enjoying the river and the landscape, then suddenly realize that you do not know where you are. To avoid this problem, note the passing of the various creeks as you work your way downstream.

All boaters who do not plan to cruise Toogoodoo Creek will need to turn south at

Shrimper on Adams Creek

flashing daybeacon #106 and enter the broad waters of the North Edisto. About .8 of a nautical mile downstream, the mouth of Tom Point Creek will come abeam on the western shore.

Tom Point Creek Enter the creek on its mid-width and continue to hold the middle ground as you cruise upstream. The area with the most swinging room is found after the stream makes its first turn to the west. Here you can anchor in some 8 to 12 feet of water with fairly good protection. The old naval craft spoken of earlier are found on the port shore a bit further upstream. Discontinue your cruise before reaching Park Island.

On the North Edisto South of Tom Point Creek the next sidewater encountered is Dawho River. This stream is part of the ICW and will be covered later in this chapter.

Stick to the mid-width of the North Edisto and it is a straightforward run south to the mouth of Steamboat Creek.

Steamboat Creek The entrance of Steamboat Creek is marked by unlighted daybeacon #2. Pass #2 to its southerly side and enter the creek on its mid-width. Continue holding to the mid-width and you can cruise as far as the the intersection of Russel and Long creeks with 10-foot minimum depths. Watch the southerly shore as you cruise along and you will catch sight of the octagonal steamboat house about halfway between the entrance and the split.

Under no circumstances should you consider cruising farther upstream than the confluence of Russel and Long creeks. At the time of this writing, shoaling not noted on the latest edition of chart 11522 had raised depths to dangerous levels on both creeks. Discontinue your passage of Steamboat Creek before reaching the forks.

On the North Edisto It is another straightforward southerly run of about 1.5 nautical miles to a point abeam of Leadenwah Creek to the east and Westbank Creek to the west. Again, hold to the mid-width of the river and don't allow leeway to ease you onto the small shoal near Wadmalaw Point.

Westbank Creek For best depths, favor the port shore a bit when entering Westbank Creek. As the stream begins to bend to the west, good depths open out almost from shore to shore. Watch the port banks and you will spy the two historic plantations on the creek's southern banks as the creek bends to the north. This is an excellent spot to drop the hook. While good depths continue for some distance, the creek's upper reaches border extensive mud flats and protection is minimal. The upper reaches of the stream are not recommended for cruising craft.

Leadenwah Creek Successful navigation of Leadenwah Creek calls for cautious cruising. As you can see from a quick study of chart 11522, the stream's entrance is flanked by unmarked shoals. The interior sections are also plagued with shallow areas. If you choose to enter, feel your way along at slow speed and watch the sounder.

Be careful to avoid the considerable shoal protruding from the northwest point when entering. You must also take care to bypass the shallow water abutting the eastern shore. Study chart 11522 carefully to familiarize yourself with the necessary maneuvers.

For best depths, proceed south down the North Edisto far enough to turn back north and enter the creek's mid-width. Once inside, good depths open out from bank to bank as far as the creek's first split.

Do not try to enter the western branch of the first fork. It is shoal and narrow. Favor the eastern bank when entering the easterly arm. This maneuver will avoid the shoal on the western shore, clearly shown on chart 11522.

One of the best spots for overnight anchorage is found between this point and the stream's next loop. Here you can drop the hook in 9 to 13 feet of water with fair protection.

Upstream the creek takes a hairpin turn back to the south. Begin favoring the starboard shore as you enter the bend. You will spy several houses on the eastern shore in this section. This is another good anchorage, though it does not have as much swinging room as the first location. The high starboard banks do give better protection, however, particularly in southwesterly blows.

Continued passage upstream is not recommended except for very adventurous skippers. Unmarked shoals abound, and it is all too easy to run aground just when you think all is well. If you do choose to proceed, study the shoal areas marked on chart 11522 carefully. According to this writer's on-site research, the chart is accurate in this section. Cruise at idle speed and keep a steady watch on the sounder.

Bohicket Creek To enter Bohicket Creek, pass well to the southeast of the forward North Edisto Inlet lighted range marker. Point to pass unlighted daybeacon #2 to starboard and set course to come abeam of unlighted daybeacon #4 well to its northwesterly side. These two markers will lead you past the mouth of Adams Creek to the west.

As you pass #4 you will observe the town of Rockville to the northwest. Take a few moments to admire the beauty of the town's historic homes. You can cruise to within 50 yards of the shore and continue holding good depths.

The creek now takes a long loop to the south and then back to the north. Unlighted daybeacon #5 marks an area of very shallow water on the northern shore. Favor the southern banks heavily through the bend.

Just before the creek takes another jog to the east, unlighted daybeacon #6 warns of shoal water on the easterly shore. Pass #6 well to its westerly side.

Favor the southerly shore just a bit as you swing out of the loop. Continue cruising upstream and Bohicket Marina will soon come abeam to starboard.

Further exploration of Bohicket Creek is not for the faint of heart. While 7-foot minimum depths are held for the most part on the stream's mid-width, there are numerous unmarked shoals waiting to trap the unwary boater. This area is strictly not recommended for craft drawing more than 4 feet. Otherwise, if you are the adventurous type who has to see it all, feel your way along, strenuously avoid points of land, and, as always in suspect waters, watch the sounder.

Those who do proceed upstream will soon encounter the Girl Scout camp, mentioned earlier, on the port banks. About 4 nautical miles further upstream, two beautiful white homes with a wide expanse of green grass will be observed on the western banks. All but small craft should discontinue their cruise once abeam of the two houses. Local knowledge is needed to cruise further.

Botany Bay Marina, Adams Creek

ICW to South Edisto River

The ICW leaves the western mouth of Wadmalaw River and follows the North Edisto to the southwest for 1.5 nautical miles. The waterway then enters the easterly reaches of Dawho River and follows this stream till it intersects Watts Cut. The cut leads in turn to South Edisto River.

This section of the ICW is remarkable only for its unusual navigational difficulty. Frequent shoaling not always noted on chart 11518 combines with improper placement of some markers to create a hazardous passage. During research this writer watched two large pleasure yachts come within several yards of running hard aground. Make no mistake, this short portion of the waterway has caused more than its share of headaches for cruising boaters. You are urged to read the navigational information presented in the next section and proceed with all due caution.

A quick study of chart 11518 would probably lead most boaters to think that a variety of good anchorages are available on Dawho River. Unfortunately, shoaling not noted on the chart has raised bottoms on all but one of these sidewaters to bare low tide mud flats. Except for Fishing Creek, the boater is strictly warned against any exploration of waters outside of the waterway channel in this area.

The shoreline is marsh grass for the most part, but here and there some higher banks do exhibit light residential development. There are also a few commercial fishing docks along the way.

The visiting boater will not find any facilities along this stretch of the waterway. In fact, the ICW traveler is pretty much on his own until reaching Beaufort, still many miles to the south.

Fishing Creek

Fishing Creek is found north of unlighted daybeacon #132 just west of the Dawho River swing bridge. This small but deep stream provides the only opportunity for sheltered overnight anchorage on Dawho River and Watts Cut. Even so, swinging room is sufficient only for boats under 34 feet in length. Minimum depths are between 8 and 10 feet, and much of the stream is deeper. The shoreline is composed entirely of marsh grass, which would not give enough protection for heavy weather. Even so, Fishing Creek is a good bet for overnight anchorage if there is sufficient swing room for your craft.

ICW to South Edisto River Navigation

Set course from flashing daybeacon #106 at the westerly extreme of Wadmalaw River to come abeam of flashing daybeacon #110, at the easterly entrance of Dawho River, to its southerly side. Swing to the west and set a new course to come abeam of unlighted can buoy #111 to its fairly immediate northerly side.

The short run between #111 and the area between the next two aids, unlighted daybeacon #112 and unlighted can buoy #113, is the first tricky section on this run. The shoals to the northwest have encroached on #112. Favor the southerly side of the channel and come abeam of #113 fairly close to its northerly side.

Set a new course to come abeam of unlighted daybeacon #116 to its fairly immediate southerly side. Ignore flashing daybeacon #115 found near the southern banks. An area of shoal water between these two aids, shown on chart 11518 as a patch of 5-foot water, has apparently worsened. To avoid the shallows, favor the northern side of the channel a bit when heading toward the next set of markers. However, you must not compensate too much or you will strike the shoal to the north and west of #116.

Point to come between flashing daybeacon #119 and unlighted daybeacon #118. The most hazardous stretch of the entire route is found between #119 and the next upstream aid, unlighted daybeacon #120. Do not attempt to run a straight course from the area between #119 and #118 to #120. Extensive oyster shoals have encroached on the northerly side of the waterway channel on this run. To avoid this hazard, continue due west from #119 for some 40 yards. Only then should you turn to the northwest and set course to come abeam of #120 by some 25 yards to its southerly side. Be careful not to let excessive leeway ease you onto the shoal to the north.

Past #120 the waterway becomes easier to follow and is generally free of shoals. Don't attempt to enter the loop to the north of unlighted daybeacon #126 or by its alternate entrance north of unlighted daybeacon #128. Both entrances have shoaled to bare mud at low tide. Also, the small loop south of #128 holds only some 1 to 2 feet of water at low tide.

The Dawho River swing bridge is soon sighted past flashing daybeacon #130. The span opens on demand. Proceed through at idle speed.

Fishing Creek The entrance to Fishing Creek is found just west of the bridge. To enter, favor the port shore heavily and pass unlighted daybeacon #132 to starboard. Once on the interior portion of the creek good depths are found from shore to shore. The long, straight stretch of the creek encountered after its first sharp turn to port is one of the best spots to anchor. Another good choice is found just before reaching the creek's split. For the explorers among us good depths continue far upstream.

On the ICW From Fishing Creek the ICW follows Watts Cut to South Edisto River. A continuing account of the waterway route will be presented in the next chapter.

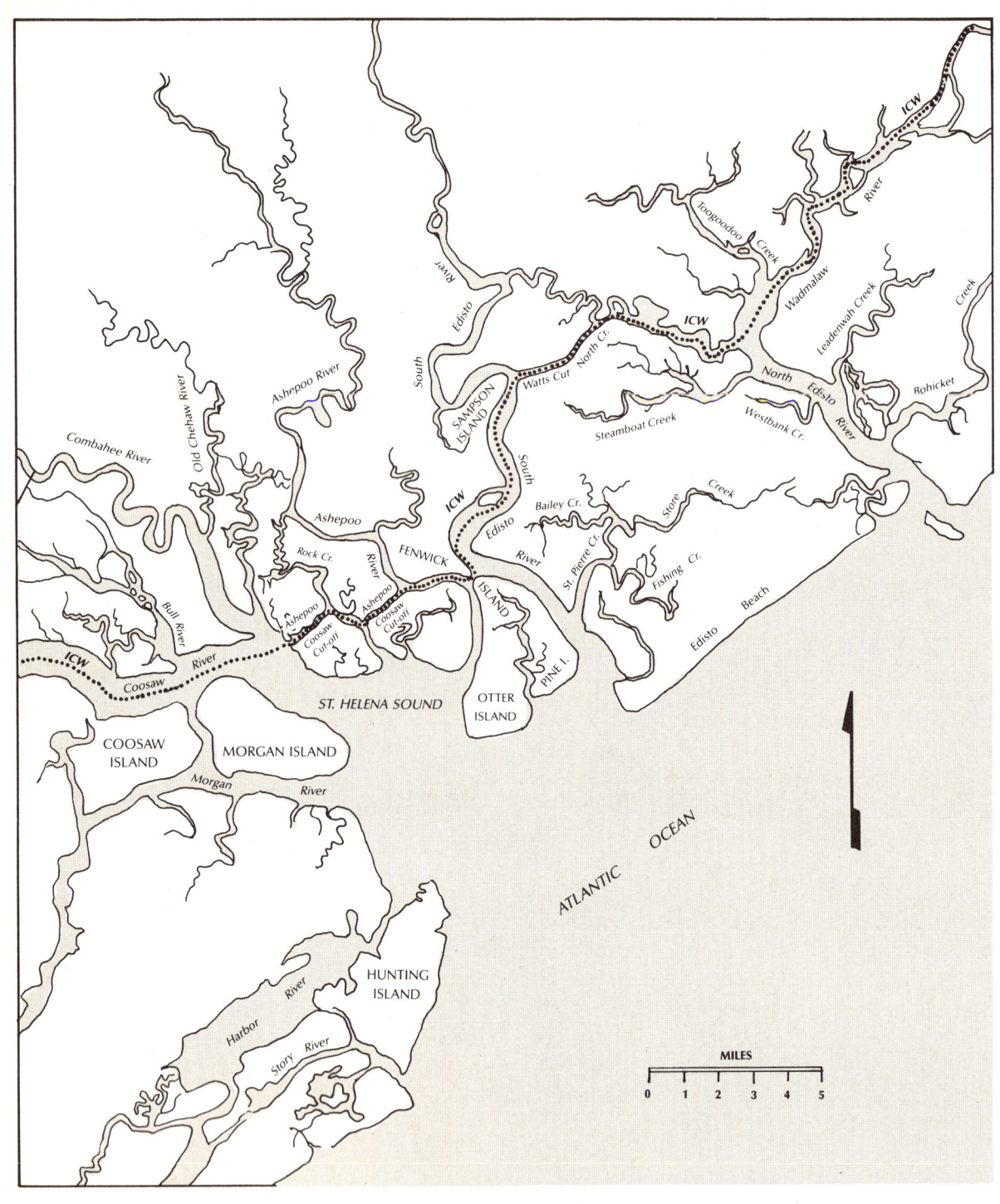

CHAPTER VI

South Edisto River to St. Helena Sound

A definite change in character becomes evident as one enters the waters of South Edisto River from the western mouth of the Dawho. Except for the ICW, friendly, well-traveled tracts give way to some of the most forlorn waters in all of coastal South Carolina. This condition persists all the way south to the beautiful port city of Beaufort.

Between the Dawho River and St. Helena Sound, three major bodies of water comprise the vast majority of the accessible cruising grounds: South Edisto River, Ashepoo River, and Rock Creek. All are traversed for a short distance by the ICW. Outside of the waterway's familiar confines, however, the boater will discover waters seldom visited by the passing cruiser. Those boaters who thrive on waters off the beaten path will find much to interest them here, while the cruiser who enjoys the lively atmosphere of coastal marinas may wish to put this stage of his journey quickly behind him.

Sunken skipjack on South Edisto River

Facilities are almost nonexistent in this section of coastal South Carolina. With only one exception, there is not a single establishment that welcomes the cruising boater between the Dawho and Beaufort River, far to the south. Be sure to have plenty of fuel on board before beginning your cruise.

On the other hand, anchorages abound. Several small streams and creeks stand ready to provide pleasant overnight stops, miles from the most remote vestige of civilization. In a few cases it is even possible to anchor within sight of a historic plantation for a truly memorable stay.

The area waters are relatively free from navigational hazards. The South Edisto, the Ashepoo, and Rock Creek are all mostly deep. There are exceptions, however, so be sure to consult the navigational sections in this chapter before venturing far off the ICW.

Much of the shoreline of the three streams consists of undeveloped saltwater marsh grass. A few small villages are to be found along the way, but the passing boater will not encounter a single major town on the water between Dawho River and Beaufort.

The ICW follows the course of South Edisto River for a short distance, then ducks across Ashepoo River and Rock Creek on its way to wide Coosaw River. This section of the waterway is relatively straightforward, with excellent shelter. The passing cruiser need not fear choppy waters unless the fickle wind exceeds 20 knots.

The waters of the South Edisto, the Ashepoo, and Rock Creek provide excellent, often historical cruising ground for the interested boater. Take your time and have the chart ready at hand, and some fascinating sights may well be your reward.

Charts Two charts are required to cover the waters discussed in this chapter:
11518 details the ICW to St. Helena Sound and covers portions of the South Edisto and Ashepoo rivers.
11517 covers the upper and lower sections of the South Edisto and Ashepoo rivers.

South Edisto River

South Edisto River provides excellent cruising grounds for the pleasure boater, though there are several unmarked shoals to be avoided. Don't be put off. Basic coastal navigation should see you through without any major difficulty.

Like its northern sister, the South Edisto boasts a wide inlet with several charted aids. While local knowledge is, as always, certainly desirable, it should be possible for cautious strangers to run the inlet successfully.

Numerous historical sites are found along the banks of the South Edisto and its auxiliary creeks. Most of the river's eastern banks are comprised of the western shores of storied Edisto Island. Several of the island's magnificent plantation homes can be seen from the waters of the South Edisto.

Only two creeks offer overnight anchorage opportunities on the lower South Edisto.

SOUTH EDISTO RIVER TO ST. HELENA SOUND

North of Watts Cut, only one small sidewater offers a protected haven. There are no marinas anywhere on the river. There used to be a small facility on Big Bay Creek near Edisto Beach, but this establishment is now closed. It is to be hoped that some enterprising individual will consider reopening this well-placed marina sometime in the future.

The ICW enters South Edisto River from Watts Cut and follows its course south for some 6 nautical miles before the waterway darts to the west on Fenwick Cut. The river is navigable for a considerable distance both north and south of the waterway channel. This account will first review the upper reaches of South Edisto River north of Watts Cut, then the ICW section, and finally the stream's southern reaches.

Upper South Edisto River

Upper South Edisto River is plagued by several shoals, but they are well defined on chart 11517 for the first 5 nautical miles, and careful navigation should see you through. Farther upstream, depths become too unreliable, and this section of the river should not be entered except by very small craft. While the undeveloped shores are lovely, particularly on a calm, bright autumn day, this is frankly a side trip which can be recommended only to adventurous see-it-all boaters.

Anchorages are very few and far between. One small sidewater offers a spot for craft under 28 feet to anchor. Another possible anchorage is found further upstream between a small island, which bisects the river near its practical cruising limits, and the western shore. Here the boater, surrounded by a beautifully undeveloped natural setting, can drop the hook in 10 to 17 feet of water. Protection is adequate only for light winds.

Sampson Island Creek

Sampson Island Creek is a small stream that makes into the western shores of the South Edisto about 2 nautical miles north of Watts Cut. The creek holds at least 8 feet of water until it splits into two branches. Good depths continue upstream for some distance on the southern fork, and there is enough swing room for craft under 28 feet to anchor. The shores are the usual undeveloped marsh grass, and no facilities are available. Protection would not be adequate for a heavy blow.

Upper South Edisto River Navigation

Those adventurous souls who choose to cruise the upper portion of South Edisto River should cut to the north once through the western mouth of Watts Cut. The river soon takes a sharp turn to the west. Begin heavily favoring the southern shore as you enter the turn. As chart 11518 clearly shows, there is shallow water on the northern shore.

The river now takes another sharp jog to

the north. You can cruise back to the stream's mid-width as you pass through this bend. The mouth of Sampson Island Creek will soon come abeam to the west.

Sampson Island Creek Enter Sampson Island Creek on its mid-width and follow the left-hand branch. Consider dropping the hook before proceeding too far upstream, as the small creek becomes even narrower.

On the South Edisto North of Sampson Island Creek hold to the mid-width until the river takes a sharp turn to the east. Begin favoring the southern shore heavily as you come out of the turn. As shown on chart 11517, there is very shoal water on the northern shore. Next, the South Edisto takes a sharp bend back to the north. There is very shoal water on the eastern banks in this area. Favor the western shore heavily to avoid this hazard.

Continue favoring the western banks as the river takes a slow jog to the east. You will soon sight a small island bisecting the river. It is possible to cruise between the small island and the western shore and hold minimum 8-foot depths, but you must halt your progress before reaching the island's northeastern tip. You might consider anchoring between the island and the mainland if winds do not exceed 15 knots. Past this anchorage, depths quickly fall off, and the twisting channels are much too treacherous for cruising craft.

ICW and South Edisto River

The ICW section of South Edisto River runs through fairly open water until the channel darts to the west at Fenwick Cut and leaves the river. With winds above 15 knots the chop can make for a dusty crossing. There are also several shoals along the way, but all are well marked. Be sure to observe all daybeacons carefully to avoid any unwelcome encounters with the bottom.

There are no sheltered anchorages between Watts and Fenwick cuts. As is true along the entire river, no facilities are available.

In fair weather, the cruising boater should enjoy this small section of the waterway. However, in heavy breezes, the visiting cruiser may remember this stretch for an entirely different reason.

Prospect Hill Plantation

East of unlighted daybeacon #152 Prospect Hill Plantation is readily visible from the water. This fascinating structure, which dates from 1790, is clearly designated as a point of reference on chart 11518 as "House."

Ephraim Baynard was the plantation's first owner and the stately design has been credited to James Hoban. Today Prospect Hill makes a truly spectacular sight from the water. Few other coastal South Carolina plantations are so readily observed from the waterway.

Prospect Hill Legend Many ghostly tales have been told about the wandering spirits that inhabit Prospect Hill. Ephraim Baynard was a great horse lover. Nell Graydon writes that "when the wind is high . . . the sound of wheels, the crack of a whip, and the beat of horses' hooves" can be heard "sweeping up the driveway."

Another tale relates the complaints of a long-time black caretaker who complained to the new owners about being bothered by Mr. Baynard's ghost. According to the old servant, the ghost incessantly rapped on his bedroom door, calling loudly to him and disturbing his sleep.

The plantation's most famous tale relates how Ephraim Baynard lost one of his favorite mounts. One fine day, so the story goes, Baynard had ridden alone to the nearby landing to collect several parcels he had ordered from Charleston for his wife and daughter. On the way home he stopped by a friend's house for a few drinks, and it was quite dark before he again set out on the road home. Mr. Baynard was passing the Presbyterian churchyard when a sudden gust of wind caused him to look at the path behind. Much to his astonishment, he saw a large white mass billowing directly behind his horse. In his fright the planter set his spurs to the fiery horse and fled down the road like the wind. When he dared to look back, his hair stood on end. Not only had he not left the phantom behind, but it seemed to be closer than ever. Baynard urged

Prospect Hill Plantation, South Edisto River

his prize horse on to even greater speed. As he entered his driveway the horse collapsed, giving his master a nasty fall. The noble beast was dead, his heart burst asunder by the great race. It was only then that the thoroughly bewildered planter realized that a long bolt of white linen had worked loose from one of the packages and had been trailing behind him. Ephraim Baynard must have been an embarrassed man when he realized that he had been frantically running from a few yards of cloth.

ICW and South Edisto Navigation

From flashing daybeacon #143, which marks the western exit of Watts Cut, swing sharply to the south and set course to pass unlighted daybeacons #147 and #149 fairly close to their westerly sides. With this procedure you will favor the eastern banks and avoid the shoals, clearly shown on chart 11518, which line the western shore.

From #147 a set of range markers on the western shore helps you stay to the channel. Swing to the south some 50 yards before reaching the range markers and point to come abeam of flashing daybeacon #151 to its westerly side. Don't allow leeway to ease you towards the large charted shoal on the eastern shore.

Continue on course and point to come abeam of unlighted daybeacon #152 to its easterly side. Look to the east and you will catch sight of Prospect Hill Plantation. If you avoid the shoal water to the north, it is possible to cruise to within 100 feet of the eastern banks for a better view.

Continue on the waterway by setting course to come abeam of unlighted daybeacon #152A to its easterly side. Look towards the southern shore and you will spy a pair of range markers. Cruise toward the markers until you are within about 50 yards of the pair. Swing to the southwest and set a new course to come abeam and pass unlighted daybeacons #154 and #156 to their southeasterly sides. Be sure to avoid the shallow water on the western shore, clearly shown on chart 11518.

From #156 another set of range markers leads you past unlighted daybeacon #157 to its northerly side. Swing to the south as you approach to within 75 yards of the range markers and set a new course to come abeam and pass unlighted daybeacons #159 and #161 to their westerly sides. The shoal area shown on chart 11518 east of #159 and #161 covers completely at high tide. You must be careful to avoid this area or a most unpleasant grounding will be the result.

Flashing daybeacon #162 marks the entrance to Fenwick Cut, where the waterway skirts to the west and enters Ashepoo River. This discussion will now turn to the cruising possibilities of the lower South Edisto River, abandoned by the waterway. A continuing account of the ICW route will be presented later in this chapter.

SOUTH EDISTO RIVER TO ST. HELENA SOUND 165

Lower South Edisto River

South Edisto River below Fenwick Cut is a delightful stream with only a few shoals, all of which are well marked. The attractive shores are undeveloped for the most part and alternate between low marsh and higher wooded shores. Several hospitable sidewaters offer safe haven for the night and interesting historical sites easily viewed from the water. As already noted, there are no facilities available in the area. Boaters would do well to include this inviting stream in their cruising plans.

St. Pierre Creek

St. Pierre Creek makes into the eastern banks of South Edisto River south of unlighted daybeacon #3. This stream is the largest sidewater on the lower South Edisto and leads to several smaller creeks and numerous historical points of interest. Cruising upstream, minimum depths of 10 feet are held to the intersection with Fishing Creek. As St. Pierre begins its first slow swing to the east, the western banks border the higher land of Bailey Island. This area can readily serve as an overnight anchorage for craft of almost any size. The waters are a little too broad for a comfortable stay if the winds exceed 15 knots, but otherwise boaters can drop the hook here with confidence.

Another anchorage possibility is found just after the creek loops back to the north. Here good depths open out from shore to shore and high ground fronts onto the eastern banks. This is a more sheltered spot than the downstream anchorage and has sufficient swinging room for craft up to 40 feet in length.

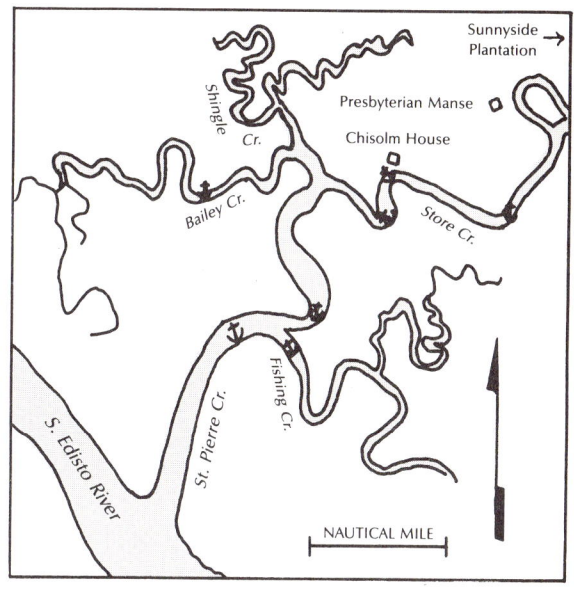

Fishing Creek

Fishing Creek splits off from St. Pierre Creek at Peters Point and wanders off to the south. The stream holds minimum 7-foot depths at least as far as its intersection with the small creek, shown on chart 11518, that leads to the north. Swinging room is sufficient for craft up to 35 feet. One of the best anchorages is found just upstream of the split, where the higher ground of Peters Point borders the eastern banks.

Until World War II a large oyster cannery was located on the shores of Fishing Creek. Here the famous Lady Edisto Oysters were canned. Longtime island residents will tell you they never tasted better canned oysters.

Bailey Creek

Bailey Creek branches off from St. Pierre about 1 nautical mile north of Peters Point.

The stream carries minimum depths of 7 feet for most of its length, but there are two small, unmarked shoals to be avoided. This would be a good spot to drop the hook for craft up to 35 feet. Consider anchoring in the section that fronts onto the northern shore of Bailey Island. The higher ground gives good protection.

The stream's shores alternate between the usual marsh grass and higher ground exhibiting light residential development. All in all, Bailey Creek can be recommended as an excellent anchorage or side trip.

In the 1880s Bailey Creek enjoyed the distinction of being one of the few areas of coastal South Carolina where subtidal oyster cultivation was practiced. At one time as much as twenty watery acres of the creek were under cultivation. There is no evidence left today of this once thriving industry. Like so many of the accomplishments of those days, it has faded into the fabric of the distant past.

Shingle Creek

Shingle Creek is a small offshoot of Bailey Creek. While the stream holds minimum depths of 5 to 6 feet for a short distance upstream, it is really too narrow for anchorage by any but very small craft and should probably be bypassed by the cruising boater.

Store Creek

Store Creek, probably named for an old store once located along the stream, branches out to the east from the intersection of St. Pierre and Bailey creeks. This creek is a real cruising find. With only a few small unmarked shoals to avoid, good depths of 8 feet or more continue well upstream. Anchorages abound and three historical sites can be observed from the creek's waters.

While it is possible to drop the hook almost anywhere on Store Creek, there are three areas worthy of special consideration. The first is found within the body of the hairpin loop that is encountered soon after entering the creek. There is enough swing room for craft up to 45 feet, and the high southern shores give good protection.

Another good spot is found as the creek takes a bend and heads back toward the southeast. Here the stream borders on high ground to the north and is overlooked by historic Chisolm House. Protection is adequate even for heavy weather, and the view of the old homeplace as the evening fades is a considerable bonus.

Boaters can also anchor in the creek's third bend, just before the stream heads northeast. Here the higher southern banks support moderate residential development and give good protection.

Before entering, be sure to read the navigation information presented on Store Creek later in this chapter. With this elementary precaution in mind, I highly recommend the extraordinary cruising opportunities of this remote stream.

Chisolm House Legend Historic Chisolm House is located on Store Creek's northern banks as the stream enters its second major turn. This beautiful home was built by Dr. Robert Chisolm for his wife, Mary Eddings, in 1830. After many years of happiness and pub-

SOUTH EDISTO RIVER TO ST. HELENA SOUND

lic service the good doctor contracted an incurable disease. Wracked with pain, Chisolm committed suicide. His body was interred in a nearby churchyard, but only a few weeks had passed before an official of the church informed Mary Chisolm that the church did not allow the burial of suicide victims within that hallowed ground.

Saying little, the grieving widow ordered the plantation's largest boat to be made ready for a trip to Charleston the next day. On her trip to the Holy City she purchased bricks and mortar. Returning to the island in the dead of night, Mrs. Chisolm instructed her slaves to build a thick masonry wall around her husband's grave. The next day she defied anyone to disturb the late doctor's rest. No one ever did, and some years later the faithful widow was laid to rest beside her husband.

Presbyterian Manse

The old Presbyterian Manse is visible to the northwest as you approach the practical cruising limits of Store Creek. Only very small, shallow draft boats can approach the house, but you can gain a good view of the old parsonage from the main body of the creek. Built in 1790, the home is a beautiful sight from the water.

Sunnyside Plantation

Sunnyside Plantation can be seen in the distance to the east just as depths begin to decline on Store Creek. While it can be viewed only from a distance by cruising craft, the house is yet another magnificent sight on this historic creek.

Sunnyside, constructed by Townsend Mikell in 1875, is one of the few plantation houses built on Edisto Island after the Civil War. There are tabby ruins of a much older structure in the front yard. Tabby was a popular building material in coastal South Carolina before the Revolution. It was made by burning limestone and seashells in an intricate process. The art of tabby-making has been

Sunnyside Plantation on Store Creek

lost over the years and is now only a distant memory.

Big Bay Creek

Big Bay Creek is a large sidewater of the South Edisto, found on the river's eastern shore near flashing daybeacon #2. Minimum depths of 7 to 10 feet extend far upstream, and good anchorage possibilities abound. Most sections provide sufficient swinging room for craft of up to at least 45 feet. Much of the creek is bounded by marsh grass, which gives only minimal protection, but there are several fortunate exceptions.

As you enter Big Bay Creek from South Edisto River, the planned community of Oristo lines the southern banks. Extensive residential development is encountered here, and a marina, now out of business, will also be sighted. The large shrimping fleet that calls Big Bay Creek home can usually be seen along this section of the creek. The picturesque shrimpers make for interesting viewing.

It is quite possible to anchor in this portion of the creek, though the waters here are a bit wider than those further upstream, and strong winds could raise an unwelcome chop. The extensive small craft and commercial fishing traffic in the area could also be a nuisance. However, the high southern banks render good protection, and this spot is certainly worthy of consideration.

Upstream the creek takes a long but sharp turn to the north. Soon after passing through the loop you will spy an area of high, wooded land on the eastern banks. This area is known as "the Mound" and is thought to be the site of a sixteenth-century Spanish Jesuit mission. It is often forgotten that the Spanish were the first European residents of South Carolina and an influence in the state until the early 1700s. The section of Big Bay Creek adjacent to the Mound is another good anchorage.

Above the Mound the high ground that continues to border the eastern shore is known as "the Neck." Tradition holds that a

Shrimpers on Big Bay Creek

SOUTH EDISTO RIVER TO ST. HELENA SOUND 169

large plantation house once looked out on the creek from these banks but has long since washed away. Local residents claim that the Neck is one of the most haunted spots in all of coastal South Carolina. According to the Sea Grant Consortium, such ghostly apparitions as "boo-daddies, plat-eyes, and drolls that take shape and cry in the night" are supposed to make regular appearances. This writer was not privileged to meet any of these supernatural visitors during his research, but perhaps you will be more (or less) fortunate.

Unless you are concerned about ghostly visitations, this portion of the creek also makes a good spot to drop the hook for the night. Depths finally drop off as the creek splits into several forks further upstream.

Below Big Bay Creek the generally reliable South Edisto Inlet runs seaward. If you plan to attempt this cut, read the navigational suggestions later in this chapter before proceeding.

Lower South Edisto River Navigation

South of Fenwick Cut successful navigation of South Edisto River remains quite straightforward until you reach unlighted daybeacon #3. Set course to come abeam and pass #3 well to its easterly side. On-site research reveals that there has been some shoaling on the western shore in this area.

Hold to the mid-width as you continue downstream. Soon the entrance to St. Pierre Creek will come abeam on the eastern banks.

St. Pierre Creek Enter St. Pierre Creek on its mid-width. Be on guard against the small shoal extending into the river from the creek's northern point. Once inside, favor the western shore slightly.

Some 1.3 nautical miles upstream the higher ground of Bailey Island will begin lining the northern banks. You can drop the hook here and be assured of a restful night unless the wind exceeds 15 knots.

The creek soon takes a swing to the east and intersects with Fishing Creek.

Fishing Creek Enter Fishing Creek on its mid-width. If you choose to anchor here, your best bet would be to drop the hook where the higher ground of Peters Point borders the eastern shore. Depths begin to fall off as you approach the intersection of Fishing Creek and the small stream, shown on chart 11518, that breaks off to the north. Cease your exploration well before reaching this point.

On St. Pierre East of the intersection with Fishing Creek, St. Pierre takes a long turn to the north. This is another good spot to drop the hook. Hold to the mid-width through the bend, but begin heavily favoring the western shore as you enter the straight stretch leading northwest. With this maneuver you will avoid the shoal on the eastern shore clearly shown on chart 11518.

As the creek enters another bend, this time to the northeast, begin favoring the eastern shore. There is shoal water abutting the northwestern banks. St. Pierre Creek soon ends at the forks of Bailey and Store creeks.

Bailey Creek Favor the eastern shore a bit as you enter the mouth of Bailey Creek. Take the port branch at the fork with Shingle Creek. Hold to the mid-width until you approach the first bend to the west. Chart 11518 marks a "Tree" on the northern shore in this turn. On-site research did not reveal any tree, but there is certainly very shoal water adjoining the northern banks. Favor the eastern and southern banks as you pass through the turn.

Good depths continue well downstream until the creek splinters into several small branches. Simply select a likely spot before reaching this point and drop the hook for a quiet, uninterrupted evening.

Store Creek Enter Store Creek on its mid-width, but begin favoring the southwestern shores slightly as you approach the creek's first hairpin turn to the north. After coming through the bend, begin immediately to favor the western banks. As shown on chart 11518, there is very shoal water on the eastern shore. The creek then takes a turn to the east. Watch the northern shore as you are passing through the turn and you will catch sight of Chisolm House. The area abeam and just past the house is an excellent spot to drop the hook for the evening.

As the creek takes a sharp jog to the northeast, begin to favor the northwestern shore heavily. A small but shallow shoal abuts the southeastern banks. Watch ahead and you will spy the old Presbyterian Manse, seemingly dead ahead. Discontinue your cruise as you approach the small marsh island bisecting the creek. Past this point depths become much too uncertain for larger cruising boats. Look to the northeast and you will see the Sunnyside Plantation house in the distance.

On the South Edisto South of St. Pierre Creek, set course to come abeam and pass unlighted daybeacon #2A and flashing daybeacon #2 well to their westerly sides. These two aids mark a large shoal on the eastern shore. At #2 you may choose to enter Big Bay Creek to the east.

Big Bay Creek To enter Big Bay Creek, continue on course past flashing daybeacon #2 for some 150 yards as if you are putting out to sea. Only then should you turn back to the north and set a new course to pass #2 by some 100 yards to its easterly side. Follow the eastern shore on around and enter the creek on its mid-width. From this point until the creek finally splinters far upstream, successful navigation is a simple matter of holding to the mid-width. Pick out a spot to your liking and settle in for the evening.

South Edisto Inlet If you choose to run the inlet, study chart 11517 carefully be-

SOUTH EDISTO RIVER TO ST. HELENA SOUND 171

fore making the attempt. If possible, follow in the wake of a local shrimper as he runs the cut. Otherwise, take your time and proceed with great caution.

Ashepoo River

The ICW quickly darts through Fenwick Cut and enters the waters of Ashepoo River. The Ashepoo is quite frankly rather a "plain Jane" in the scheme of coastal South Carolina rivers. There is only one sidewater on the stream's entire navigable length that offers enough protection for overnight anchorage, and only one historic site is visible from the water. Even this single point of interest calls for a very long cruise from the waterway channel.

While most of the Ashepoo is deep and free of shoals, there are several unmarked patches of shallow water to be avoided. Except for these hazards the river can be easily navigated from St. Helena Sound to Airy Hall Plantation.

The Ashepoo's shoreline alternates between saltwater marsh and higher, wooded banks. There is very little development along the river and sighting a house is a rare occurrence.

Many boaters will choose to follow the Ashepoo only so far as the waterway channel traverses its length. Adventurous captains, on the other hand, may want to consider the cruising possibilities both above and below the ICW channel.

Lower Ashepoo River

South of Fenwick Cut, Ashepoo River is abandoned by the ICW, but the stream remains deep and almost entirely free of shoals. The river leads to a marked deepwater entrance to St. Helena Sound. The boater wishing to enter the sound can use this route with confidence.

There are no sidewaters offering anchorage on this section of the Ashepoo, nor are there any facilities. Most of the shore is undeveloped marsh grass. Fenwick and the Otter Islands, both located on the eastern banks, are exceptions.

Fenwick Island

Fenwick Island is today a rather isolated tract with only a few buildings in the village of Seabrook. The island is cut into two parts by Fenwick Cut. This passage through the narrow part of the island was opened many years ago to shorten the water passage from South Edisto River to the Ashepoo.

Before the boll weevil's unwelcome arrival, the Jenkins family, residents of nearby Edisto Island, planted Sea Island cotton on Fenwick. The Jenkins' fortune was decimated when the entire crop was destroyed, soon after the Civil War, by a sudden plague of caterpillars. This writer has not been able to learn of another single instance of such an occurrence during the Sea Island cotton agricultural dynasty.

Otter Islands

The Otter Islands are several small patches of higher ground found to the east of Ashepoo River near its entrance to St. Helena Sound. A very grim story of human cruelty is attached to these sad little islands. During the Revolutionary War, the British forces occupying South Carolina marooned captured slaves here and left them to die without food or drink. It is pitiful to read the accounts of the abandoned slaves swimming desperately after the English skiffs only to be turned back or wounded by sword thrusts from the British soldiers.

ICW and Ashepoo River

From Fenwick Cut, the ICW follows the course of Ashepoo River for just over 1 nautical mile as the river winds its way to the northwest. At flashing daybeacon #166 the waterway again cuts to the west on the Ashepoo-Coosaw Cutoff and leaves the river behind. This is a very straightforward, easily navigable section of the ICW. There are no accessible anchorages on this stretch.

Upper Ashepoo River

North of the Ashepoo-Coosaw Cutoff, Ashepoo River winds its way northward for almost 8 nautical miles before it is spanned by the Settlement Island fixed bridge, which has only 20 feet of vertical clearance. Craft that can clear this height will find a pleasant anchorage near the one spectacular historical

Airy Hall Plantation, Ashepoo River

SOUTH EDISTO RIVER TO ST. HELENA SOUND

site the Ashepoo offers, while other boats can enjoy a night on a well-protected sidewater, Mosquito Creek.

Mosquito Creek

Mosquito Creek enters the eastern banks of Ashepoo River as the stream takes its first westward bend north of the ICW cutoff. The creek has one unmarked shoal but otherwise maintains minimum depths of 7 feet until its path is blocked by a low-level fixed bridge. The creek is an excellent anchorage possibility for any craft up to 45 feet in length. Protection is adequate for all but the heaviest of weather.

The northern shore near the creek's entrance supports some moderate residential and commercial development, as do the southern banks near the low-level fixed bridge. Otherwise the shoreline is composed of the usual marsh grass.

Mosquito Creek offers the best anchorage on Ashepoo River. Waterway boaters should consider putting in here at the end of the day if it does not seem advisable to continue westward to the Rock Creek anchorages.

Airy Hall Plantation

Airy Hall Plantation house overlooks the western shores of Ashepoo River from a high bluff about 2 nautical miles upstream from the Settlement Island Bridge and 1 nautical mile downstream from the power line shown on chart 11517. The old home is a magnificent brick structure that dates from around 1825. It is surrounded by a collection of moss-draped oaks that lend an air of mystery and age to the grounds. Happily, the house has apparently been lovingly restored and presents a magnificent sight from the water. Consider anchoring abeam of the plantation for the evening. You may find it an evening to remember.

Ashepoo River Navigation

Flashing daybeacon #164 marks the western entrance of Fenwick Cut, which is the ICW's entrance into Ashepoo River. The waterway channel turns sharply to the northwest, while the river's lower reaches split off to the south.

Lower Ashepoo River Simply stick to the mid-width on the lower Ashepoo as you move toward the intersection with St. Helena Sound. As Otter Islands come abeam to the east, set course to come abeam of unlighted daybeacon #A1 by some 75 yards to its westerly side. Set a new course to come abeam of unlighted daybeacon #A2 by some 75 yards to its easterly side. #A2 marks the entrance into St. Helena Sound. A wide, easily followed channel leads south into the deep waters of the sound.

ICW-Ashepoo River Continue on course once past flashing daybeacon #164 until you are on the river's mid-width. Swing 90 degrees to the northwest and follow the mid-width past flashing daybeacon #165. Watch to the north thereafter for flashing daybeacon #166. Come abeam of #166 well to its southerly side. At this point the Ashepoo-Coosaw Cutoff will be directly abeam to the south. Cut into its mid-width and continue through to Rock Creek. Unlighted daybeacon #172 marks the cutoff's western entrance into the Rock Creek area. A continuing account of the ICW will be presented later in this chapter.

Upper Ashepoo River If you choose to visit the upper Ashepoo River, continue cruising to the north past flashing daybeacon #166 and the Ashepoo-Coosaw Cutoff. Hold to the mid-width and you should not encounter any difficulty. As the river enters its first westward bend north of #166, the entrance to Mosquito Creek will come abeam to the east.

Mosquito Creek Enter the creek on its mid-width. Be careful to avoid the shoal water extending out into the Ashepoo from Bennetts Point. Continue on the mid-width until the stream takes a sharp turn to the south. Begin heavily favoring the western shore as you enter the bend. There is very shoal water on the eastern shore, as this writer's bent props can readily attest.

Past this small shoal the creek widens a bit. This is an excellent spot to drop the hook. Soon after the stream takes a second turn to the south, the low-level fixed bridge is visible in yet another bend to the east.

On the Upper Ashepoo North of Mosquito Creek simply hold to the mid-width until you begin to approach the northerly entrance of Rock Creek on the western shore. As shown on chart 11518, a shoal is located on the eastern shore in this area. Favor the western banks to avoid the hazard, but don't approach this shoreline too closely either.

Do not attempt to enter Rock Creek. Its entrance is guarded by several unmarked shoals and is far too tricky for cruising craft.

Continue favoring the western shore as you move upriver. As shown on chart 11517, a large area of shallow water abuts the eastern shore between Rock Creek and the river's next bend to the west.

You must begin favoring the eastern shore beginning about .5 of a nautical mile before you reach the western bend. Again, as shown on chart 11517, there is a small area of very shallow water on the western banks at the turn.

Beyond the turn, Ashepoo River opens out into a bay-like area. Chart 11517 shows a marsh island in the middle of the stream, but this small mass covers completely at high tide. To avoid this hazard, favor the western shore heavily until the creek again narrows.

From here to the area marked "Hole in the Wall" on chart 11517, stick to the mid-width. At "Hole in the Wall"—which you should not attempt to enter—the main body of the Ashepoo takes a sharp bend to the north. Favor the port side banks heavily as you round the sharp turn. Begin cruising back to the mid-width as you approach the

SOUTH EDISTO RIVER TO ST. HELENA SOUND 175

Settlement Island Bridge. From here to Airy Hall, stick to the mid-width and you should not have any problems.

Watch to the west after cruising some 3 nautical miles upstream from the bridge. You will spot Airy Hall Plantation atop a high bluff of land. Discontinue your cruise at this point. Depths fall off upriver and the stream soon leaves the chart.

Rock Creek

The ICW enters Rock Creek from the western exit of the Ashepoo-Coosaw Cutoff and follows the stream north for less than 1 nautical mile before it again cuts to the west on another man-made channel, also known as the Ashepoo-Coosaw Cutoff. This section of the waterway calls for caution. While the section is well marked, there is one large shoal

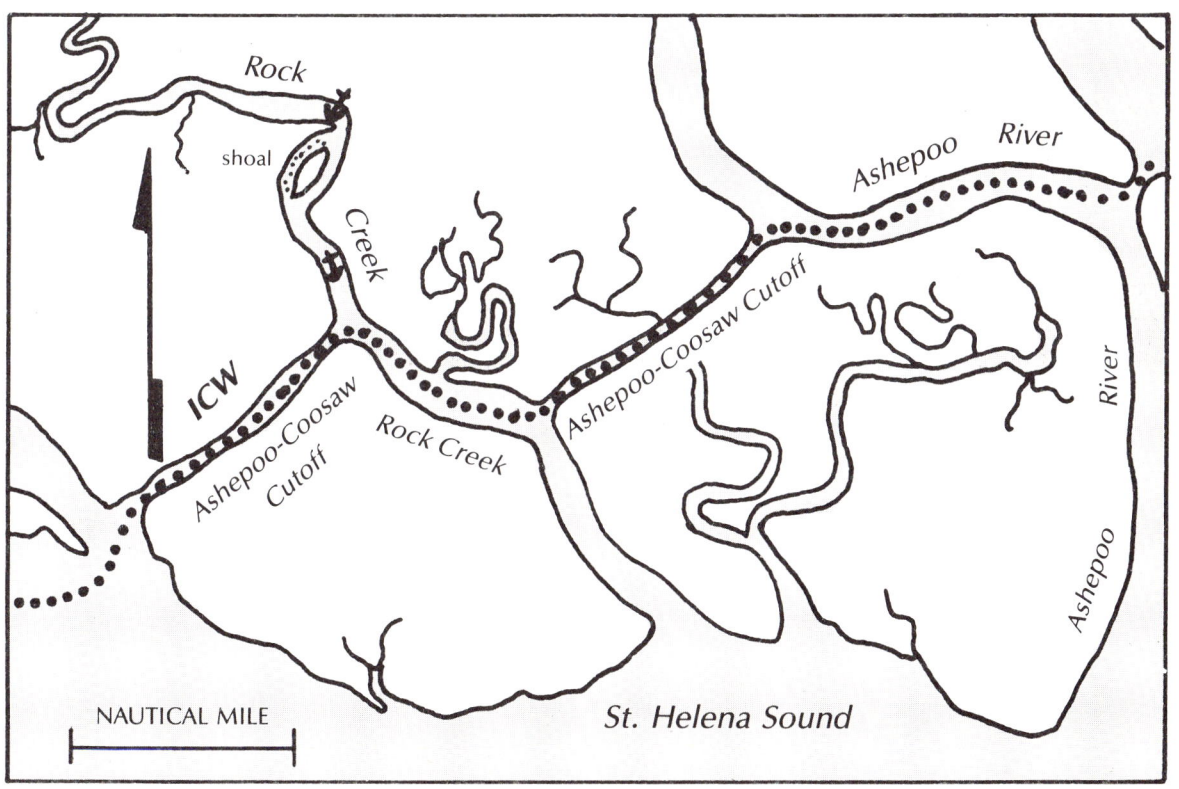

area that, if not avoided, could quickly bring the unwary boater to grief.

South of the waterway channel Rock Creek flows to join St. Helena Sound. This portion of the stream should probably be avoided by cruising boaters. There are several unmarked shoals in the area, and the creek's entrance into the sound is flanked by numerous shallows. This section of Rock Creek is too open for effective anchorage.

On the other hand, north of flashing daybeacon #177 and the upper cutoff, Rock Creek can provide excellent anchorage for craft up to 45 feet in length. There is one unmarked shoal but it can easily be avoided. Otherwise the creek holds minimum 6-foot depths, with most of the channel being much deeper.

One of the best spots for anchorage is found as the creek takes its first sharp bend to the west. The eastern shores border high ground in this area and protection should be excellent, particularly from northeasterly breezes. There are many other choices as well. Just select a spot that seems to be sheltered and settle in for an undisturbed evening.

Adventurous boaters can follow Rock Creek for quite a distance upstream and hold good depths. Eventually a small marsh island, clearly shown on chart 11518, bisects the stream. Above this small land mass Rock Creek begins to narrow and should probably be avoided by larger cruising boats.

Rock Creek Navigation

ICW to Coosaw River Come abeam of unlighted daybeacon #172, at the western mouth of the Ashepoo-Coosaw Cutoff, to its southerly side. Set course directly for flashing daybeacon #173 on the southern shore of Rock Creek. Don't let leeway ease you onto the shoals to the north.

Swing sharply to the west just before reaching #173, then carefully set course to pass the northernmost of the two range markers (set up for northbound craft) just to its northerly side and come abeam of unlighted daybeacon #176 by some 30 yards to its southerly side. As you can see from a quick study of chart 11518, these maneuvers will help you avoid the considerable area of shallow water abutting the northern shore of Rock Creek.

Come abeam of flashing daybeacon #177 to its northerly side, then swing 90 degrees to the west and enter the mid-width of the upper Ashepoo-Coosaw Cutoff. Continue holding to the mid-width until you come abeam of flashing daybeacon #184. Here the waterway enters the wide waters of Coosaw River and the St. Helena Sound area. Continued description of the ICW route will be presented later in this chapter.

Upper Rock Creek If you choose to make use of the excellent anchorage opportunities of upper Rock Creek, abandon the waterway once abeam of flashing daybeacon #177. As you continue upstream, heavily favor the eastern banks to avoid the shoal, shown on chart 11518, that borders the western shore.

Soon the creek makes a slow bend, first to the west and then to the east. Cruise back to the mid-width as you enter this turn. From here the visiting boater need only hold to the mid-width for good depths at least as far as the small island described earlier, where the creek begins to narrow.

Consider dropping the hook in the creek's first hairpin turn to the west. The higher ground found here on the eastern shore should give good protection. Otherwise just select a spot to your liking. Discontinue your cruise at the small island unless your craft is less than 25 feet in length.

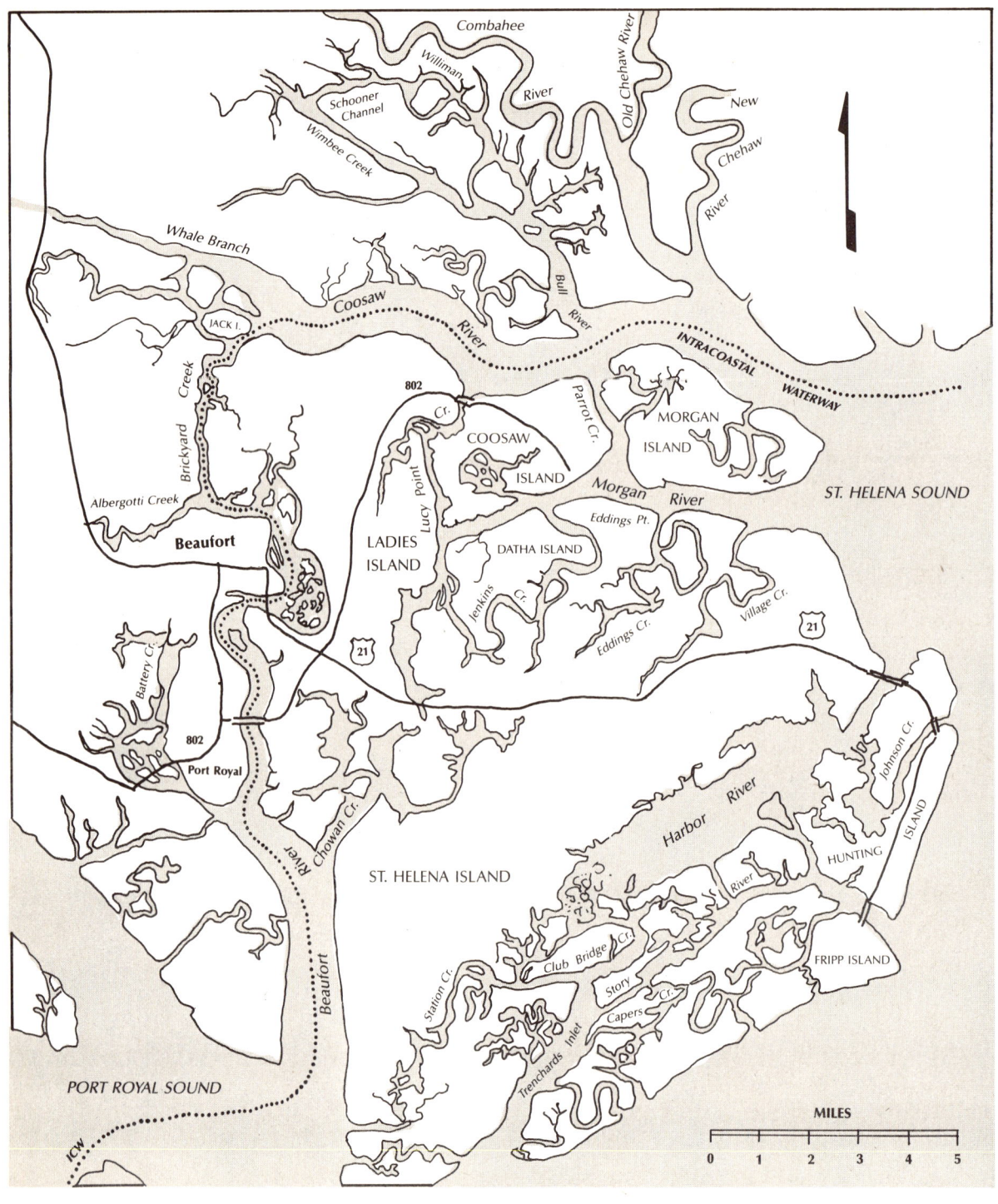

CHAPTER VII

St. Helena Sound to Beaufort

At flashing daybeacon #184 the southbound waterway traveler will come upon the broad waters of Coosaw River and St. Helena Sound. Suddenly the boater finds himself on mighty rivers and wide waters. Here, fresh winds can quickly set up a nasty chop, which often leads to rough crossings. This openness can be quite a shock after the mostly sheltered sounds and streams to the north. However, on days of fair breezes, the waters of St. Helena Sound and its many auxiliary streams offer some of the finest cruising in all of coastal South Carolina. Nevertheless, many are the boaters who have wisely taken a second glance at their charts—and the weather forecasts—before leaving the sheltered reaches of the Ashepoo-Coosaw Cutoff. You would do well to approach the area with similar respect.

The St. Helena area is host to many, many streams and rivers. From the sound itself to little-known Trenchards Inlet, the visiting boater can contemplate a palette full of cruising opportunities. To the south, Morgan, Harbor, and Story rivers beckon. These waters are seldom visited by the cruising boater and can provide many a fine hour of pleasant gunkholing. To the north, Combahee, New Chehaw, Old Chehaw, and Bull rivers offer exciting off-the-beaten-path cruising opportunities of their own. Meanwhile, the ICW route works its way west on broad Coosaw River until it enters Brickyard Creek and begins its approach to the beautiful port city of Beaufort. This stretch is one of the most unprotected portions of the entire South Carolina ICW. Successful passage calls for great caution.

Marina facilities are practically nonexistent. One friendly establishment does welcome transients on Fripp Island, but the visiting boater must follow a tortuous route to reach this isolated haven. As stated in the last chapter, you should make sure your tanks are topped off and your craft in perfect working order before beginning a cruise south of North Edisto River.

Anchorages abound on all the area streams. While most of the shoreline is the usual saltwater marsh, some of the myriad Sea Islands found along the way exhibit high ground and provide a pleasing contrast where their heavily wooded banks overlook the waters. It is often possible to anchor near one of these small oases, miles and miles from the nearest civilization. The adventurous souls among us may want to contemplate a quick trip ashore on one of these isolated islands, which may not have known the foot of man for many years.

Shoreside development in the St. Helena area is very sparse indeed. A few of the sound's streams exhibit light residential development, but many look as if they have remained in the same pristine condition for the last several hundred years.

Coosaw and Morgan rivers and St. Helena Sound are all relatively deep and free of hazards, while Combahee, Bull, Harbor, and Story rivers are peppered with shoals and obstructions. The cruising boater should give long and careful consideration before leaving the safe waters of the ICW channel in this area. To be sure, there are many interesting cruising opportunities, but almost all of them constitute some hazard. Many boaters will find the risk to be more than justified. Others will wish to hurry on to the considerable charms of Beaufort. Whichever course you choose, take your time and practice good navigation.

This chapter will first review the waters of St. Helena Sound and the rivers south of the waterway channel. Next, the rivers to the north—Combahee, New Chehaw, Old Chehaw, and Bull rivers—will be explored. Finally, the ICW route will be followed until it begins its approach to Beaufort.

Charts Several charts are required to cover the wide-ranging waters discussed in this chapter:
11518 details the ICW to Beaufort and covers portions of the Combahee and Bull rivers. It also encompasses all navigable sections of the New Chehaw and Morgan rivers.
11517 covers all of St. Helena Sound, Old Chehaw, Harbor, and Story rivers.
11519 provides coverage of the upstream portions of the Combahee and Bull rivers.
11516 details the Trenchards Inlet area.

St. Helena Sound

St. Helena Sound is a very impressive body of water. When one is cruising in its central section, the surrounding shores are barely visible. The sound also provides reliable access to the open sea. The inlet channel is wide, relatively deep, and well marked. Most of the inlet's aids are charted, which greatly facilitates successful navigation of the seaward passage.

The sound can quickly give rise to a very sharp chop in winds over 15 knots. Smaller cruising craft should consult the latest weather forecast before venturing on St. Helena's wide waters. The same holds true for its major sidewaters, particularly Morgan and Coosaw rivers.

The St. Helena shrimping fleet can often be seen plying the waters of the sound for the abundant shellfish found here. If you choose to cruise the sound or its large sidewaters, you may well be joined by several of these classic trawlers.

With one small exception St. Helena Sound itself offers few cruising opportunities to the visiting boater other than its reliable seaward passage. Fortunately, the same cannot be said of its sidewaters. Both the Harbor and Morgan River areas present multiple off-the-track cruising grounds.

Morgan Island

Morgan Island comprises the southern banks of upper St. Helena Sound and the northern banks of Morgan River. The island was named for Captain Joshua Morgan, a sea captain who settled on nearby St. Helena Is-

ST. HELENA SOUND TO BEAUFORT   181

land. Today, according to the South Carolina Sea Grant Consortium, monkeys are raised here for experimental purposes.

Morgan Back Creeks

A group of small streams known as the Morgan Back Creeks are found south of the unnumbered flashing daybeacon at Marsh Island Spit, on the northern shore of Morgan Island. Navigation of these small streams is quite tricky, but there is sufficient swing room on the various creeks for craft from 30 to 40 feet to anchor in fairly good protection. If you can avoid the unmarked shallows, minimum depths in the channel run around 7 feet. This area should be visited only by adventurous skippers who are willing to take a gamble in order to explore these little-traveled waters. On-site research reveals that the charted marshy area northwest of the unnumbered flashing daybeacon no longer exists. Instead, the area is now covered with just enough water to trap the trusting boater. For this reason the channel that chart 11518 shows running northwest from the unnumbered daybeacon should not be attempted.

The central branch of the creek affords the

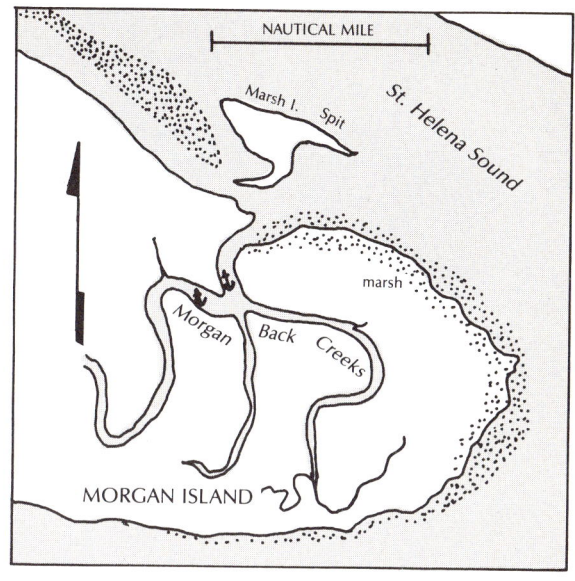

most swing room. Here craft up to 40 feet can anchor flanked by marsh grass on both shores. The starboard fork has some 5-foot depths, but for those that can stand these readings, there is room for craft up to 35 feet to anchor.

The port fork is the deepest of the three, but also the narrowest. There is only enough room for boats of less than 28 feet to anchor.

St. Helena Sound Navigation

Unless one's cruising plans call for a visit to Combahee River, all boaters entering Coosaw River from the Ashepoo-Coosaw Cutoff at flashing daybeacon #184 must turn south and set course to come abeam of flashing buoy #186 to its southeasterly side. From here the ICW continues westward, while a turn to the south leads to the upper reaches of St. Helena Sound.

If you are making for the sound's seaward passage, set course from #186 for unlighted nun buoy #12, located to the southwest of Combahee Bank. This is a long run of 3.6 nautical miles, but it passes through deep water and you should not have any difficulty.

Morgan Back Creeks   To visit the Morgan Back Creeks, set course from #186 to bring abeam, by some 150 yards to its easterly side, the unnumbered flashing daybeacon marking Marsh Island Spit. Continue on course until the mid-width of the creeks' central branch is directly abeam to starboard; then turn in toward the stream's mouth, passing the unnumbered aid well to starboard. As you approach the entrance, favor the starboard shore in order to avoid a small shoal guarding the southern banks.

Once on the stream's interior, stick to the mid-width until the creek forks. The best swinging room is found in this central section before the forks.

Only those craft that can stand 5-foot depths should consider entering the starboard fork, and only boats under 28 feet should enter the port branch. Don't cruise very far upstream on either creek, as depths soon begin to decline.

On St. Helena Sound   From unlighted nun buoy #12, set course to pass between the unnumbered flashing daybeacon to the north, which marks Combahee Bank, and unlighted can buoy #A3, which marks Pelican Bank to the south. Bend your course a bit to the south and point to pass unlighted can buoys #11 and #9 well to their northerly sides. Come abeam of unlighted can buoy #7 well to its northeasterly side.

From #7 point to pass between unlighted nun buoy #6 and unlighted can buoy #5. Continued seaward navigation is well documented on chart 11517. Be sure to consult the latest edition of the chart before attempting the inlet.

Morgan River

Morgan River is a wide, deep stream that enters St. Helena Sound west of Egg Bank. This mighty river stretches westward between St. Helena and Datha islands to the south and Morgan and Coosaw islands to the north. Eventually the stream takes a sharp turn to the south and becomes much too tricky for cruising boaters. Along the way, however, numerous auxiliary creeks afford many anchorage opportunities and fascinating side trips.

The river is marked by a single aid to navigation that warns of the extensive shoals guarding the entrance's northern flank. Otherwise, successful navigation of the Morgan is a simple matter of sticking to the mid-width.

The Morgan is bounded by a pleasant mixture of marsh grass, mostly undeveloped, and higher ground. This writer was struck time and time again by the great natural beauty of this stream. Few will count a cruise of Morgan River as a waste of time.

Coffin Point Plantation

Coffin Point Plantation is visible to the south at the eastern entrance to Morgan River. Built in 1801 for Thomas A. Coffin, this is one of the very few St. Helena Island plantations to survive the turmoil of the Civil War. Following the close of the war the elegant house was used by northern missionaries who came south as part of the "Port Royal Experiment," an effort to educate the freed slaves. Sea Island cotton continued to be grown here by the missionaries until the coming of the boll weevil.

St. Helena Island

Before the Civil War, St. Helena was the richest Sea Island south of Edisto. Numerous cotton plantations once dotted the landscape. Following the fall of Port Royal in 1861, the planter families fled, leaving their slaves behind. Most of the beautiful plantation homes were subsequently destroyed by Union troops. Northern missionaries established the Penn School soon thereafter, with the intent of educating the emancipated blacks in academic, domestic, and craft skills.

Attempts were made to continue the cultivation of Sea Island cotton after the war to support the various educational efforts. The South Carolina Sea Grant Consortium comments that, "Although there were abuses and mistakes . . . valuable lessons were learned . . . . Today the Penn Center continues to be an important cultural and community center for the people of St. Helena."

Datha Island

Datha Island, which lines Morgan River to the south, was once the cotton empire of the wealthy Sams Family. According to James Rice, writing in *Glories of the Carolina Coast*, the family manse "has long crumbled and no trace remains; but the live oak grove speaks with mute eloquence of taste and care in days gone by. Near it is another grove, where rest the dead of the family."

Coosaw Island

Coosaw Island flanks Morgan River to the north near its westerly cruising limits. Tradition holds that the island once supported large groves of orange and olive trees. The cultivation of these fruits was not commercially successful, but there are some reports of scattered trees surviving to this very day.

Fishing on Edding Creek

Village Creek

Village Creek is a small offshoot that makes into the southern shore of Morgan River to the east of Pine Island. In spite of depths shown on chart 11518, the entrance has shoaled to 3 feet. Don't attempt to enter.

Edding Creek

Edding Creek enters the southern shore of Morgan River not far to the west of Village Creek. While some caution must be exercised in order to avoid several shallow areas, most of the stream carries minimum 7-foot depths well downstream. The western shore around Edding Point supports moderate residential development. The houses on the point itself are particularly pleasing to the eye. Otherwise the shoreline consists mostly of saltwater marsh. There are no facilities on the creek.

Edding Creek offers excellent anchorage for craft up to 45 feet. For best protection consider dropping the hook where the creek fronts onto high ground just south of the small unnamed creek that enters the eastern banks. This is a very sheltered spot and is one of the best anchorages on all of Morgan River.

Parrot Creek

Parrot Creek flows north from Morgan River between Coosaw and Morgan islands. The stream provides reliable access from Morgan to Coosaw River and features at least one anchorage opportunity on a small sidewater. The entire shoreline is composed of undeveloped marsh grass and there are no facilities in the area.

Charts 11518 and 11519 both note a shoal adjacent to unlighted daybeacon #2 near the creek's northern mouth. However, on-site research reveals that 6-foot minimum depths can now be held all the way into the deeper waters of Coosaw River. Apparently, recent dredging not shown on the charts has considerably improved depths in the channel. There are two other unmarked shoals to avoid, but good navigation should see you through. However, this cut is not recommended for craft over 38 feet or those that draw more than 4 feet. Be sure to review the navigational information presented later in this chapter before attempting to run the cut.

Bass Creek

Bass Creek, a small sidewater of Parrot Creek, makes into the larger stream's eastern shore. Minimum depths of 7 feet are carried on the creek's mid-width as far as the first small bend to the north. Swinging room is sufficient for craft up to 36 feet to anchor. The

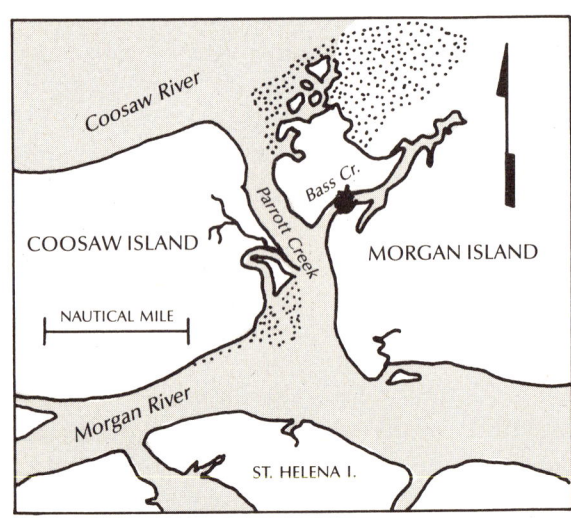

marsh grass shores do not provide enough protection for heavy weather, but otherwise this is an excellent spot to drop the hook.

Jenkins Creek

Jenkins Creek is located on Morgan River's southern shore east of Datha Island. The stream is home to a small fleet of shrimpers, which docks on the eastern shore below the creek's first bend to the south. Anchorage abeam of the commercial piers would be a definite possibility for boats under 36 feet in length. Most of the western shore is marsh, but the higher eastern banks should give good protection in strong northeasterly blows.

Several unmarked shoals render navigation of Jenkins Creek a bit tricky. If you stay in the channel, you can expect 8-foot minimum depths, but a navigational error could land the hapless boater in 2 to 3 feet of water. Because of these difficulties, Jenkins Creek is not recommended for boats over 35 feet or those drawing more than 4½ feet. Be sure to read the Jenkins Creek navigation section presented later in this chapter before attempting entry.

Lucy Point Creek

Lucy Point Creek flows to the north as Morgan River takes a sharp turn to the south and heads for Warsaw Island. The creek is wide and mostly deep and offers reliable passage to Coosaw River for boats that can clear a fixed bridge with 14 feet of vertical clearance. The stream boasts many possible anchorages. There are a few unmarked shallows, but if you take your time, you should encounter no undue difficulty.

Unlike many creeks in this area, most of this stream's western shore borders on high ground. Attractive, modern houses watch over the creek from much of this shore. The eastern banks are mostly marsh, but even these are backed by higher land on Coosaw Island further to the east.

Because of its higher shores, Lucy Point Creek makes an excellent anchorage for almost any craft that can find sufficient swinging room. The creek's broad lower reaches can accommodate boats up to 40 feet, while the narrower upper sections can shelter craft as large as 32 feet. Simply select a spot that looks right for your size of craft and settle in for the night.

The old and the new on Lucy Point Creek

Sams Point Bridge spans Lucy Point Creek just south of the intersection with Coosaw River. The fixed span has only 14 feet of vertical clearance, which effectively bars most sailcraft from using this route to reach the Coosaw. Just north of the bridge there is a small dock on the eastern shore, but there are no facilities for transients.

Lucy Point Creek is a particularly attractive sidewater. The modern homes on the western shore, interspersed with woodlands, make for very pleasant viewing from the water. Coupled with the stream's many anchorage possibilities, this creek can be unreservedly recommended as a side trip for all craft and as a route to the Coosaw for all boats that can clear the fixed bridge.

Morgan River Navigation

To enter Morgan River from St. Helena Sound, set course from unlighted can buoy #9 northeast of Harbor Island to pass well to the south of unlighted nun buoy #A4, which warns of shallow water to the north on Pelican Bank. Be careful not to shift too far to the south, since you must also avoid the shallows around Egg Bank.

Enter the river on its mid-width between the eastern points of Morgan and St. Helena islands. From here to the stream's eventual turn to the south, you can cruise on the Morgan's middle ground with confidence.

As you begin your approach to the river's mouth, look to the south and you will catch sight of the Coffin Point Plantation house on the northeastern point of St. Helena Island. Do not approach the old home, as the adjacent shores are shoal and dangerous.

Soon after you pass into the Morgan's main body, both Coffin and Village creeks will come abeam on the southern shore. Avoid both creeks, as entrance depths have shoaled to 3 feet or less.

Continue on the mid-width, but take care to avoid the shoals on the southwestern tip of Morgan Island. Watch to the south and Edding Creek will come abeam on the southern shore.

Edding Creek If you choose to enter Edding Creek, carefully set course to cruise into the stream's mid-width. Shallows guard both the eastern and western flanks of the entrance. Take your time and watch the sounder.

Once on the creek's interior, favor the western shore slightly for best depths until the stream's first small jog to port. Here the deeper water is found on the eastern shore, which fronts onto high ground. This may also be the best place on the creek to drop the hook.

To continue, follow the mid-width through the sharp bend to starboard. Once through this turn, begin favoring the northern shore to avoid the charted shoal on the southern banks.

As Edding Creek takes a sharp bend to

port, it leaves chart 11517. Discontinue your cruise at this point.

Parrot Creek Favor the eastern shore heavily when entering the southern reaches of Parrot Creek. As clearly shown on chart 11519, a large patch of shallow water guards the western shore. As you begin to approach the mouth of Bass Creek on the eastern shore, cruise to the opposite bank and begin favoring the western shore. Again as shown on chart 11519, shoals line the eastern banks north of Bass Creek.

Point to come abeam of unlighted daybeacon #2 fairly close on its easterly side. Set a new course to bring unlighted daybeacon #1 abeam by some 10 yards to its westerly side. Remember, you can expect some 5- to 6-foot readings between the two markers. Once abeam of #1 the broad and deep waters of Coosaw River open out on all sides.

Bass Creek To make use of the anchorage on Bass Creek, enter the stream, from the southern deepwater section of Parrot Creek, on its mid-width. Exercise caution and watch the sounder in case you accidentally approach the surrounding shallows. Once inside, drop the hook at any likely spot west of the stream's first swing to port. Don't cruise past this turn, as depths begin to decline.

On Morgan River It is a simple, straightforward run down Morgan River to the area abeam of Jenkins Creek to the south. Continue on the mid-width and enjoy the sights.

Jenkins Creek Cruising Jenkins Creek calls for caution and careful navigation. Favor the eastern shore slightly when entering. As the creek takes a sharp swing to port the waters widen and extensive shoals line the southwestern shores. Cruise to within 50 feet or so of the port banks and set your course parallel to the shoreline. Maintain this distance from the shore and follow the land until the creek narrows. Good depths open out from shore to shore where several private docks abut the eastern banks. Don't attempt to cruise past the creek's next sharp bend to starboard. Depths quickly fall off past this point.

On Morgan River Morgan River takes a sharp turn to the south at its intersection with Lucy Point Creek. While good depths continue for a short distance upstream, extensive unmarked shoals are soon encountered. Boaters who cruise this far on Morgan River are advised either to retrace their path or to use Lucy Point Creek to enter Coosaw River.

Lucy Point Creek Even though Lucy Point Creek is used on a daily basis by local craft of all sizes, navigation of the stream does call for some caution. One of the trickiest sections is the entrance from Morgan River.

To enter the creek, continue on the mid-width of the river until you are just past coming abeam of the stream's southern point. Turn 90 degrees to starboard and enter the creek by heavily favoring the eastern banks. As you will quickly note from a study of chart 11519, this procedure will avoid both the shallows around Coosaw Island's southeastern point and the large shoal on the creek's western shore.

Hold scrupulously to the mid-width and you should not have any problems until reaching the stream's first bend to port. Be sure to avoid both shorelines before reaching this first turn. Some are quite shoal.

As you enter the bend, favor the western shore heavily. An oyster bank lines the eastern banks.

Soon the creek takes a turn to the east. From here to the Sams Point Bridge you need simply stick to the mid-width for good depths.

Once through the span, set course to come abeam of unlighted daybeacon #2 fairly close to its easterly side. From #2 the wide waters of the Coosaw River open out on both sides.

Harbor-Story River Area

The Harbor-Story River area comprises the southernmost sidewaters of St. Helena Sound. Besides the two major rivers, a vast network of smaller streams and two inlets infiltrate the area around the various Sea Islands. The principal land masses are Hunting and Fripp islands. Both are the scene of extensive resort development.

There are perhaps no other waters in coastal South Carolina that present such a variety of navigational difficulties for the visiting boater. Some of the channels carry only 6 feet of water. At high tide many of the mud flats, which bare at low water, are completely covered and it becomes almost impossible to determine just where the deep water is located. A single error can quickly result in a hard grounding on the many oyster banks lining the shores, even when the boater is trying to navigate carefully.

Due to these various navigational problems, the entire area should be entered only by adventurous skippers who pilot craft of less than 38 feet in length and drawing no more than 4 feet. Even then, boaters should attempt entry only at *low* tide, when it is possible to identify the channels.

Interestingly enough, the only marina between North Edisto River and Beaufort is found among these difficult waters, on Old House Creek near Fripp Inlet. Associated with the resort development on Fripp Island, this facility offers safe haven for the visiting cruiser.

Both Fripp and Trenchards inlets are surrounded by extensive shoals that render the two cuts impassable by the cruising boater. Neither is marked, and boaters who stray on their breaker-tossed waters do so at their own peril.

Several of the area creeks do offer overnight anchorage, but almost all are lined by unde-

ST. HELENA SOUND TO BEAUFORT

veloped saltwater marsh, where protection would be minimal in strong winds. The marsh grass can become quite boring after a while and one often wonders if it's ever going to end.

Most boaters, except those interested in visiting the island resorts, will probably wish to bypass this entire area. However, if you are the adventurous type who is willing to risk touching bottom, there are many isolated streams that can be visited, miles away from the usual treks. If you are numbered among these hardy souls, please proceed with the greatest caution and keep one person watching the sounder at *all* times.

Harbor River

Harbor River is the deepest body of water in the area. In spite of the depths, you must enter the river from St. Helena Sound by a narrow but well-marked channel. This cut is used on a regular basis by local shrimpers and should not prove too taxing.

The river is spanned by a swing bridge near the easternmost point of St. Helena Island. The bridge has a closed vertical clearance of only 15 feet but does open on demand.

Upper Harbor River is too wide for effective anchorage and offers only one sidewater that may be entered by larger pleasure craft. Eventually, depths begin to decline as the river peters out into extensive mud flats and salt marsh to the southwest. Here a narrow channel can lead the courageous captain south to Fripp Inlet. Chart 11517 shows an area of 3- and 4-foot depths east of the cut leading to Fripp Inlet. This area has apparently been dredged. On-site research here revealed 6-foot minimum depths.

West of the cut-through to Fripp Inlet, good depths are maintained for a short distance on Harbor River as the stream snakes its way to

Shrimper on Wards Creek

the northwest. Here boats up to 38 feet can anchor, but the marsh shores provide only minimal protection in winds over 15 knots. Do not approach the stream's first sharp turn to port. Contrary to depths shown on chart 11517, 3- and 4-foot readings will be encountered at low tide well before reaching the bend.

Wards Creek

Wards Creek enters the western banks of Harbor River south of the swing bridge. While successful entrance can be a bit tricky, the stream is used on a daily basis by local shrimpers and carries minimum 6-foot depths on its mid-width as far as the commercial docks on the northern banks of the creek's upper reaches. There is enough swing room on the creek for craft up to 32 feet to anchor, but you may be obliged to move aside early in the morning by the shrimp fleet that calls Wards Creek home.

A fairly large commercial dock, used by the shrimpers, is located on the upper reaches of Wards Creek. Here it may be possible to anchor abeam of the docks and take the dinghy ashore for an unexpected dining treat.

A fairly long walk from the shrimpers' piers will bring you to a small restaurant on the main highway with the unlikely name of The Shrimp Shack. The building lives up to its name. It is merely a screened porch where visitors eat on picnic tables and benches. The food is served drive-in style through small windows. Don't be put off! The shrimp served here are some of the finest this writer has ever enjoyed. I suspect that the restaurant's shrimp supply is garnered daily from the docks on

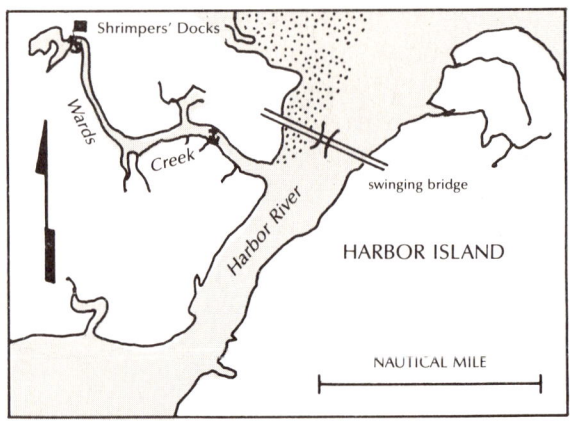

Wards Creek. Don't be a late arrival. The unusual eatery closes at 7:30 P.M.

Hunting Island

For many years Hunting Island, which borders the eastern reaches of Harbor River, was owned by several wealthy St. Helena Island planters. They used the land as a private hunting preserve and would often spend weeks camping and hunting during the fall months. Until the Civil War, hunting was one of the chief leisure occupations of the Sea Island planters.

In recent years Hunting Island has become the northernmost of the resort developments that stretch south from St. Helena Sound to Hilton Head Island. Five thousand acres of the island have been set aside as Hunting Island State Park and are protected from commercial construction.

While cruising Harbor River you may be able to catch a glimpse of the Hunting Island Lighthouse to the east. Built in 1875, the tower was cleverly constructed of movable

ST. HELENA SOUND TO BEAUFORT

parts so that the light could be moved if beach erosion threatened its base. The structure, although located a quarter-mile from the surf line, did indeed have to be moved in 1889. The old light remained in operation until 1933. It is now open to the public and commands an imposing view of the surrounding islands and streams.

Fripp Inlet

Fripp Inlet is an impassable seaward cut. The only access for pleasure boats to the interior of the inlet is via the small, twisting cut from Harbor River. This channel is marked by one unlighted daybeacon, but it still calls for careful navigation.

The inlet branches into several streams that might serve as overnight anchorages for visiting cruisers. Almost without exception the various creeks have undeveloped marsh shores, which would not afford much protection in winds over 15 knots. The fork leading from Harbor River maintains minimum depths of 7 feet once past the entrance shoals and has sufficient swinging room for craft up to 36 feet.

Northwest of the Harbor River cut, another branch of the inlet offers a wide, deep channel and swing room for boats as large as 45 feet. This stream eventually forks. The left-hand creek carries minimum depths of 8 feet until it begins its first sharp jog to starboard. Craft up to 35 feet will probably find enough swing room here for safe anchorage. The right-hand stream has swing room for craft up to 40 feet and minimum depths of 6 feet, but there is one unmarked shoal to avoid.

An unnamed creek enters the eastern shore

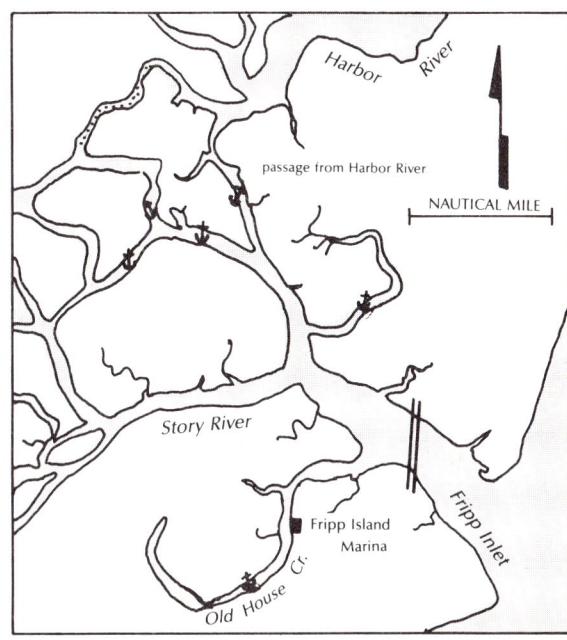

of Fripp Inlet northeast of unlighted daybeacon #A16. This small stream holds minimum low tide depths of 8 feet well upstream and can accommodate boats of up to 35 feet for overnight anchorage. Eventually depths begin to rise as the creek takes its first sharp bend to port.

Old House Creek

Old House Creek makes into the western shore of Fripp Inlet north of the bridge. The visiting cruiser must avoid several unmarked shoals, but prudent navigation should see you through without any undue difficulty. The channel carries minimum depths of 8 feet and is deeper for most of its length.

Fripp Island Marina is found on the shores of Old House Creek where the higher ground of Fripp Island abuts the southern banks. The management of the marina has informed this writer that it would be glad to accept transients for overnight dockage, although, being so far from the usual path, they have had few visiting craft up to this point. Floating berths offer all power and water connections. Gasoline and diesel fuel are readily available. The marina maintains a well-stocked ships' store and offers both mechanical and below-the-waterline repairs. There is even a restaurant within walking distance. Don't forget! If you are seeking a marina, this facility is the only one of its kind between North Edisto River and Beaufort.

Fripp Inlet Channel

Good depths continue on Fripp Inlet for some distance southeast of the fixed bridge that crosses the channel south of Old House Creek. The span has a vertical clearance of only 15 feet, and the channel soon becomes much too treacherous for anyone without the aid of specific local knowledge. The wise cruiser will discontinue his exploration a short distance southeast of the bridge.

Fripp Island

According to Nell Graydon, "It is possible that there are more legends connected with this lovely little island than any other on the South Carolina coast." Tradition has it that Fripp Island was one of the favorite hiding places of the notorious pirate Blackbeard. The many twisting creeks and small inlets that regularly indent Fripp's shores were ideal for the brigand's purposes. Legend tell us that he buried many chests of his ill-gotten booty under the island's shifting sands. None has ever come to light, but if you are the adventurous type, you might try your luck.

Another story tells how Blackbeard brought his new, unwilling wife, whom he had kidnapped in Charleston, to Fripp Island and left her there under heavy guard while he continued his buccaneering on the high seas. Some say that she remained a prisoner till the end of her days, but others claim that eventually she became a loving wife and at last joined her pirate husband in the West Indies.

Story River

Story River leads the adventurous boater from Fripp to Trenchards Inlet and its several creeks, which split off to the north. At low tide the river's channel is fairly easy to follow and holds minimum depths of 7 feet. However, at high tide many of the surrounding mud flats become covered with a foot or two of water, and it is virtually impossible to pick your way along the unmarked channel. If you decide to attempt passage of the river, enter and exit the area at *low tide*.

The river is relatively sheltered and would make a good anchorage for craft of up to 40 feet. One of the best spots is the area where the higher ground of Old Island borders the southern shore. Protection from southerly blows should be quite good, though winds from the north could raise an unwelcome chop.

Just east of Old Island, a branch of Story River splits off to the north. This wayward fork holds minimum depths of 9 feet for quite a distance upstream and affords enough swing

ST. HELENA SOUND TO BEAUFORT

room for anchorage by craft of up to 38 feet. As usual, the marshy shores would give minimal protection in strong winds.

Trenchards Inlet

Trenchards Inlet is another of the several impassable seaward cuts located in this area. This writer was struck by the very real isolation of the inlet. From the main body there was no sign of civilization, and one could easily imagine that the shores had not changed at all in the last three hundred years. If this sounds appealing, you might wish to exert every effort to reach this isolated water body, but bear in mind that successful passage is not easy.

The interior portion of Trenchards Inlet holds good depths but is too open for effective anchorage. If the wind is not blowing, you might consider dropping the lunch hook anyway just to savor the stream's wild character a bit longer.

To the north, Trenchards Inlet splits into two large creeks. Both offer cruising opportunities of their own, and one leads to a small community.

Club Bridge Creek

Club Bridge Creek comprises the eastern fork of upper Trenchards Inlet. While the creek's lower reaches are far too wide for anchorage in any but the lightest of airs, the upper portion offers several opportunities to drop the hook far from the beaten path. Most of the shores are the usual salt marsh and there is no development on the creek's banks.

The warning beacon shown on chart 11516 at the stream's intersection with its first sidewater consists of only a few pilings located near the eastern shore. The creek opposite the marker maintains good minimum depths of 9 feet for some distance upstream and has enough swinging room for craft up to 35 feet.

Further upstream Club Bridge Creek splits into three branches. Between the old warning beacon and the forks, craft of almost any size can anchor on the creek's mid-width in light to moderate airs. Again, the grassy shores do not afford enough protection for a really heavy blow.

Each of the three upstream forks holds good depths for a short distance. These offer a bit more protection than anchorage on the main stream, but all must be entered with caution. Pick out a branch that appears appropriate for your size of boat and carefully feel your way in.

Station Creek

Station Creek leads west from Trenchards Inlet to the small village of County Landing. Most of the stream is quite deep, with one spot holding a surprising depth of 60 feet. Several sidewaters as well as the upstream portion of the main creek offer anchorage opportunities.

The easterly reaches of Station Creek near Trenchards Inlet are a bit too open for anchorage except in very light airs, but a wide sidewater leads off to the north less than 1 mile from the creek's mouth. This stream has minimum depths of 10 feet and affords plenty of swinging room for almost any size craft to drop the hook in safety.

Further upstream Station Creek splits into three branches. The northernmost fork is the main body. The southernmost stream is shoal and should not be entered. The middle cut holds low tide depths of around 8 feet or more. There is enough room for boats of less than 36 feet to anchor. Do not try to reenter the main body at County Landing from this stream, as depths drop off to 3 feet or less.

The northerly branch has minimum depths of 7 feet, and most of the channel is deeper. The stream eventually curves around to the south and borders the small village of County Landing on its western banks. Anchorage by boats up to 38 feet is a practical possibility on the creek as far as County Landing. Once past the village depths quickly decline.

Harbor-Story River Area Navigation

Remember, navigation of this entire area calls for the most exacting use of chart, compass, log, sounder, and the information contained in this section. Enter the waters south of Harbor River at *low tide only*. Go slowly and exercise extreme caution at all times.

Harbor River Enter Harbor River by the marked channel west of Egg Bank. The direct route from St. Helena Sound calls for local knowledge and is too tricky for visiting cruisers.

Proceed from St. Helena Sound as if you plan to enter Morgan River, until unlighted daybeacon #A6 comes abeam well to the south. Continue on this course for another 100 yards, then turn back to the southeast and set course to come abeam of #A6 fairly close to its easterly side. Immediately set a new course to come abeam and pass unlighted daybeacon #A8 to its immediate easterly quarter, and to come abeam of unlighted daybeacon #A10 by some 10 yards to its easterly side. Continue on course for 100 yards or so. You can then swing to the southwest and enter the broad Harbor River channel without any difficulty. Stick to the mid-width; excellent depths are carried well upstream to unlighted daybeacon #A13.

Wards Creek Favor the northern shore heavily at the entrance to Wards Creek. Once on the stream's interior, swing back to the mid-width. If you hold scrupulously to the middle, you can expect good depths as far as the shrimpers' docks far upstream. If you choose to anchor, just select a likely spot and drop the hook. If possible, try to leave enough room for passing shrimpers.

On Harbor River South of unlighted daybeacon #13 unmarked shoals guard the western shores. Favor the eastern banks as you approach the cut-through to Trenchards Inlet. If you choose to enter the upper reaches of Harbor River west of unlighted daybeacon #A14, stick to the mid-width, and be sure to stop before reaching the stream's first sharp bend to port.

ST. HELENA SOUND TO BEAUFORT

South to Fripp Inlet In order to enter the small cut leading south to Fripp Inlet, you must pass unlighted daybeacon #A14 immediately to its eastern side. Avoid the eastern banks, where an extensive shoal juts well out into the creek. Once past #A14 swing back to the mid-width. Good depths continue on the creek's middle until its intersection with the main body of the inlet.

If you choose to proceed inland from the cut-through's junction, avoid the point of land separating the two streams. No difficulties will be encountered until the creek splits into two branches.

Enter the southern fork on its mid-width. Be sure to stop before reaching the stream's first sharp bend to starboard.

To enter the northern branch you should also hold to the mid-width initially. After proceeding for some 75 yards, begin favoring the eastern banks, and continue to favor them until the stream cuts sharply to port. Cruise back to the mid-width when you have rounded the turn. Discontinue your exploration before reaching the area where the creek splits into several small branches.

Lower Fripp Inlet Hold to the mid-width as you cruise to the southeast, toward the bridge, on the main body of Fripp Inlet. Unlighted daybeacon #A16 will be passed west of your course. This aid marks the entrance to Story River and will be covered in the next section. Watch to the west and you will soon spy the entrance to Old House Creek and Fripp Island Marina.

Old House Creek Be careful to avoid the large shoal flanking the northern banks at the entrance to Old House Creek. Favor the southern banks when entering, but don't approach this shoreline too closely either. Watch to the north for the first point of land extending into the creek. As this point comes abeam, alter your course and begin to favor the northern shore as you approach the stream's first turn to the south.

Once around the turn, cruise back to the mid-width. From this point successful navigation of the creek's practical cruising limits is a simple matter of holding to the mid-width.

As the creek takes a sharp turn to starboard, begin watching the southern shore; Fripp Island Marina will soon come abeam. Good depths continue until the stream swings sharply to the northeast and finally peters out. If you decide to anchor rather than make use of the marina, consider the long, straight section past the docks.

Story River Pass unlighted daybeacon #A16 well to its southerly side and enter Story River on its mid-width. Some 1.3 nautical miles upstream, Story River divides. As described earlier, the northerly branch can provide good anchorage. Enter on the mid-width and drop the hook at any likely spot. Depths fall off rapidly where the creek splits into three branches. Stop well south of this area.

The southerly branch of Story River runs southwest to Trenchards Inlet. Hold strictly to the mid-width and you should not have any difficulty. At high tide this section of the river is particularly susceptible to the problem of covered mud flats. During on-site research this writer repeatedly failed to find the channel at high water. Plan your cruise to correspond with low tide.

As Story River makes its entrance into Trenchards Inlet the stream broadens appreciably. Hold strictly to the mid-width and you should be able to maintain 6 foot depths. Very shallow water flanks the river's mouth on both sides of the channel. This section calls for caution. Feel your way along and keep a weather eye on the sounder.

Trenchards Inlet Trenchards Inlet holds excellent depths as far as Bull Point, on the southwestern tip of Capers Island. Further seaward passage is strictly not recommended without specific local knowledge.

To cruise north and enter either of Trenchard's two northerly streams, continue cruising west from the mouth of Story River until you come abeam of the inlet's mid-width. Turn 90 degrees to the north and point for the middle of the split.

Club Bridge Creek Favor the southern shores of Club Bridge Creek a bit when entering. Good depths soon spread out again from shore to shore. Hold to the mid-width until you encounter the three pilings near the eastern banks that serve as the charted warning beacon. Here the creek's first sidewater will come abeam to the west.

If you choose to make use of this first creek, enter on the mid-width. Drop the hook anywhere you like, but be sure to stop well before reaching the stream's hairpin turn to the north. Depths of 3 feet or less are encountered in this area.

From north of the warning beacon to the split, the main section of Club Bridge Creek is a good spot to drop the hook in all but the heaviest of weather. Don't attempt to enter the next large sidewater, which makes into the western banks. Depths are too uncertain on this changeable stream for larger cruising boats.

Eventually Club Bridge Creek splits into three forks. Adventurous skippers may enter any of these branches on the mid-width, but shallow depths are soon encountered on all three creeks.

Station Creek Station Creek features unusually deep readings on its mid-width from its intersection with Trenchards Inlet until it splits into three branches well upstream. If you choose to enter the first sidewater on the northern shore west of the split, do so on its mid-width, and don't cruise any further upstream than the area where the stream splits into several branches.

Remember not to enter the southernmost fork of Station Creek. It is shoal and treacherous.

The center fork holds good depths until it encounters the waters of the northern branch looping south at County Landing. Here depths of 2 feet or less wait to greet

ST. HELENA SOUND TO BEAUFORT

the unfortunate cruiser. Drop your hook well before reaching the intersection, and retrace your path to the east when it is time to leave.

Enter the northern stream's mid-width and continue on the middle course until the small village of County Landing comes abeam on the western shore. Watch to starboard and you will spy a concrete launching ramp near the town's southern border. In spite of readings shown on chart 11516, depths drop off to 4 feet or less past this point.

Combahee River

The Combahee River is one of the two major streams that enter the eastern reaches of mighty Coosaw River before it joins St. Helena Sound. The Combahee has two major auxiliary waters of its own, New and Old Chehaw rivers. These two streams will be reviewed later in this chapter.

Despite its impressive size and rich history, Combahee River presents surprisingly few cruising opportunities other than those offered by the two Chehaw rivers. No other sidewaters offer a safe haven for the night, and the river itself is much too wide for anchorage. Most of the shores are salt marsh except where the higher ground of Fields Point borders the northern banks east of Gunboat Island. There are no facilities on the river. Finally, the Combahee has a number of unmarked shoals to be avoided, and the stream leaves the charts north of Gunboat Island.

Quite frankly, the only reason visiting cruisers should consider entering Combahee River is for its fascinating sidewaters. However, for those brave, hardy cruisers who simply must see it all, a navigational sketch of the river as far as Gunboat Island is offered.

Combahee River History Before the Civil War the banks of Combahee River hosted one of the richest rice cultures in South Carolina. Sadly, there is very little left today of this once-thriving agricultural dynasty. An occasional sluice gate is sometimes spotted by adventurous explorers along the shore, and hunters still frequent the fields during the fall months, but the beauty and grandeur that once graced the river's banks are now only a distant, haunting memory.

Combahee River Navigation

It is a simple matter to enter the main body of Combahee River from the western mouth of the Ashepoo-Coosaw River Cutoff. Cruise past flashing daybeacon #184 on the ICW channel for some 50 yards, then turn 90 degrees to the north, and you will find yourself in the river's lower reaches.

Favor the eastern shore to avoid the small, extremely shallow patch of water on the entrance's western quarter, clearly shown on chart 11518. Once past this area, cruise back to the mid-width. If you intend to enter New Chehaw River, you should begin to make your way toward the eastern banks as you cruise upriver.

To continue upstream on the Combahee, begin heavily favoring the western shore as you approach the first point on that shore. A large patch of shoal water bisects the river just to the north, and it is easiest to maneuver around this shallow area by hugging the western banks.

Watch to the east for a sharp point of land jutting out into the river. As soon as this area comes abeam, ease back to the mid-width. Continue on the middle course and you can hold good depths for some distance upstream, until the river takes a hairpin turn to the south. The entrance of Old Chehaw River will come abeam on the eastern banks some .8 of a nautical mile before you reach this turn.

As you round the sharp bend to the south, immediately begin to favor the eastern banks. As shown on chart 11519, a very shallow stretch of water lines the western shore. Soon the Combahee takes another 90-degree turn, this time to the north. You can hold to the mid-width as you pass through this bend.

Favor the eastern shore slightly when approaching Fields Point. Follow the river around its next turn to the west and begin favoring the southern banks. You will soon sight Gunboat Island dead ahead. Continue favoring the southern shore and you can cruise to the south of the island in at least 20 feet of water.

Further passage upstream is not recommended for larger cruising boats. Numerous unmarked shoals wait to trap the too-adventurous boater, and the river soon leaves the chart. It might be possible to anchor in the southern lee of Gunboat Island, but it would be an uncomfortable night unless the fickle winds are quite calm. Otherwise, it would be much better to retrace your route down the Combahee and explore the fascinating cruising possibilities of Old and New Chehaw rivers.

New Chehaw River

New Chehaw River is a lovely stream with at least two inviting anchorages. However, the river's entranceway is a bit tricky and holds minimum depths of only 5 feet. For this reason the New Chehaw is recommended only for boats under 38 feet that draw less than 4 feet.

Once past the troublesome entrance, good depths of 7 feet or more are found along the mid-width. The lower reaches of the river are

ST. HELENA SOUND TO BEAUFORT

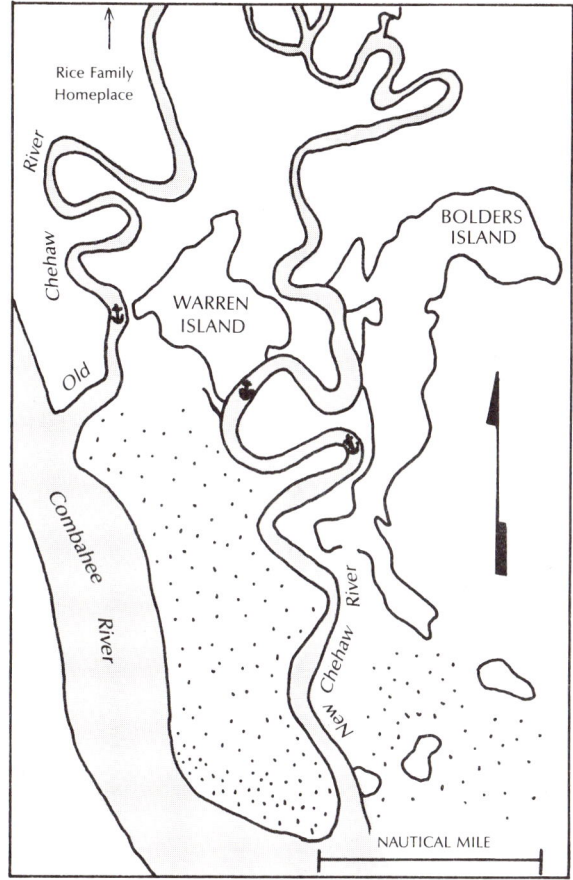

lined by marsh and would be suitable only for light air anchorage. Further upstream there are two more sheltered areas that could make for a memorable overnight stay. The first is found where Bolders Island flanks the eastern banks in a hairpin loop to the west. This is an excellent place to drop the hook, with good protection and attractive scenery.

This writer's personal selection for overnight anchorage, however, is the spot where the heavily wooded banks of Warren Island line the river's northern shore. Here good depths run almost to the island's banks, and there is plenty of swing room and excellent protection. The undeveloped woodlands of Warren Island seem to beckon the adventurous visitor to come ashore and explore. I gave in to the temptation and found the remains of an old logging camp. Whether you stay on your boat and simply admire the area's beauty or heed the pioneering instinct and go ashore, this is an anchorage you will not soon forget.

New Chehaw River Navigation

Entrance of New Chehaw River calls for caution! Don't be in a hurry! Proceed at idle speed and feel your way through the river's mouth. Keep a weather eye on the sounder to quickly spot any encroachment on the surrounding shoals.

Begin heavily favoring the eastern shores of Combahee River well south of the New Chehaw's entrance. Stay about 75 feet from the banks and follow the shore into the interior of the river. Expect some 5- to 6-foot readings in this area at low tide. Take care not to drift to port. As shown on chart 11518, a shoal flanks the mid-width of the river's mouth.

Continue favoring the eastern banks until the river narrows perceptibly. As the stream passes through its first small jog to port, cruise back to the mid-width. From here to Warren Island, you need only stick to the middle, where you can expect minimum low tide depths of 7 feet with most of the channel being deeper.

Upstream of Warren Island, good depths continue for some distance. However, as the river takes a sharp turn to starboard north of Bolders Island, depths finally decline. Wise cruisers will terminate their explorations soon after passing Warren's shores.

Old Chehaw River

Old Chehaw River, another fascinating sidewater, makes into the eastern banks of Combahee River. Like its southerly sister, New Chehaw River, the stream offers a multitude of anchorage opportunities and one historic site of great interest. Unlike its sister river, however, the Old Chehaw is easy to enter and maintains minimum depths of 8 feet on its mid-width to the stream's charted upstream limits. There are a few unmarked shoals to be avoided, but basic navigation should see you safely by these hazards without any difficulty. Boats of up to 40 feet that draw less than 5 feet can enter Old Chehaw River with confidence.

Most of the shores lining the Old Chehaw's lower reaches are the usual marsh grass. This area is suitable only for light air anchorage. Protection is much improved where the river briefly borders the western limit of Warren Island. Another excellent anchorage is found on the long, straight stretch of the river bounded by the high ground of Big Island.

The Old Chehaw's most exciting anchorage is located just east of the small community of Wiggins (clearly marked on chart 11517) where high ground fronts onto the western banks and a "Tank" is noted on the chart. Here it is possible to anchor, with excellent protection and solid holding ground, within sight of a historical point of interest.

It is quite possible to cruise further upstream on Old Chehaw River past the Wiggins area, but there are several unmarked shoals to avoid, and the river leaves chart 11517 near the abandoned course of the old South Carolina Railroad. The navigation is not difficult, however, so if you are of a mind, don't hesitate to continue your cruise as far as the old railroad. Be sure, though, to read the navigational information presented in the next section before proceeding.

Rice Family Homeplace

Just east of Wiggins the Rice Family homeplace gazes boldly out on Old Chehaw River from a high bluff. This beautiful home was once the abode of James Henry Rice, Jr., whom this writer has had frequent occasion to quote in this guide. It is not difficult to picture Mr. Rice sitting on his porch with the magnificent river panorama before him, penning his immortal *Glories of the Carolina Coast*. With such inspiration it is no wonder that Rice's phrases so vibrantly reflect the wondrous qualities of coastal South Carolina. The visitor's imagination is fired by the romantic word portraits Rice painted of the land he loved so deeply.

During research I had occasion to anchor in the shadow of the Rice homeplace for a special evening. Nature cooperated by providing a breathtaking sunset behind the old house, and I came a bit closer to a true understanding of why so many are lured back to this dreamlike land. That evening will always remain my fondest memory of traveling the South Carolina coast.

Rice Family homeplace on Old Chehaw River

Old Chehaw River Navigation

Favor the northern shore a bit when entering Old Chehaw River from the Combahee. As shown on chart 11517, a small patch of shoal water guards the entranceway's southern point. Once past the river's mouth you need only hold to the mid-width as far as the Rice homeplace for successful navigation of the stream.

Soon after passing the Rice home, the river takes a 90-degree bend to the east. Begin favoring the southern shore and continue to do so until the stream again turns to the north. By this procedure you will avoid an area of very shallow water lining the northern banks in this section.

As the Old Chehaw turns to the north, cruise toward the western banks and favor this shoreline until the stream's next jog to the east. Past this last turn, simply hold to the mid-width as far as the old railway for good depths.

Bull River

Bull River flows into the northern banks of the Coosaw several miles west of Combahee River. An impressive stream for its size, the Bull also affords a number of overnight anchorage possibilities. Surprisingly, there is not a single historic site visible from the water. The many cotton plantations that once dotted the river's banks were entirely destroyed by Sherman's ruthless northern march during the latter stages of the Civil War.

As Bull River winds its way to the north, it soon splits into two large branches, Wimbee and Williman creeks, which in turn exhibit numerous sidewaters of their own. Williman Creek eventually leads to Schooner Creek. Anchorage opportunities abound on all these streams. Additional overnight stops are also afforded by several smaller streams that break off from the river's main body.

Bull River and its two main offshoots hold excellent depths for the most part. Several of

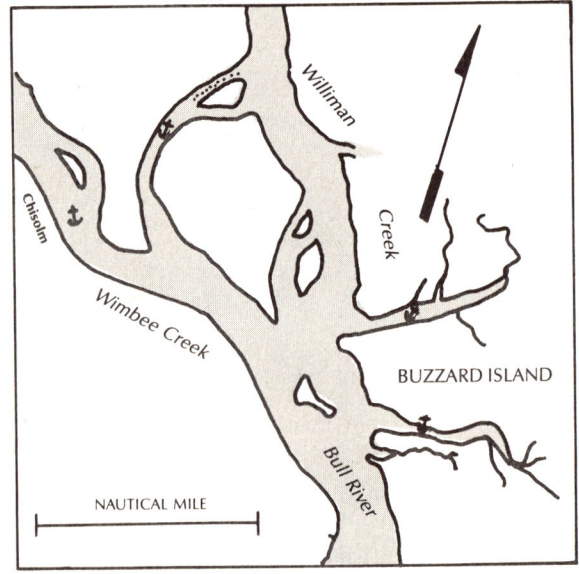

the Wimbee and Williman Creek sidewaters are shoal and much too treacherous for larger cruising boats. If you choose to enter any of these auxiliary waters, proceed with caution and keep a steady watch on the sounder.

With only a few exceptions, Bull River and its various creeks are surrounded by marsh grass. High ground reaches the river's banks in only a few places. These uniform shoreside conditions render minimal protection for overnight stops. None of Bull River's anchorages is particularly recommended for heavy weather.

Main Body Anchorages

Two small sidewaters on the Bull's eastern shore south of Williman Creek afford good anchorage for craft up to 34 feet in length. The southernmost creek is located south of Buzzard Island. This small stream carries only 6-foot minimum depths, and there is a large unmarked shoal to be avoided at the entrance. Past this hazard the stream's interior provides visiting cruisers the opportunity to drop the hook in a primitive setting. Depths drop off in this creek sooner than a study of chart 11519 would lead you to believe. Be sure to discontinue your exploration before proceeding too far upstream.

The northernmost of the two creeks is somewhat larger and also holds 6-foot minimum depths in its unmarked channel. Here, too, there is a large shoal that must be avoided at the stream's entrance, but the careful cruiser should be able to bypass this danger without too much difficulty. Select a likely spot on the mid-width of the inner creek and drop the hook for an undisturbed evening.

Wimbee Creek

Wimbee Creek, the southern fork of Bull River, leaves the main body north of Summerhouse Point. The creek holds good depths as far as the small village of Chisolm on the western banks. Here almost any craft can anchor abeam of several private docks, but the creek is a bit wide for comfortable conditions in winds over 15 knots. Don't attempt to enter the branch of Wimbee Creek that flows south from Williman Creek. This stream can be entered from Williman Creek and offers good anchorage in its northern reaches, but shoals guard its intersection with Wimbee Creek, rendering the southern reaches treacherous for the boater who lacks specific local knowledge. For the same reason, you should avoid the small offshoot northeast of Chisolm.

West of Chisolm frequent unmarked shoals render conditions too uncertain for larger cruising boats.

Williman Creek

Williman Creek is a deep stream and affords good anchorage in light to moderate airs. For more protection, boats of 34 feet or less can enter this end of the small stream that flows south to Wimbee Creek. The sidewater holds 8-foot minimum depths on its mid-width before reaching the shoals that guard its southern exit. If you choose to enter, be sure to use the lower of the two entrances from Williman Creek. The upper entrance is quite shoal.

Eventually, Williman Creek splits. The deep northerly branch becomes Schooner Channel, while the southerly fork affords additional anchorage opportunities. The southern stream eventually leads to a large area of shallow water that effectively bars reentry into Schooner Channel from this quarter. Before reaching the shoals, however, this stream affords an excellent anchorage opportunity for boats up to 36 feet as it rounds its first sharp turn to starboard. Here the higher ground of Williman Island to the west gives good protection.

Schooner Channel

Schooner Channel holds 8 foot minimum depths on its mid-width until the creek rejoins the northerly reaches of Wimbee Creek. Boats up to 40 feet can easily anchor anywhere along the creek's length in light to moderate winds. Protection is not adequate for strong blows.

Though a channel continues upstream from this point, there are numerous unmarked shallows that can readily bring the visiting boater to grief. This writer highly recommends that you cease your exploration where Schooner Channel and Wimbee Creek meet.

Bull River Navigation

Exercise caution when cruising Bull River. While most of the river is deep, many sidewaters are blinds and traps waiting to surprise the careless boater. Be sure to research any creek with the information in this guide before attempting entry.

Enter Bull River on its mid-width from the Coosaw. Avoid the shallow water extending southeast from Bull Split, marked by an unnumbered and unlighted red and green junction daybeacon north of Parrot Creek.

Begin favoring the eastern banks just a bit as you cruise upriver. This procedure will help you avoid the large shoal, clearly shown on chart 11519, that lines the western banks south of Summerhouse Point. The charted warning beacon north of the shallows was absent during on-site research.

You will soon observe an island bisecting the Bull. Don't approach this small land mass. It is surrounded by shallow water. You must now make a choice. If you want to visit Wimbee Creek, pass to the west of the island. If, on the other hand, you intend to explore Williman Creek or make use of the two small unnamed anchorages on the eastern banks, set your course to pass the island's eastern quarter.

Bull Sidewater Anchorages The entrance to the unnamed southern creek is flanked by very shallow water to the north. Favor the southern banks heavily when entering. Set the hook on the interior at any likely spot. Don't attempt to cruise past the stream's first turn to starboard. Despite readings recorded on chart 11519, 3- and 4-foot depths will be immediately encountered in this area.

The northerly stream's mid-width is blocked by a shoal, which bares at low water but is covered at high tide. Favor the southern banks heavily at the entrance to avoid this hazard. Select any likely spot on the interior to anchor. Depths eventually begin to fall off as the stream splinters into several smaller creeks to the east.

Wimbee Creek Stick to the mid-width of broad Wimbee Creek as you cruise upstream. Remember not to attempt entry of the branch connecting Wimbee with Williman Creek or of the small offshoot that is separated from the main body by a marsh island northeast of Chisolm.

Watch to port and you will spy several private docks and a few homes on the southwestern shore. This is all that is visible today of Chisolm Island, once virtually covered by rich Sea Island plantations. Anchor a respectful distance from the piers.

Don't attempt to cruise further up Wimbee Creek than the small island bisecting the stream east of Keans Neck. Unmarked shoals lie beyond this point. You should also bypass South Wimbee Creek. It is too narrow for larger boats, and depths quickly drop off.

Williman Creek Favor the eastern shore of Williman Creek a bit when entering the stream from Bull River, but don't approach the eastern banks too closely either. Don't be fooled by the false entrance behind a marsh island on the western shore. This area is choked with shoals and oyster banks.

From its southerly entrance until it splits, Williman Creek carries minimum 8-foot depths on its mid-width, and most of its channel is significantly deeper. Anchorage on this section of the creek would be a consideration in light to lower-moderate airs, but winds over 15 knots could raise an uncomfortable chop.

Williman Sidewater Anchorage If you choose to make use of the more protected anchorage on the small stream running south to Wimbee Creek, be sure to use its southern entrance. Hold to the mid-width and drop the hook at your convenience. Discontinue your cruise well before reaching the bend to port where the creek begins to make its way into Wimbee's northern banks.

Southern Williman Creek Exercise caution when entering the southerly branch of Williman Creek. Favor the port shores until the stream makes a sharp bend to starboard. Cruise back to the mid-width at this point.

Consider anchoring after passing around the bend. Further upstream, numerous shoals guard the creek's intersection with Schooner Channel.

Schooner Channel Deep Schooner Channel does not present any navigational difficulties as far as its intersection with the northern reaches of Wimbee Creek. Simply stick to the mid-width and drop the anchor anywhere you choose.

Be sure to cease your exploration at the intersection of Schooner Channel and Wimbee Creek. Further passage upstream calls for local knowledge and is strictly not recommended for larger cruising craft.

ICW to Beaufort

From the western reaches of the Ashepoo-Coosaw Cutoff, the ICW follows mighty Coosaw River until it intersects the headwaters of Brickyard Creek, which in turn lead south to the Beaufort area. The Coosaw section of the waterway is broad and unsheltered. It is one of the most open stretches on the entire South Carolina ICW. Winds over 10 knots can quickly give rise to a sharp chop, and blows over 20 knots can make for a very rough crossing indeed. The waterway traveler would be well advised to check on the latest weather conditions before tackling the Coosaw.

At unlighted daybeacon #209 the waterway turns south into Brickyard Creek and begins its approach to the port city of Beaufort. This section of the waterway boasts good protection and easy navigation. Several sidewaters offer convenient overnight anchorage.

The cruising boater would do well to approach the run from the Coosaw to Beaufort with a healthy amount of respect. With the proper caution, however, you can enjoy your cruise to Beaufort and gain a broader perspective of the beautiful South Carolina Low Country.

Coosaw River

The broad Coosaw seems more like a sound than a river. More than one boater visiting South Carolina for the first time has sailed calmly out of the Ashepoo-Coosaw Cutoff only to stop short, amazed by the wide swath of waters before him. Don't be put off. In fair weather your passage of the Coosaw can be a very pleasurable experience.

The only Coosaw sidewaters offering protected anchorage are the Combahee and Bull rivers, just described, and the two smaller creeks leading south to Morgan River that were reviewed earlier in this chapter. If you seek shelter, consider one of these auxiliary streams. Otherwise you must reach the protected waters of Brickyard Creek before finding safe haven.

While the vast majority of Coosaw River is quite deep, there are some shoal areas. The smart boater will stick to the marked waterway channel unless he decides to visit one of the area sidewaters. It is often a long run between aids to navigation on the Coosaw. It is an excellent idea to run compass courses between the various markers to avoid possible error. Practice sound coastal navigation and you should not have any undue difficulty.

This portion of the ICW does present a certain challenge to the cruising boater. The river's open waters can indeed provide a most humbling experience in foul weather. Still, this writer cannot help feeling a genuine fondness for this stretch of the waterway. There is a very real sense of adventure that comes from the successful navigation of such broad waters with only undeveloped, natural shorelines within your range of vision. This is an experience sometimes absent along the well-marked waterway and one which passing cruisers should not dismiss too lightly.

Whale Branch

At flashing daybeacon #203 a broad fork of Coosaw River breaks off to the northwest and becomes Whale Branch. While it is possible to enter Whale Branch from Broad River to the west, the eastern entrance from Coosaw River is littered with unmarked shoals and is much too dangerous for cruising craft. Visiting boaters are strictly advised to bypass this section of Whale Branch. The entrance from Broad River will be covered in the next chapter.

Brickyard Creek

A well-marked, easily followed channel leads south down Brickyard Creek to the Beaufort area. Several small auxiliary waters along the way can provide good anchorage for boats under 40 feet. Stick to the channel in Brickyard Creek. Outside of the marked cut numerous shoals await the unlucky boater.

Jack Island Anchorage

West of unlighted daybeacon #209, an unnamed creek south of Jack Island offers very protected anchorage for craft of less than 36 feet that draw less than 4 feet. A large, unmarked shoal guards the entrance, but careful navigation should see you through. Otherwise the creek's channel carries 6-foot minimum depths until the stream takes a sharp bend to the north. In spite of soundings shown on chart 11519, shallow water is quickly encountered past this turn.

The creek's southern banks support moderate residential development. The best anchorage is located abeam of the several private docks that serve the shoreside homes.

Loop Anchorage

A small, unnamed loop of Brickyard Creek, east of unlighted daybeacon #217, provides one of the best overnight stops on this stretch of the waterway. Minimum depths of 8 feet on the creek's southerly reaches combine with excellent protection from the surrounding shores to make a superior anchorage.

Entrance from the north, though possible, is a tricky passage not recommended for cruising boaters. The southern entrance is easily navigated and provides reliable access to the stream's protected areas.

Watch to starboard as you enter the creek and you will eventually spy a large private dock on the eastern shore, just before the stream begins to curve back to the ICW. During on-site research this writer was fascinated by a huge old wreck beached on the mud flats beside the pier. Consider anchoring abeam of the old derelict. This is the most protected area on the creek. Further to the north depths become uncertain.

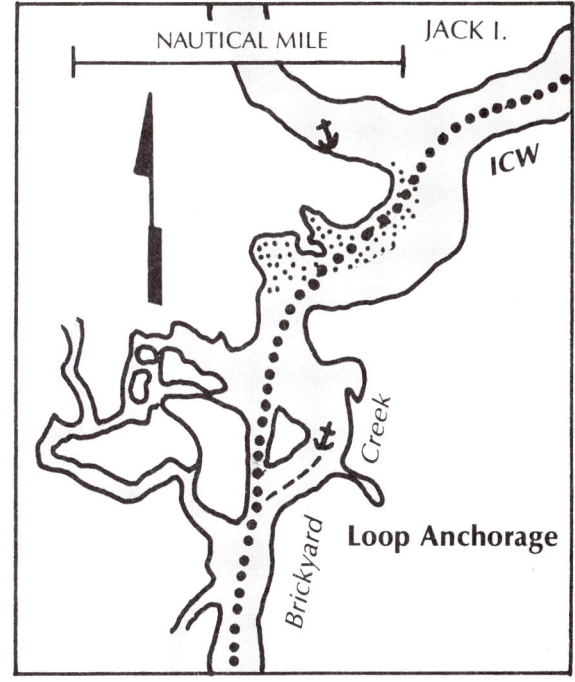

Albergottie Creek

West of unlighted daybeacon #226 two small buoys mark the entrance to Albergottie Creek. In spite of these markers the cruising boater is advised to bypass this stream. Questionable depths of 4 feet or less render Albergottie unusable by larger craft.

Pleasants Point

Just across Brickyard Creek from unlighted daybeacon #226, a beautiful home on Pleasants Point overlooks the stream. This property was originally owned by "Tuscarora Jack" Barnwell, one of the historical heroes of Beaufort. The present house was built in the 1920s, but it does reflect the style of earlier times.

Brickyard Creek Anchorage

An offshoot of deep water abuts the northern banks of Brickyard Creek near unlighted

Airplane flying over Brickyard Creek

daybeacon #229A. While this area is rather exposed, it can be used as an overnight anchorage in light to moderate airs by craft up to 40 feet. However, you will be exposed to the wake of all passing vessels, which could make for a rude awakening during the night.

On to Beaufort

South of unlighted daybeacon #229A the waterway flows around Pigeon Point, once a favored spot for duels, and begins its approach to the lovely city of Beaufort. This marvelous port of call will be reviewed in detail in the next chapter. A continuing account of the ICW to Savannah River will be presented in the last chapter.

ICW to Beaufort Navigation

Coosaw River presents some navigational circumstances seldom encountered on the South Carolina ICW. Markers are widely spaced, and the often choppy waters can make it difficult to hold a steady compass course. Practice sound coastal navigation at all times.

Brickyard Creek, on the other hand, is a typical section of the South Carolina waterway. The creek fairly bristles with markers; passing boaters would almost need to be asleep at the helm to encounter trouble. Stranger things have happened, though, so be sure to stay alert.

Coosaw River Begin bending your course slightly to the south as you exit the Ashepoo-Coosaw River cutoff at flashing daybeacon #184. After proceeding for some 50 yards, swing to the south and set a new course to come abeam of flashing buoy #186 to its southerly side. *Do not* try to shortcut your entrance into Coosaw River by passing between #189 and the southwesterly point of Combahee River. This point is building outward and could trick you into a most unpleasant grounding.

From #186 set a careful compass course for flashing daybeacon #189 north of Coosaw Island. Along the way you will pass flashing daybeacon #187 south of your course. Set a new course from #189 to come between flashing daybeacon #191 and unlighted nun buoy #192. From here to flashing daybeacon #203 the waterway channel is well marked and generally easy to follow.

Between #203 and the next westerly aid, unlighted daybeacon #206, a spoil bank flanks the southern tier of the waterway channel. Set course to come abeam of #206 to its immediate southerly side. West of #206 a pair of range markers helps you to avoid the spoil bank. Line the two markers up and stay on course until you begin your entrance into Brickyard Creek at unlighted daybeacon #209.

Jack Island Anchorage To hold best depths when entering the unnamed creek south of Jack Island, come abeam of unlighted daybeacon #209 and then turn 90 degrees to the west. Continue on course, favoring the northern banks heavily as you pass through the stream's mouth. Take care to avoid the large shoal, marked on chart 11519, that flanks the southern section of the creek's entrance.

Watch the southern shore and you will soon spy a series of private docks. As you begin your approach to these piers, slowly cruise toward the southern banks. Drop the hook as you come abeam of the docks.

Don't attempt to follow the creek past its first sharp bend to the north. In spite of depths shown on chart 11519, 3- and 4-foot readings are quickly encountered past the turn.

Loop Anchorage If you choose to enter the loop stream east of unlighted daybeacon #217, remember to use the southerly entrance. Cruise into the creek on its mid-width and continue on the middle ground. Set your hook at any likely spot before the stream begins to bend back to the west. Past this point depths become too uncertain for cruising craft. To rejoin the waterway, retrace your route to the south.

Cruising on Coosaw River

On the ICW On-site research reveals that dredging has apparently removed the large shoal on the waterway's western banks between flashing daybeacons #221A and #224. As you approach #224 you will see a large commercial dock facility on the western shore. Slow down and proceed at idle speed if any barges should be loading.

Brickyard Creek Anchorage If you choose to make use of the open anchorage on Brickyard Creek north of unlighted daybeacon #229A, continue on the ICW channel until you are well to the east of #229A; then turn sharply to the north and cruise toward the shore. This procedure should help you avoid the finger of shoal water that extends east from unlighted daybeacon #229.

Some 100 feet before reaching the banks, swing sharply to port and cruise back upstream, hugging the shoreline. Good depths continue within 40 yards of shore until unlighted daybeacon #229 comes abeam to the south.

Do not attempt to rejoin the waterway by cruising to the west. Retrace your steps to the ICW channel.

On the ICW As you round Pigeon Point, be sure to set course to come abeam and pass unlighted daybeacon #232 to its easterly quarter. Shallow water is found to the west of this aid.

A continuing account of the waterway in the Beaufort area will be presented in the next chapter.

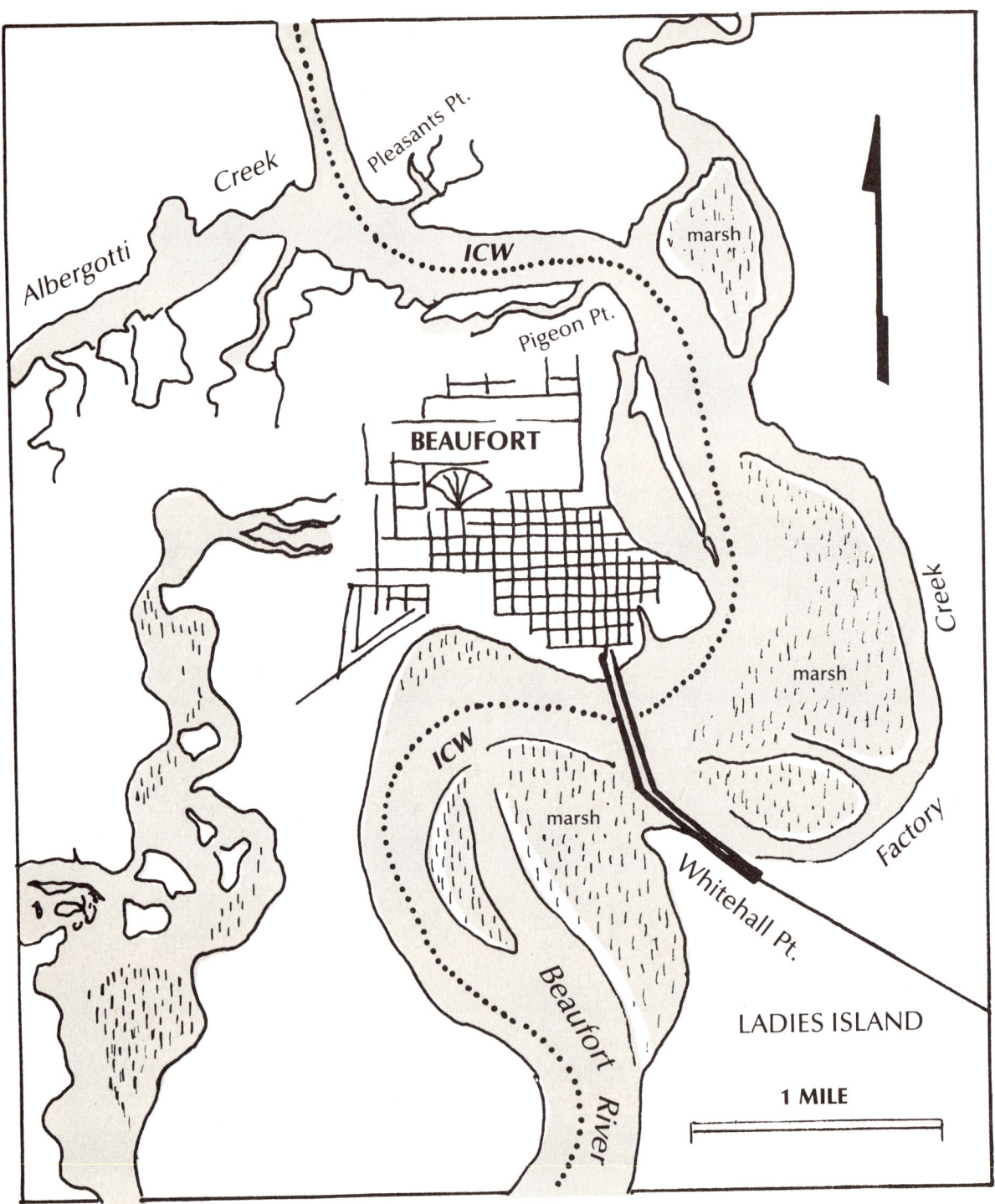

CHAPTER VIII

Beaufort

"Just after sunset . . . the writer, with several friends, viewed a beautiful phenomenon from the terrace of the Gold Eagle Tavern, Beaufort, S. C.

"With the heavens for a canvas, from zenith to the southwest horizon, the greatest of Artists, Nature, had painted another glorious masterpiece, the motif being continuous areas of variable size and contour, in a soft medium tone of ultramarine or lapis lazuli blue, each framed in clouds of brilliant silver, copper and gold, while the restless waters of Beaufort Bay were mirrored in exquisite pastel shades.

"On a pale pearl azure background, Luna, the Queen of Night, appears in luminous splendor, wearing, in honor of the Harvest Month, a royal robe of turquoise blue beneath a shimmering gossamer veil of silvery grey.

View of Beaufort River from Bay Street

"The radiant picture now in its entirety presents an entrancing ensemble of color and beauty, suggesting in its enchantment an approach to the celestial Gates of Paradise—and adds another glory to the Carolina Coast."

Thus wrote Gilbert Augustus Selby in 1934 as a preface to a new printing of James Rice's *Glories of the Carolina Coast*. The Golden Eagle Tavern is gone now, but the breathtaking scene described above can still be witnessed when nature chooses to cooperate. Just across the street from the old tavern site, Bay Street Inn still welcomes the weary traveler. From its second story balcony my mate and I were privileged to watch the sunset in a scene very much like the one described by Selby many years ago. The beauty of that sunset will remain with us always.

Charleston may be the Holy City of coastal South Carolina, but this writer contends that Beaufort is certainly the coast's most romantic community. The many stately homes and the mysterious old oaks that surround them impart an air of romance and wonder that must be experienced to be understood. The atmosphere of age, coupled with a yearning for the simpler, more gracious life of bygone years, is a pervasive presence. The sensitive visitor sometimes feels that he can almost reach out and touch those far-removed days.

Beaufort is a "must" stop for those cruising the waters of coastal South Carolina. Those who pass by without stopping to make the acquaintance of this unique city will be less for the omission. And just in case you are not yet enticed, take a moment to listen to the haunting words of Robert W. Barnwell, one of Beaufort's many famous citizens of another era.

"Called Back"

I think if I could see once more
The tide at Beaufort sweep,
Just as the crimson fades to gray,
Just as the shadows creep.
Just as the star of evening glows
And the skimming swallows seek repose
There where the oleanders grow
Before my boyhood's home,
Stumbler and groper that I've been,
Panting on the mountain path,
Lost in the forest green,
Wrecked by the Ocean's wrath,
Stifled in throngs of men;
Come for the wanderer's rest
Come to the home loved best . . . .

Charts You will only need one chart to cover all navigation in the Beaufort area: **11518** covers the ICW through Beaufort and all surrounding waters.

Beaufort

Beaufort sits poised on the banks of Beaufort River, waiting to greet the cruising boater. The town boasts three excellent marinas. A number of noteworthy restaurants are within walking distance of the various shoreside facilities, and several inns wait to shelter those who have seen one wave too many. One particularly well-placed marina is located in the heart of the city's historical district. It is indeed fortunate that this fascinating town has such excellent accommodations for passing boaters.

Moving north to south, Beaufort's first facility, Marsh Harbor Marina, is located on an unnamed creek that makes into the eastern shores of Beaufort River north of unlighted daybeacon #233. This marina is primarily a service facility. Both mechanical and below-the-waterline repairs, as well as a first-rate parts store, are featured. Marsh Harbor is one of the only marinas this writer has ever encountered that specializes in trawler repair. If you are the captain of such an excellent cruising craft and need repairs, Marsh Harbor is the place to stop.

Minimum approach depths on the well-marked entrance channel run between 7 and 8 feet. You can expect 6 to 7 feet of water at dockside during low tide. If there is room, Marsh Harbor will accept transients, but the management has informed this writer that only a few boats stop just for the night. Should you berth here, you will find all power and water connections at the floating docks. The marina does not offer gasoline or diesel fuel.

Beaufort Marina is located on the southern shores of Factory Creek, south of the Ladies Island Bridge. This large, modern facility gladly accepts transients for overnight dockage and offers berths at floating docks with all power and water connections. Gasoline and diesel fuel are readily available. There is an on-site ships' store, and a number of grocery retailers are well within walking distance.

This marina has a 50-ton railway and offers below-the-waterline repairs. If you have prop

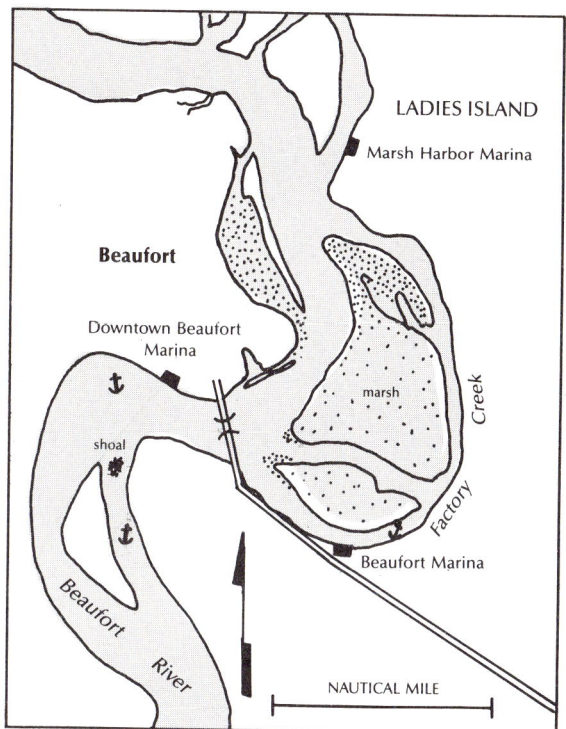

or shaft damage, it would be an excellent idea to have your craft serviced here.

Several small restaurants are located within walking distance of the marina. One of these, The Dutch Treat, offers an excellent selection of sandwiches and is highly recommended. To reach the eatery, begin walking back toward the Ladies Island Bridge on the main highway. You will soon spy the restaurant on the left-hand side of the road.

Perhaps the most famous restaurant on Ladies Island is the WhiteHall Inn. This fine restaurant is known up and down the ICW for its fresh seafood and continental cuisine. The visitor can be assured of a satisfying meal. Though a bit too far for walking, the inn will be glad to provide courtesy transportation if you give them a call.

Factory Creek may also be used for anchorage east of Beaufort Marina. The best spot is found after the creek passes through a sharp bend to the north. Here, the starboard shores border high ground and give good protection. Boats up to 45 feet should find plenty of swinging room. Do not try to rejoin the waterway through the creek's northerly entrance. Depths are much too uncertain in this area for cruising craft.

The Beaufort Downtown Marina is located in the heart of the city's historical district, north of unlighted daybeacon #239. This facility gladly accepts cruising boaters and offers ultramodern floating docks with all power and water connections. Gasoline and diesel fuel are readily available, and there is a very attractive ships' store on the premises. Several grocery stores and a host of shoreside businesses are located within a short walk of the docks.

The Downtown Marina is adjacent to a lovely riverside park. Passing cruisers are welcome to berth at the park's docks. During the early evening hours, many local residents gather here to watch the spectacular river sunsets that nature thoughtfully provides from time to time.

There is a local mooring area west of the Downtown Marina where visting craft are welcome to drop the hook. Be sure to leave plenty of swing room for nearby boats. Anchor well away from the ICW channel to avoid any passing traffic.

A number of dining establishments are located within a short walk of the Downtown

Beaufort Downtown Marina

Marina. Among these are the Dolphin Dining Room, associated with the Best Western Sea Island Motel, and the John Cross Tavern on Bay Street. The Dolphin's fresh seafood has been well known for many years. The John Cross often features live entertainment and draws a warm, lively crowd. The tavern features seafood, sandwiches, and steaks.

The Anchorage House, this writer's choice for Beaufort's most distinguished dining spot, is also just a short step from the marina's docks. The restaurant is housed in a magnificent three-story mansion that presents a striking facade to passing boaters. Built by William Elliott during the pre-Revolutionary period, the old house has passed through many different phases. At one time it was used as an exclusive club, complete with gambling casino. Some years later, the commander of the nearby Parris Island Marine Base, Admiral Beardsley, came to admire the house greatly during his tenure, and he purchased it upon retirement. Having spent several years in Japan, the admiral imported many pieces of heavily carved oriental furniture. Though some of these rare articles were lost in an auction sale many years later, others can still be seen today. Following the admiral's death, the house was operated as a tourist home for many years, until it was finally converted into an elegant restaurant.

The Admiral would most likely have approved of the fine food and spirits served in his one-time home. Entrées range from the finest continental seafood to fowl and beef dishes. All appetizers and desserts are of the same excellent quality. The fortunate visitor to Anchorage House will not soon forget the

View of Ladies Island Bridge from balcony of Bay Street Inn

succulent offerings of this one-of-a-kind restaurant.

The Anchorage House is not the place for a quick meal. The unhurried pace of simpler times, when dining was an event to be remembered, is preserved here with painstaking accuracy. The service is impeccably correct, but you should plan to set aside several hours during the evening for this memorable gastronomic event.

Beaufort Lodging

Beaufort is a wonderful choice for weary cruisers who are ready for a break from their waterborne life. The town boasts a number of fine lodging establishments. Two of these are particularly convenient to the passing boater.

The Best Western Sea Island Motel is located just across Bay Street from the Downtown Marina. This modern hostelry occupies the same site as a much older inn of the same name. The renowned reputation of the old Sea Island lives on in its well-managed modern counterpart. The motel is located in the heart of the historical district and is convenient to all the city's major attractions.

The Bay Street Inn is found four blocks north of the Downtown Marina docks. This notable inn is housed in one of Beaufort's historic homes. The house is readily visible from the water and many a passing boater has no doubt admired its cool white porches and columns, never guessing that they were welcome to spend the night. The management will be glad to provide transportation from the area marinas for cruise-weary guests. The proprietor is a boater himself and well understands the waterborne traveler's needs. Lodging rates are most reasonable and include a splendid continental breakfast. If you're lucky, a mace-flavored blueberry coffeecake may be a part of the morning's fare.

The two-story inn was built by Lewis Sams in 1852. Apparently Mr. Sams was very fond of sitting on the porch in the evenings, as he built his house with not one, but two porches, one above the other. Both offer a magnificent view of the river. The breathtaking panorama provided by the upper balcony has already been alluded to in the opening section of this chapter. I cannot imagine a more peaceful evening than taking one's ease in the balcony's rocking chairs and watching the day's light slowly fade from the surrounding waters.

The inn's interior fulfills the promise of its external view. Few will be unimpressed by the inn's elegant appointments. The house has 14-foot ceilings and is impeccably furnished in period antiques. From the huge piano in the parlor to the lush oak paneling of the library, the old home is an elegant reminder of the bygone days of gracious Southern living.

To say the least, this writer is more than a little enthusiastic about the Bay Street Inn. I hope you have the time to enjoy its many charms.

Beaufort History The long and colorful history of the Beaufort area stretches back to early exploration and colonization by the Spanish Empire. The first European to visit the area was apparently Francisco Cordillo, who landed at Port Royal Island in 1520. It was he who named the nearby cape "St. Elena," which, with the passage of the years, became St. Helena. In 1557 the Spanish attempted to establish a base in the area, but the colony failed, and little is known of this early attempt at settlement.

In 1562 an adventurous Frenchman, Jean Ribaut, led a group of French Protestants to the New World. The colonists built a settlement on nearby Parris Island and named their small town "Charlesfort." For a time all went well, but the colony was doomed to end in tragic and grisly failure.

Promising to return as soon as possible, Ribaut sailed back to France to obtain needed supplies. When the dynamic leader arrived in his mother country, he found the French nation torn asunder with religious conflict. Despairing of aid from his native land, Ribaut traveled to England, where for a time it appeared that he might obtain the aid he needed. Finally, though, he was thrown into prison, and he vanished from the canvas of Beaufort's early history.

Meanwhile, the Parris Island colonists were quickly running through their inadequate supply of stores. Despite generous aid from

Anchorage House Restaurant, Beaufort

nearby Indian tribes, starvation began to loom as a very real fear in the colonists' minds. It is curious that they could have feared hunger surrounded by forests teeming with game and waters jumping with fish, but for whatever reason, the settlers determined to build a small ship and sail for France. The vessel was finished and the desperate group quickly abandoned Charlesfort. But when the little boat was becalmed in the doldrums, food supplies were soon exhausted. It is whispered that the crew even resorted to cannibalism to fend off their hunger. At last a passing English ship rescued the survivors, and France's colonization attempts along the South Carolina coast were brought to an abrupt end.

Spanish soldiers returned to Parris Island in 1566 and built Fort San Felipe. This small outpost was temporarily abandoned some years later and then reoccupied for a single year. With the burning of St. Augustine, Florida, by Sir Francis Drake in 1566, Spanish efforts to maintain a foothold in the Beaufort area were brought to an end. Many more years were to pass, however, before the threats of Spanish intervention and attack were no more.

In 1660, following the restoration of the English Monarchy, Britain sent out an expedition under William Hilton to explore the Carolina coast. Hilton wrote glowingly of the Beaufort coastline: "The Ayr is clear and sweet, the countrey very pleasant and delightful; and we would wish, that all they that want a happy settlement of our English Nation, were well transported thither."

The English colonization party that was eventually to found Charleston first put ashore at Port Royal in 1679. The local Indians were

Beaufort Marina, Factory Creek

able to persuade the expedition's leader, Robert Sayle, that better lands were to be found to the north. This advice led to the removal of the party to the banks of Ashley River.

Some historians have labeled this series of events as a crafty move on the part of the Cacique of Kiawah. However, it seems plain from later history that the Indians' advice was quite sound. For all their many qualities, neither Beaufort nor Port Royal could ever have become as great a port as Charleston.

In 1648 a group of adventurous Scotsmen established "Stuarttowne" near the present site of Port Royal. This ambitious settlement was completely wiped out by a Spanish raid in 1688, though the invaders were later soundly beaten at Charleston. By 1712, successful expeditions against the Spanish and the Indians of Florida had lessened the threat of attack. In 1712 the South Carolina colonial legislature laid out plans for a new settlement in the area, to be known as the town of Beaufort.

Beaufort had been officially established for only a few years when the great Yemassee uprising broke out. Allied with the Creeks and other Indian tribes, the Yemassees slaughtered every white settler they could find in the Beaufort region. Peace finally returned in 1717 after the Cherokees became allied with the English settlers, but continued fear of Indian and Spanish attacks retarded the development of Beaufort into the 1720s.

Indigo provided the first basis for agricultural wealth in the Beaufort-Port Royal area. Beginning about 1740, this cash crop brought continuing progress and prosperity to the area. Nevertheless, this was a time of small farms and simple dwellings. The great plantations and town houses that we admire today were to come much later.

As reported earlier in this guide, the British government paid a sizable bounty for indigo. For this reason more than any other, the citizens of Beaufort showed a marked dislike for the patriot cause at the outbreak of the Revolution. It seemed to them that the American leaders were doing all in their power to remove their greatest single source of prosperity.

Beaufort and Port Royal were occupied by British forces in 1779. The entire area became a staging ground for raids by rival parties of patriots and tories.

Prosperity returned around 1790 with the rise of Sea Island Cotton. Until 1860 the long-staple plant brought fabulous wealth to Beaufort as it did to the surrounding Sea Islands. Great plantations sprang into being on nearby St. Helena Island, and the wealthy planters built sumptuous summer residences in Beaufort, where the cool river breezes helped to alleviate the sweltering heat.

Beaufort took a decidedly secessionist stance during the tragic train of events that led to the Civil War. One of the town's citizens, Robert Barnwell Rhett, gained the title of "Father of Secession." Other Confederate leaders actually considered Rhett too fiery and unrestrained, and he was denied a place in the new Southern government.

In November of 1861 a strong Union fleet, under the command of Commodore S. F. Dupont, smashed the Confederate forts defending the entrances to Port Royal Sound. Under the orders of Robert E. Lee, the area was quickly abandoned by the few Southern forces left, and Beaufort remained under Union occupation for the rest of the war.

The area planters were caught by surprise. They had been told that the forts guarding the water approaches to the sound were impregnable. Most of the white population fled in panic, leaving their homes and possessions behind. Many of these estates were confiscated as abandoned lands and redistributed to freed blacks. Few residences were actually destroyed, and as a consequence Beaufort still boasts many beautiful homes built in the lavish antebellum style. Following the war, some properties were returned to their rightful owners, but others were never recovered.

The Reconstruction period was a difficult time in Beaufort as in all of South Carolina. Sea Island cotton was again grown, but the coming of the boll weevil erased this final mark of prosperity.

In 1893 a hurricane of astonishing violence struck Beaufort. The town and nearby islands were covered with twelve feet of water, and winds of more than one hundred miles per hour wrought havoc. According to one report, the receding waters left a large ship aground in the middle of present-day Bay Street.

Prosperity finally began a long awaited return to Beaufort during World War I with the establishment of the Parris Island Marine Base nearby. This event was followed by the establishment of the Port Royal Port Authority in 1955 and the opening of a major shipping terminal at Port Royal in 1958. Improved roads and bridges further added to the development of Beaufort. Moving into the 1960s and 1970s the town began to enjoy the fruits of a thriving tourist trade. With recent historic restorations and a newly landscaped waterfront, Beaufort's future as a tourist attraction appears bright.

Every visitor to this beautiful port city should be thankful that the good sense and foresight of Beaufort's leaders have led to controlled development that has carefully preserved the town's historic character. In "A Brief History of Beaufort," John Duffy comments, "It is heartening to note that much of Beaufort's wealth in the third quarter of the twentieth century has been used to restore the grandeur of old homes and buildings dating from its 'Periclean Age.' As a result Beaufort is one of the most attractive towns on the Atlantic coast."

Beaufort Attractions

The many period homes of the Beaufort Historical District are clearly the city's star attraction. Thanks to the lack of extensive damage during the Civil War and to the diligent efforts of the local historical society and many private citizens, Beaufort still teems with lovely nineteenth-century homes. It is a very special treat to view these old homeplaces from the town's shady lanes. A walking tour of the historical district is not to be missed.

The map on the following page points out some of the more prominent homes. For more information you should acquire *A Guidebook to Historic Beaufort,* published by the historical society. This fine publication gives a detailed history of most of Beaufort's historic homes and other points of interest. For those interested in the area's rich folklore, always a worthwhile concern, Nell Graydon's *Tales of*

Beaufort relates many a touching story.

Begin your tour at the local chamber of commerce office just behind the Downtown Marina's ships' store. Here you will find all sorts of information that will help to make your tour a more meaningful experience. The books listed above can also be purchased at the office.

You will find that it is a good idea to choose which homes you wish to view before setting out. It is a rather long walk—though undeniably a pleasant one—from one end of the district to the other. By planning your tour, you can avoid unnecessary steps.

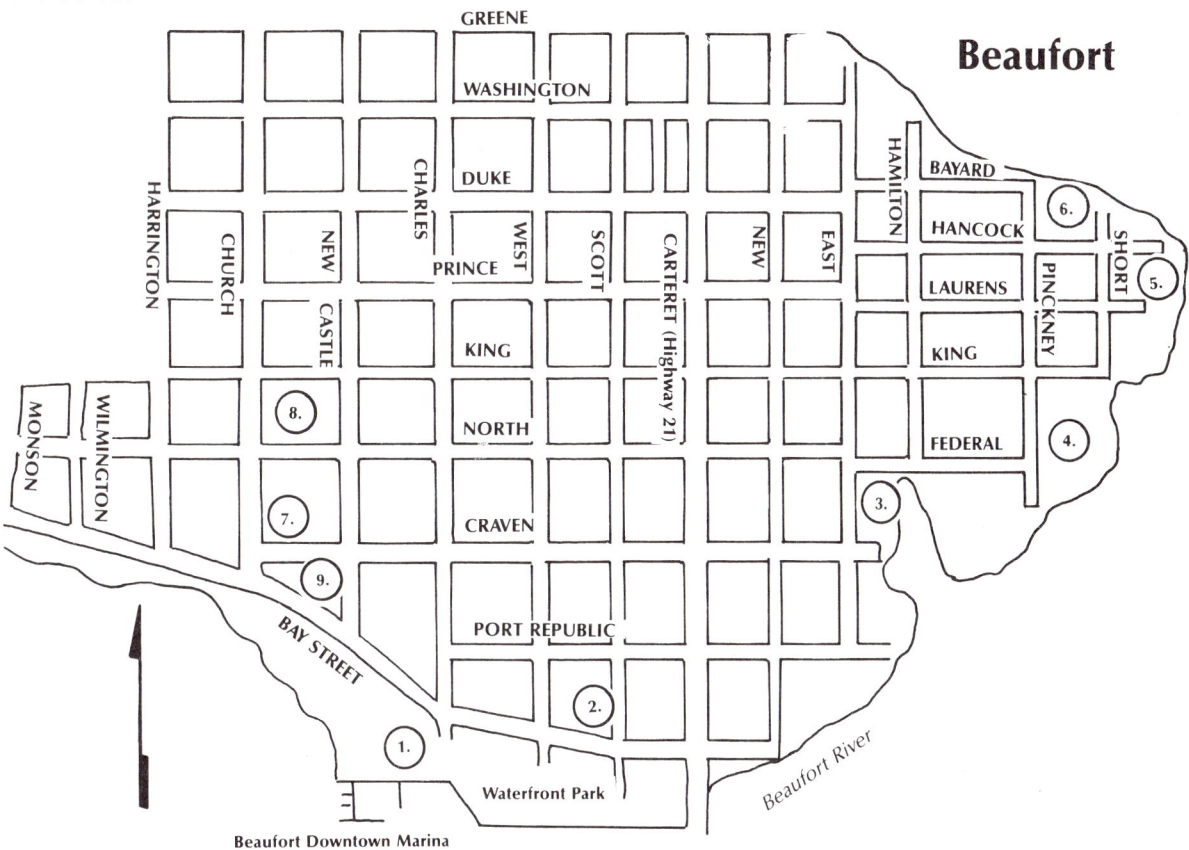

1. Chamber of Commerce
2. John Mark Verdier House Museum ("Lafayette House," 1790)
3. Joseph Johnson House ("The Castle," 1850)
4. James Robert Verdier House ("Marshlands," 1814)
5. James Fripp House ("Tidalholm")
6. Hext House ("Riverview" c. 1720)
7. Milton Maxey House ("Secession House")
8. St. Helena Episcopal Church, 1724
9. William Elliott House (The Anchorage)

224 CRUISING GUIDE TO COASTAL SOUTH CAROLINA

It would be impossible to list all of Beaufort's many historic homes or relate any reasonable portion of their history within the confines of this guide. For complete information I suggest one of the publications recommended above. However, some of the more prominent homes and their fascinating stories will be reviewed in the following pages.

Lafayette House

The "Lafayette House," or the John Mark Verdier House (801 Bay Street), was built in 1790. The structure was raised on a tabby foundation and styled in the Federalist manner. John Verdier was a very successful merchant and factor. He did not hesitate to spend whatever sum was necessary to insure that his home would stand the test of time. Verdier would be quite pleased, I am sure, to know that his proud homeplace has so well withstood the rigors of the passing years.

The Marquis de Lafayette paid a brief visit to Beaufort during his tour of the United States in 1825. For many days before the scheduled

Secession House, Beaufort

arrival of the marquis, preparations went forward at a feverish pace for a grand reception. As the time for Lafayette's arrival drew near, huge crowds gathered at the city's wharves.

The crowds were destined to be disappointed. Lafayette was unavoidably delayed on Edisto Island for several hours. Tradition claims that his steamboat was stranded on the bottom by the ebbing tide. When he finally arrived in Beaufort, it was the dead of night. A messenger, sent on ahead, breathlessly informed anyone he could find that the marquis was just a short distance away. The crowds were hastily reassembled, and they cheered the steamboat as it appeared around a bend of the river.

Lafayette was well behind schedule and did not really have the time for a stop in Beaufort. Being a true gentleman, however, he refused to disappoint the gathered multitude. He descended the gangplank and delivered a speech from the balcony of the Verdier home. The venerable residence has been known ever since as "the Lafayette House."

Today, after many successful and dedicated restoration efforts, the house is open to the public on weekdays and serves as the headquarters of the Beaufort Historical Society. The home has been magnificently furnished in period antiques and is certainly one of the premiere attractions of the historical district.

During your visit to the Lafatette House, be sure to inquire about special events sponsored by the Historical Society. In October the society usually promotes a tour of homes. If you are in the area, don't miss this very special chance to visit Beaufort's historic homes.

Secession House

The foundation of Secession House (1113 Craven Street) dates to the 1740s. During the early 1800s the present structure was built atop the old tabby base. In 1861 Edmund Rhett rebuilt the two upper floors in a modified Greek Revival style. He installed marble steps at the entrance and imported Italian marble mantelpieces, which were carefully placed above each fireplace. Today the proud home stands in all its grandeur, facing Beaufort River. This writer was struck by the vivid contrast between the house's beauty and the grim events that took place there.

Edmund Rhett, a United States Senator from South Carolina, was one of the leading advocates of secession from the Union. He held many impassioned meetings at his magnificent house on Craven Street and continually advocated the cause of state's rights. Tradition claims that the last meeting of Beaufort's delegates to the Secession Convention was held at Rhett's house, from which they went directly to their waiting boat amid the lusty cheers of many onlookers. The delegation voted for secession to a man. Little did they realize that their vote was the death knell of the life they treasured so deeply.

The Castle

The Joseph Johnson House (411 Craven Street) has been known as "the Castle" for time out of mind. The title is well bestowed. Built by Dr. Joseph Johnson in 1850, the house has few rivals for pure magnificence. Fashioned in the Italian Renaissance style, the grand structure occupies a full city block. Curiously, the house's exterior color changes with the light. Sometimes it appears gray, sometimes tan, and on rare occasions it even seems pink. The large porches are supported by six massive columns. The house contains seventy-nine windows and boasts four triple chimneys. Yet this massive structure is actually built on a crib of palmetto logs. The Castle has had the distinction of serving as the centerpiece for a 1961 United States Department of Commerce poster. Many people feel that if you have not seen the Castle, you have not seen Beaufort.

As you might well expect of a homeplace like the Castle, the house has its ghost story. While Dr. Johnson was supervising the construction of his house, he saw a strange, dwarfish figure wandering the grounds. When he went to investigate, the apparition vanished. When the good doctor questioned a gardener working nearby, the gardener nonchalantly informed him that the dwarf lived in the basement.

Many claim to have seen the ghostly figure since those early days, and the family members have reportedly learned to live with fur-

The Castle, Beaufort

niture that is moved about and doors that are opened and closed by invisible forces.

Marshlands

The James Robert Verdier House (501 Pinckney Street) is one of the loveliest homes in all of Beaufort. Nicknamed "Marshlands," this beautiful house faces south on Beaufort River at Pigeon Point. Many boaters have undoubtedly admired its striking facade as they passed by.

Built in 1814 by Dr. James R. Verdier, Marshlands is set high off the ground on a foundation pierced by multiple arches. The double entry stairway runs parallel to the second story porch and lends a very impressive look to the home's frontal view.

Dr. Verdier had a most illustrious medical career. He is credited with early successful treatment of yellow fever. This dread disease often ran rampant during the summer months and was greatly feared by whites and slaves alike. Verdier's crude but apparently effective vaccines helped to mitigate the horrors of epidemics in the Beaufort area.

Marshlands has the distinction of being the

Tidalholm ("The Big Chill" House), Beaufort

mythical home of Emily, the heroine in Francis Griswold's novel of the Civil War, *Sea Island Lady*. This fictional work remains popular in the South Carolina Low Country to this day and is highly recommended for those who wish to acquire a "feel" for the coast.

Tidalholm

The house known as Tidalholm (1 Laurens Street) presents a strikingly beautiful view to the passing visitor. Surrounded by mighty oaks and enclosed by an impressive wrought iron fence, this historic home has more than one claim to fame.

Legend tells us that following the Civil War, the old homeplace was put up for auction to be sold for back taxes. The owner, James Fripp, stood by with tears running down his cheeks because he didn't have enough money to make a bid. An unknown Frenchman visiting Beaufort attended the auction and was made aware of Fripp's plight. He bought the house and immediately presented the deed to the astonished owner. The two embraced and the Frenchman left, never to be heard from again.

In 1982 the house was the setting for the critically acclaimed motion picture *The Big Chill*. This touching story of the reunion of six college friends of the 1960s and how they deal with the reality of the 1980s seems altogether fitting with Tidalholm's romantic past. I'm sure James Fripp and the unknown Frenchmen would have approved.

Riverview

The Elizabeth Hext House, also known as "Riverview," is one of Beaufort's oldest

St. Helena Episcopal Church

homes. Though simple in comparison to many of the area's antebellum mansions, Riverview maintains a feeling of intimacy that is often absent from grander structures.

Built about 1720, the house has been added to over the years. Many of the windows still contain the original glass. The floors in most of the house are the same ten-inch pine planks that were laid so long ago. The heavy old doors still swing on their H-hinges. The house is surrounded by huge shade trees and is set well back from the street. Even without its many ghost stories, the old home would be a point of interest.

Legend tells us that in later years the owner of Riverview was strolling the grounds when she noticed her faithful gardener digging holes in apparently random spots in the yard. When questioned about this strange practice, the old servant replied that he was searching for gold as instructed by several visitors who had called on him the night before. The gardener described the strange callers' clothing, and the mistress was astonished to hear an accurate description of ancient pirate garb.

One morning the excited servant informed his mistress that the strange visitors had come again and had promised to reveal their secret that very night.

When the gardener did not appear the next morning, the mistress went to his house to see what was the matter. She found him speechless; he had suffered a stroke the night before. The old servant died soon thereafter without ever revealing whether he had learned the fateful secret.

Some may call this tale fanciful, but stories of pirates and their buried treasure have been associated with Riverview for many a year. Strange apparitions are said to haunt the night, offering riches to any who will follow their instructions. For all these ghostly visitations, however, no treasure has ever been unearthed. Perhaps the old gardener learned that it is better to be happy with what you have than to covet the treasure of those long gone.

St. Helena Episcopal Church

Not all of Beaufort's attractions are to be found among the community's historic homes. St. Helena Episcopal Church is one of the most popular points of interest in the city. Built in 1724 for a congregation organized in 1712, the handsome edifice has twice been enlarged, and the steeple has been replaced in this century. The adjacent cemetery contains some notable graves, in particular that of "Tuscarora Jack" Barnwell. Old records note the burial of a man named Perry who, in great fear of being buried alive, instructed his friends to place a jug of water, a loaf of bread, and a hatchet in his coffin. If he regained consciousness, he could then stave off hunger and thirst while chopping his way out.

During the Civil War, St. Helena was used as a hospital by Union troops. Pews were summarily removed, and gravestones were uprooted and used as operating tables. The old organ was destroyed and the walls much damaged.

The churchyard is graced by a number of unusually large oak trees, which lend a quiet, shaded atmosphere to the old house of worship. The grounds are surrounded by a wall built of brick once used as ships' ballast. It is a very peaceful place indeed and one you won't want to miss.

Beaufort Area Navigation

South of unlighted daybeacon #232, set course to come abeam of unlighted daybeacon #233 fairly close to its westerly side. Don't let leeway ease you to the west. As shown on chart 11518, a large shoal lines the western shore. Between #232 and #233, the entrance to Marsh Harbor Marina will come abeam to the east.

Marsh Harbor Marina The entrance to Marsh Harbor is well marked by two pairs of unlighted daybeacons and one lone green marker. Pass between the first two sets of aids and come abeam of the green daybeacon to port. Continue on the creek's mid-width and the docks will soon come abeam to starboard.

On the ICW The northern reaches of Factory Creek make into the eastern banks of Beaufort River at unlighted daybeacon #233. Do not attempt to enter the creek from this quarter. The stream's mouth is flanked by mud flats and oyster banks, which cover at high water. The channel is much too treacherous for visiting cruisers who lack specific local knowledge.

From #233 point to come abeam and pass flashing daybeacon #235 well to its westerly side. At #233 a sign on the eastern banks warns that all waters around Beaufort are a Minimum Wake Zone. Larger power craft should proceed at slow speed from this point to flashing daybeacon #241.

Beaufort anchorage with Bay Street in background

From #235 set course to pass unlighted daybeacon #237 to its northerly side and point for the central pass-through of the Ladies Island Bridge. Just before you reach the bridge, the entrance to Factory Creek and Beaufort Marina will come abeam to the south.

Beaufort Marina To enter Factory Creek, continue on the ICW channel until you almost reach the bridge; then swing 90 degrees to the south and point to come abeam of unlighted daybeacon #1 by some 10 yards to its westerly side. Carefully set a new course to come abeam of unlighted daybeacon #3 by about the same distance to its southerly side. Be sure to bend your course a bit to the west as you cruise between the two markers. By doing so you will avoid the very shallow water flanking Factory Creek's eastern banks. Be on guard against leeway. Watch your stern to be sure that you are not drifting to the east.

Once past #3 good depths open out almost from shore to shore. You will soon spy the marina docks to starboard. Remember to proceed at idle speed as you approach the docks.

If you choose to anchor in Factory Creek rather than to make use of Beaufort Marina's excellent facilities, continue upstream past the piers, holding to the mid-width. Once clear of the marina docks, simply drop your hook at any likely spot and settle in for the night.

Do not attempt to enter the small arm of Factory Creek that breaks off to the west just as the stream finishes its first long curve to the north. Also, be sure to discontinue your exploration of Factory Creek before it begins to curve to the west to rejoin the waterway. Depths are too uncertain in both these areas for larger cruising craft.

On the ICW The Ladies Island Bridge at Beaufort has 30 feet of closed vertical clearance. Boats that cannot clear this height must contend with restrictive opening hours. From 7 A.M. to 9 A.M. and from 4 P.M. to 6 P.M., Monday through Saturday (except for legal holidays), the span opens only on the intervening hour. Otherwise the bridge supposedly opens on demand. The operator has sometimes been known to be rather slow to open. It might be best to call ahead on your VHF to avoid any unnecessary delays.

Once you are through the bridge, the Beaufort Downtown Marina docks will come abeam to the north. Entrance into this facility should present no problem.

Past unlighted daybeacon #239, the waterway follows Beaufort River south towards Port Royal and Parris Island. A continuing account of the ICW to the Georgia line will be presented in the next chapter.

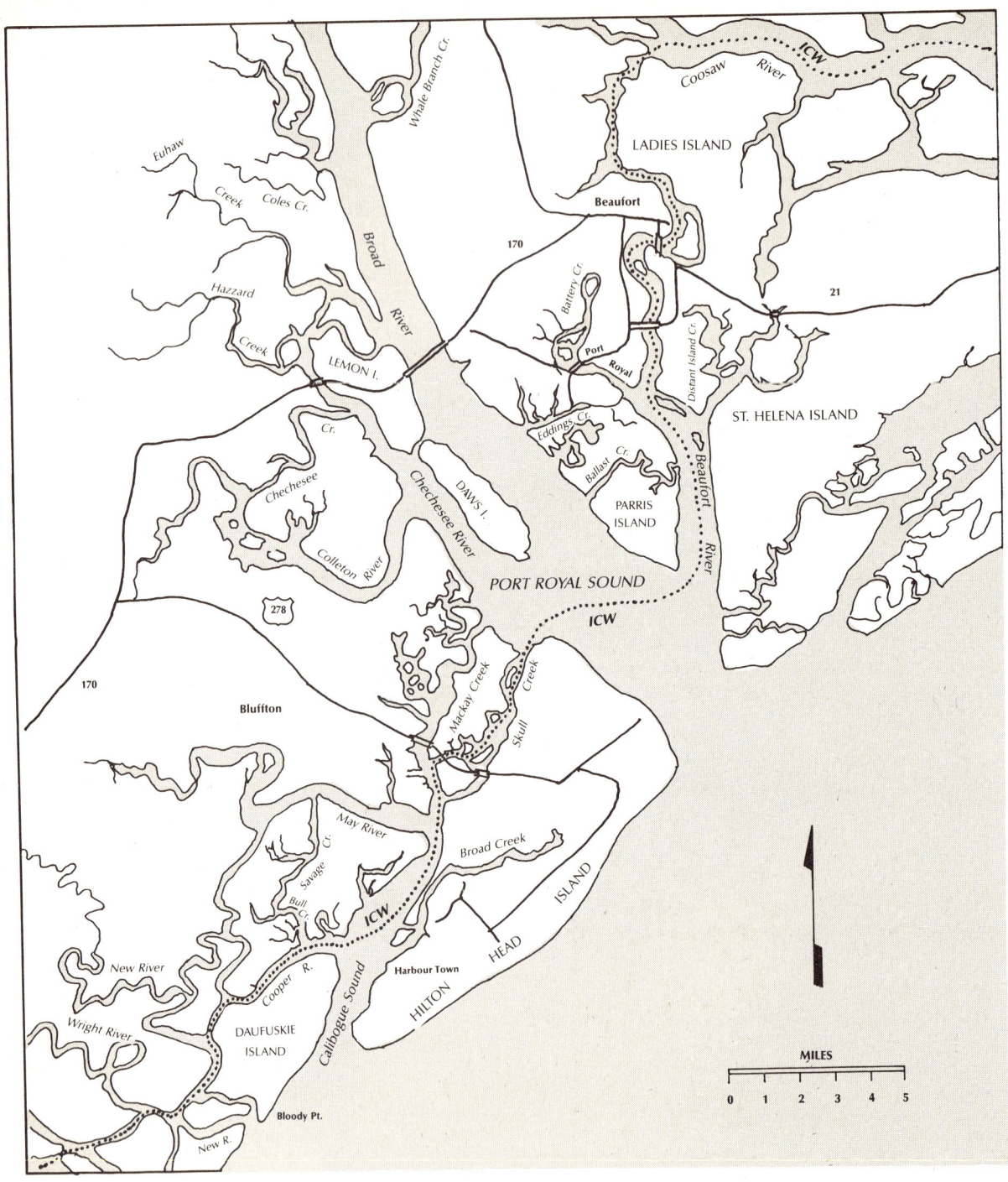

CHAPTER IX

Beaufort River to Georgia

The waters of coastal South Carolina between Beaufort and the Savannah River offer a very mixed bag of cruising opportunities to the visiting boater. To the north, Beaufort River, Port Royal Sound, and the sound's tributary streams provide cruising grounds off the beaten path. Anchorages are numerous but facilities are almost nonexistent. Further to the south, Calibogue Sound and Hilton Head Island boast no fewer than six marinas waiting to greet the transient boater. Hilton Head is the largest resort in South Carolina and its popularity seems unbounded. Several water bodies in the Hilton Head area are noted for their beauty and will appeal to those who like a bit more isolation.

Upon leaving Calibogue Sound behind, the waterway cruiser is abruptly plunged into another undeveloped area. The ICW follows the Cooper, New, and Wright rivers, joined by several man-made cuts, south to Savannah River and the Georgia state line. Along the way the waterway passes through a lonely countryside with only a few homes to break the landscape.

The waters between Beaufort River and Savannah River are some of the most interesting in the state. In few other places does one find cruising conditions that range from islands bristling with marinas to small, secret, winding creeks in such a relatively small area.

Charts Five NOAA charts are required for complete coverage of the waters from Beaufort to the Georgia state line:
11518 follows the ICW down Beaufort River as far as Port Royal.
11507 details the ICW from Beaufort River to Georgia and includes many sidewaters off the waterway.
11516 covers Chowan Creek on Beaufort River, Port Royal Sound, the lower section of Broad River and all of Colleton and Chechessee rivers, as well as the May River and Calibogue Sound (including Broad Creek).
11519 includes upper section of Broad River and all the navigable sections of Whale Branch.
11512 details the upper and lower portions of New and Wright rivers.

Beaufort River

South of Beaufort the river bearing the port's name becomes a wide stream that often spawns a healthy chop. Winds over 15 knots can make for a bumpy ride, but waves seldom reach a dangerous height. As you approach Port Royal Sound the waters widen further and are even more likely to be rough in high winds. If bad weather threatens, it would be a good idea to retreat to one of Beaufort River's anchorages and wait for fair conditions before attempting the run across Port Royal Sound to Skull Creek.

South of Beaufort there are no facilities on the river. In fact, except for one very small marina on a remote section of Chechessee River, cruising boaters are on their own until reaching Skull Creek.

Three large creeks provide good overnight anchorage on Beaufort River. Two are suitable only for light to moderate winds, while the other can be used in all but the heaviest of weather.

Being part of the ICW, Beaufort River is easily traversed. South of Port Royal a large ships' channel is well defined by numerous flashing buoys. The waterway follows this passage until cutting west across Port Royal Sound at flashing daybeacon #246. With a few exceptions, the river is mostly deep and generally free of shoals. Most boaters need have no concern about successful passage of Beaufort River.

The northerly section of the river, near Beaufort, is bordered by high banks on the western shore. In fact, most of the Beaufort's shoreline is higher ground than is usually seen along this section of the coast. One exception to this rule is the extensive marsh land of Parris Island that comprises lower Beaufort River's western shore. Some buildings associated with the island marine base are visible near flashing buoy #37. It does not take much imagination, as you view the island marsh, to understand why Parris Island is considered by many to be the toughest basic training camp in the country.

Northerly Anchorage

East of unlighted daybeacon #241A, a wide, deep stream runs between the river's banks and a small marsh island. When entered from its southerly mouth this stream carries minimum 10-foot depths for most of its length. Protection is adequate for anchorage in light to moderate winds. Depths finally drop off as the stream begins its reentry into Beaufort River to the north.

Spanish Point

West of flashing daybeacon #242, Spanish Point juts boldly out into the waters of Beaufort River. In 1686 a group of daring Scots founded Stuarttowne near the point. The settlement was later destroyed by a Spanish-Indian raid from Florida. The survivors fled to Charleston, where the attackers were soundly repulsed.

Fort Frederick

The tabby walls of Fort Frederick are clearly visible near the grounds of the large naval hospital south of the Beaufort River highrise bridge. Chart 11518 notes a "Surfaced Ramp" near the fort's position.

Fort Frederick was built between 1732 and 1734 to protect the Beaufort area from Spanish attack. It was abandoned after only a few years. The walls have survived the long years in remarkably good condition, a monument to the tabby makers of the day.

Battery Creek

The deep waters of Battery Creek lead to the modern shipping facility at Port Royal. Jean Ribaut once described Port Royal as "one of

BEAUFORT RIVER TO GEORGIA

the greatest and fairest havens . . . where without danger all the ships in the world might be harbored." The port has never really lived up to this billing, but today the town's fortunes certainly seem to be on the upswing.

The terminals here are not as large as those of Georgetown or Charleston, but several seagoing freighters can usually be seen loading or unloading cargo at the docks. The waters west of the wharves offer anchorage for pleasure boats of almost any size. The stream is rather broad at this point and bordered by marsh grass to the south. This is not a good spot to ride out heavy weather.

Further upstream a bridge with only 12 feet of closed vertical clearance bars the creek. This span is normally closed. Requests that the bridge be opened must be made to the South Carolina Department of Transportation 24 hours in advance, and even then the request will likely be denied, unless the applicant has a very good reason.

Chowan Creek

Chowan Creek makes into the eastern banks of Beaufort River north of unlighted can buoy #33. This wide stream eventually splinters into several branches. One of these forks, Distant Island Creek, is the best anchorage on the river.

Chowan Creek itself is a bit wide for effective anchorage in all but light airs. However, boats requiring a great deal of swinging room can drop the hook just south of the split in light to moderate winds. Otherwise, craft under 42 feet should proceed to Distant Island.

Chowan Creek is bordered by extensive

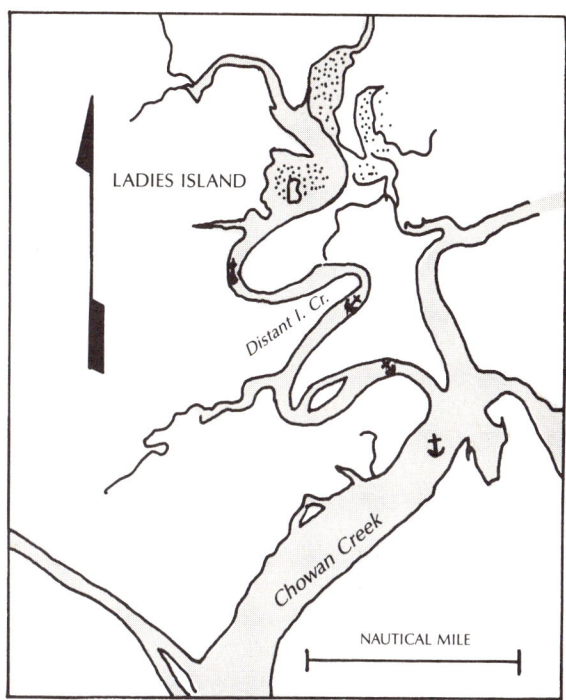

shoals to the west, but there is a wide entrance channel north of unlighted can buoy #33. Several unmarked shallows flanking the cut must be avoided, but good navigation should see you through. Because of these difficulties, Chowan Creek is not particularly recommended for boats over 45 feet or those that draw more than 5 feet.

Distant Island Creek

On this fine anchorage, swing room is sufficient for boats up to 45 feet. Certain areas of the creek are very well sheltered and could be used in heavy weather. Minimum depths are 7 feet with most of the stream being deeper.

There is one small navigational problem. At high tide, some of the mud flats in the creek's first hairpin curve to the north are submerged. While the careful boater should be able to pick out the correct passage, entry into this area at high water does call for caution.

The shoreline of Distant Island Creek is most attractive, especially where the stream borders Distant Island. Currently the banks are beautifully undeveloped with many large oaks and hardwoods overhanging the water. There are plans underway to develop a resort on the island, but it is to be hoped that the new construction will not affect these attractive shores.

Some sections of Distant Island Creek are better sheltered than others. The first well-protected area is found just upstream of the intersection with Chowan Creek. The high banks of Distant Island border the creek in this area and provide a good wind break. You need not pass the mud banks mentioned above to reach this spot.

The second superior anchorage is located in the middle of the creek's second hairpin curve. Again, the high, wooded shores of Distant Island border the creek to the east, offering excellent protection.

The third and final protected spot is encountered as the creek takes its second sharp bend to the north and begins to head into its shallow upstream reaches. A small section of high ground on Ladies Island flanks the creek to the south. This area would provide partic-

Banks of Distant Island Creek

BEAUFORT RIVER TO GEORGIA 237

ularly good protection in a hard southwesterly blow. The creek does narrow here a bit and provides only enough swinging room for craft up to 40 feet.

Ballast Creek

Ballast Creek enters Beaufort River from Parris Island west of unlighted nun buoy #36. Though the stream is marked by two aids, boaters should not enter. This is United States Marine Corps property and off limits to pleasure craft.

Station Creek

The southerly reaches of Station Creek enter the mouth of Beaufort River at its intersection with Port Royal Sound, east of unlighted nun buoy #26. The creek has two markers on its track, but the extensive unmarked shoals flanking the stream's entrance are not easily avoided. The cruising boater is advised to bypass this section of Station Creek unless he is armed with local knowledge.

Beaufort River Navigation

South of unlighted daybeacon #239 the ICW follows a broad turn in Beaufort River as the great stream bends to the south. Simply stick to the mid-width as far downstream as flashing daybeacon #242 and you should encounter no difficulty. Look to starboard as you cruise along. The high bluffs to the west are dotted with tasteful modern homes and a few larger structures. This is an attractive section of the waterway.

North of #242 the boater may choose to enter Beaufort River's first anchorage.

Northerly Anchorage To enter the broad sweep of water between the mainland and the marsh island east of flashing daybeacon #241, continue on the waterway channel until you are well past the southern tip of the marsh island; then swing slowly around to the north and enter the stream on its mid-width. Good depths stretch almost from shore to shore. Select any likely spot and drop the hook. Do not attempt to reenter Beaufort River to the north, as the passage is guarded by extensive shoals. Discontinue your forward progress before reaching this passage.

On the ICW South of unlighted daybeacon #244 the waterway begins its approach to the highrise Beaufort River Bridge. The span has a vertical clearance of 65 feet. Even the tallest sailcraft should not have any difficulty.

South of the bridge there are no further markers until reaching flashing buoy #41, which marks the intersection of the ICW and the Port Royal Shipping Channel. Fortunately there are no shoals in the area. Stick to the mid-width and you will not have any problems.

South of #41 the ICW follows the well-marked Port Royal Channel to Port Royal

Sound. Colors reverse here, red to port and green to starboard. To the northwest, Battery Creek offers anchorage opportunities.

Battery Creek From flashing buoy #41 set course to pass between flashing daybeacon #43 and unlighted nun buoy #42. Continue on the mid-width and you will soon spy the Port Royal wharves to starboard. Just past the docks, unlighted daybeacon #47 marks the southern shore. The current edition of chart 11518 notes a can buoy #47 here. Daybeacon #47 has apparently replaced this aid.

The best anchorage is found just past #47 before the creek turns to the west. Good depths stretch from shore to shore in this area. Set the hook near the lee shore and settle down for the night.

Further passage upstream to the bridge is not particularly recommended. A large shoal flanks the northern shore, and the creek widens, making for even less protection.

On the ICW Watch to the west between unlighted can buoy #39 and flashing buoy #37 and you will observe some of the buildings of the Parris Island Marine Base. Remember not to attempt entry of Ballast Creek west of unlighted nun buoy #36. North of can buoy #33 the boater may choose to enter Chowan and Distant Island creeks.

Chowan and Distant Island Creeks To enter Chowan Creek from Beaufort River, set course from #33 toward the unnumbered flashing 16-foot range marker to the northeast. Some 100 yards before reaching the range marker, swing sharply to the north and set a new course to pass the small marsh island east of flashing buoy #37 by some 35 yards to its easterly side. Proceed with caution in this area. As you will note in a quick study of chart 11516, extensive shallows border the channel to the east.

Continue past the island and enter the creek on its mid-width. Cruise upstream, holding to the middle, until you reach the area where the stream forks into four branches. If winds are light, you might consider dropping the hook here. Otherwise, cut to the northwest and enter the extreme left-hand fork, Distant Island Creek.

Cruise into Distant Island Creek on its mid-width. Larger craft may want to drop the hook within the entrance rather than continue upstream. Those who do choose to continue should approach the creek's first hairpin turn to the north with caution. Remember, at high tide some of the surrounding mud flats cover completely. If you enter at high tide, choose what will appear to be the central passage and feel your way slowly around the turn with the sounder.

Once around the bend, continued navigation upstream to both other anchorage areas is a simple matter of holding to the mid-width. Remember to stop soon after the creek takes its third sharp turn. Depths finally begin to decline.

On the ICW The ICW continues to follow the Port Royal Channel south to the sound. While the cut is very well marked, you

BEAUFORT RIVER TO GEORGIA

might find it advisable to run compass courses between markers. Some are set fairly well apart.

At unlighted nun buoy #26 the waterway abandons the large ships' channel and cuts sharply to the west. Set course to come abeam and pass flashing daybeacon #246 by some 100 yards to its southerly side.

From this aid, Port Royal Sound and its tributary streams offer many cruising possibilities to the north, while the ICW flows to the west and enters Skull Creek. This chapter will next review the waters to the north, after which a continuing account of the waterway south to Hilton Head Island will be presented.

Port Royal Sound Area

Port Royal Sound is formed by the juncture of several large streams, all of which lead into the South Carolina mainland. Broad, Chechessee, and Colleton rivers are all major bodies of water. Each offers many cruising possibilities and anchorage opportunities.

The vast waters of the Port Royal area are seldom visited by cruising boaters. Except for one small facility, there is not a single marina on any of the three rivers or their creeks. With only a few exceptions, most of the area shoreline is undeveloped. Isolated residential settlements dot the banks here and there, but in between are vast stretches of untouched marsh grass and highlands. Most of the anchorages found north of the ICW provide only minimal shelter and would not be suitable for winds over 20 knots.

Successful navigation of the three rivers is no simple matter. Numerous unmarked shoals call for careful cruising. There are only a few aids to navigation on any of the area streams. Consequently, you must practice your best coastwise navigation in order to know your position at all times and keep off the bottom.

Still, the waters of the three rivers are not lacking in positive attributes. Seldom will the cruising boater find such wide-open waters, often fronting onto lovely, undeveloped shorelines, with so few other boats in evidence. The natural beauty and splendor of these rivers will delight all those who enjoy adventurous cruising on little-traveled waters. On the other hand, those who prefer a well-marked channel with several marinas close by will probably want to forego these streams. Whether you choose to enter Broad, Chechessee, and Colleton rivers will depend on what type of cruising you enjoy.

Port Royal Sound

Port Royal Sound itself provides reliable access to the open sea via the Port Royal Channel. The cruising boater can use this well-marked seaward cut with confidence. Large ships enter and exit the channel on a regular basis. Otherwise the cruising possibilities of the sound are limited to its northern tributary streams.

Broad River

Broad River is aptly named. The waters of

the Broad are so wide that often they seem more like a sound than a river. In fact, Broad River is nothing more than the northern extension of Port Royal Sound. The river remains a substantial body of water for its entire length until it intersects its feeder streams, the Pocotaligo, Tulifiny, and Coosawhatchie rivers to the north.

Broad River is an exceptionally beautiful body of water. Both shorelines are readily visible. The southern section of the river is lined mostly by marsh grass, but much of the northern section is bordered by high, wooded banks. On a calm, clear day, passage of Broad River can be a wonderful visual treat.

Except for its natural beauty, however, Broad River is surprisingly void of cruising possibilities. Only two sidewaters make interesting side trips and offer safe haven for the night. Even these creeks call for a long cruise from the safe confines of the ICW. *None* of the several streams that enter the river's western shore and lead to Chechessee River should be attempted by the cruising boater. All are bounded by numerous unmarked shoals, and depths shown on chart 11516 cannot be trusted. To the east, several streams flow into the river from Parris Island. Chief among these is Archer Creek. Do not attempt to enter these sidewaters. They are part of the Parris Island Marine Base and are off limits to pleasure boaters.

The three northern feeder rivers are uncharted and consequently too risky for large cruising craft. This lack of charting is most unfortunate, as this writer's on-site research leads him to believe that all three rivers would make excellent cruising grounds. Perhaps some enterprising Power Squadron will undertake the charting of the three rivers in the near future.

Successful navigation of Broad River is an exacting process. There are several large, unmarked patches of shoal water on the river's mid-width and along the banks. You will need to make careful use of chart, compass, log, and the information contained in this guide to stay off the bottom.

Broad River is crossed by a long, fixed bridge some 7 nautical miles north of the intersection with Port Royal Sound. The current edition of chart 11516 shows a swing bridge at this location with only 12 feet of closed vertical clearance. However, on-site research reveals that the charted structure has been replaced by a new, fixed, highrise span. I have been unable to find any published account of the new bridge's height, but I estimate it to be at least 25 feet. Tall sailcraft might have trouble clearing the span, but most power boats should be able to pass without difficulty.

Broad River is *not* for the casual boater. The river's hazards call for a wary cruise. On the other hand, the adventurous boater who can overcome these difficulties will reap rewards that few other boaters have known.

Boyd Creek

Boyd Creek enters the western shore of Broad River north of Hogs Neck. The creek has two unmarked shoals that could prove hazardous for cruising craft. Consequently, this stream should be entered only by daring skippers piloting boats of less than 36 feet that draw no more than 4 feet.

Once these hazards are bypassed, Boyd

Creek and its several auxiliary streams offer a number of spots suitable for overnight anchorage. With one exception the various creeks' shorelines are undeveloped marsh and would not give enough protection in heavy weather.

Cole Creek breaks off to the south from Boyd Creek near the latter stream's intersection with Broad River. This small stream holds 8-foot minimum depths for a short distance. There is enough swing room for craft up to 35 feet to drop the hook. Don't attempt to cruise past the stream's first turn to port. Depths quickly become too uncertain for cruising craft.

Further upstream, Boyd Creek splits into eastern and western branches. The western fork holds 7-foot minimum depths as far as Deloss Point, though there is one unmarked shoal to be avoided. The best anchorage in the area is located on this stream. Soon after the creek splits, the southern banks of the westerly branch border the high land on Boyd Neck. Here boats up to 35 feet can anchor with good protection.

The easterly fork of Boyd Creek holds 7-foot minimum depths until the stream peters out in its approach to Pilot Island. Some of the undeveloped marsh shores are shoal, and care must be exercised to hold to the mid-width. Do not anchor here if winds exceed 20 knots. Otherwise, you can drop the hook at any likely spot.

Whale Branch

Whale Branch is the second (and last) readily navigable auxiliary water of Broad River that offers overnight anchorage. Tradition claims that the creek was named for a whale

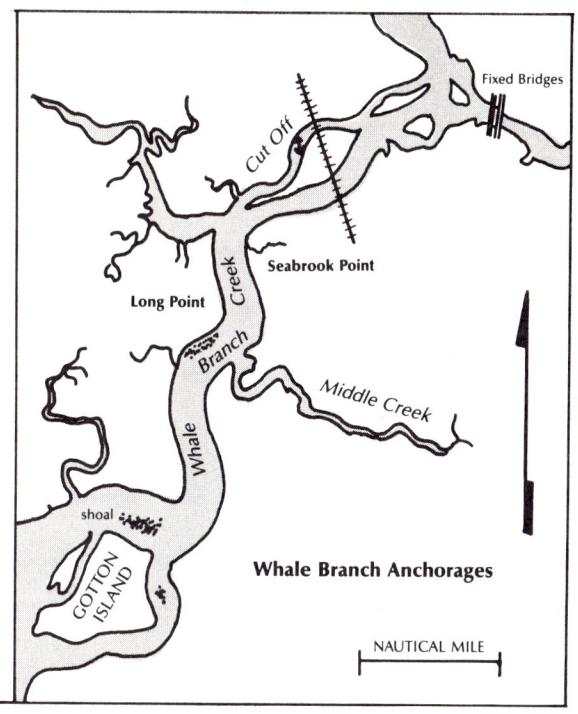

Whale Branch Anchorages

that was stranded on the stream's banks. If so, he picked a good spot to meet his end. As if to make up for the Broad's absence of navigable creeks, Whale Branch's natural beauty is enough to make any cruising boater sigh with contentment.

There are only one or two unmarked shallows to avoid. Most of the stream holds minimum depths of 7 feet between its banks. The entire area is quite sheltered, and beautiful anchorages abound. All you need do is select a spot that is to your liking and sheltered from the prevailing breezes. There you may drop the hook for an unforgettable evening.

Whale Branch's shoreline is bordered for much of its length by high, heavily wooded banks. There is just enough marsh grass to make a pleasing contrast. Several private homes overlook the creek here and there. One historical site graces the shores. It almost appears as if some landscape architect spent many months in the sky, selecting the sites for the area homes, to give the creek a perfect balance.

In heavy weather, Whale Branch offers at least one very sheltered anchorage with sufficient swing room for craft up to 40 feet. Just west of the railroad bridge that crosses Whale Branch upstream from Seabrook Point, a fork of the creek charted as "Cut Off" splits off from the main body. While care must be taken when entering this fork, interior minimum depths run about 8 feet, with most of the creek being considerably deeper. The best place to anchor is found just west of the railroad bridge. Here high ground abuts the northern shore and gives excellent protection.

Whale Branch and "Cut Off" are both eventually blocked by a railroad bridge. Even though chart 11519 shows the span crossing Whale Branch as being a swing bridge, it is usually closed. Even if you were lucky enough to find it open, the stream is again blocked by twin highway bridges a bit further upstream. The westerly highway span is a highrise fixed bridge with 20 feet of vertical clearance, but the easterly span shown on chart 11519 as a swing bridge has had its swinging section re-

Clarendon Plantation, Whale Branch

moved. It now has vertical clearance of only 5 feet. Apparently, the South Carolina Highway Department did not feel there was enough traffic on Whale Branch to justify a swing bridge.

Clarendon Plantation

The house at Clarendon Plantation is readily visible on the eastern shore of Whale Branch, near the area marked "Corning Lodge" on chart 11519. The present house was built in 1930. Even though it is relatively modern, it is an imposing brick structure and makes an impressive sight from the water.

The history of Clarendon stretches far back into the past. The property was once owned by Paul Hamilton, Secretary of War under President James Madison. Hamilton is buried on the plantation.

Whale Branch Tale In *Tales of Beaufort,* Nell Graydon relates an amusing tale about the Whale Branch Bridge. The story takes place before the Civil War, when the span was little more than a narrow wooden track. It seems that a certain gentleman from Beaufort was visiting friends to the north of Whale Branch one wintery evening. The party was warm and lively. As the gentleman prepared to return home, his host presented him with a fine bottle of Irish whiskey to be opened on a special occasion. The traveler departed and soon approached the Whale Branch bridge. Because it was a cold night, he decided to stop for a swallow from his host's gift. Finding the whiskey much to his liking, he concluded that the present was as good an occasion as any and proceeded to drink freely.

Suddenly, he heard a clatter on the bridge, and the ghostly specter of a camel appeared before the astonished traveler's eyes. This strange apparition was followed by the form of a huge elephant, and the gentleman even heard the unmistakable roar of a lion. Throwing the bottle away, he foreswore strong drink then and there and never broke his promise.

Of course, it so happened that a small traveling circus was visiting Beaufort at the time and had incurred more bills than the owner could pay. He decided to make his escape by nightfall and just happened to pass over the bridge as our hero was approaching the span from the opposite direction. The circus' owner probably never knew that he had rescued a soul from the hands of John Barleycorn.

Chechessee River

Chechessee River is a large but erratic stream that enters Port Royal Sound north of unlighted nun buoy #2, found to the east of Dolphin Head. The river is littered with unmarked shoals, and great care must be taken to avoid an unpleasant grounding. It should be entered only by adventurous cruisers with boats of less than 40 feet that draw no more (and preferably less) than 4½ feet.

The Chechessee does offer several opportunities for overnight anchorage. There is even one small facility. Lemon Island Marina, a facility mostly for small craft, is located on the river's western banks north of the fixed highway bridge (vertical clearance 20 feet) that spans the stream at Chechessee Bluff. There are no facilities for transients and no diesel fuel, but gasoline can be purchased from a lone pump adjacent to the docks.

The shores of Chechessee River are not as attractive as others in this area. Most banks are composed of the usual saltwater marsh. Higher ground is rare on the stream.

All in all, the best that can be said for the Chechessee is that it leads to several protected anchorages and to the Colleton River, a beautiful stream that will be covered later in this chapter.

Chechessee Creek

Chechessee Creek makes into the western banks of the river north of Spring Island. The stream carries minimum depths of 7 feet though there are, as usual, several unmarked shoals to contend with. These shoals are not too difficult, however, and boats up to 40 feet can drop anchor here with confidence.

One of the best anchorages is found after the creek takes a long, slow turn to port. The high ground of Manigault Neck borders the stream on its western banks in this section and offers excellent protection. Fripps Landing, a small community of resort homes, is found along this shoreline. Many private docks will be observed on the banks. Select any likely spot, but be sure to leave plenty of clearance between your craft and the nearby piers.

Another possible anchorage is found upstream as the creek runs between two undeveloped marsh banks. There is not nearly as much protection here, but there is plenty of swing room. In light to moderate airs this would be a good spot for those who prefer a more isolated anchorage.

A third consideration for anchorage is the area where the high ground of Spring Island

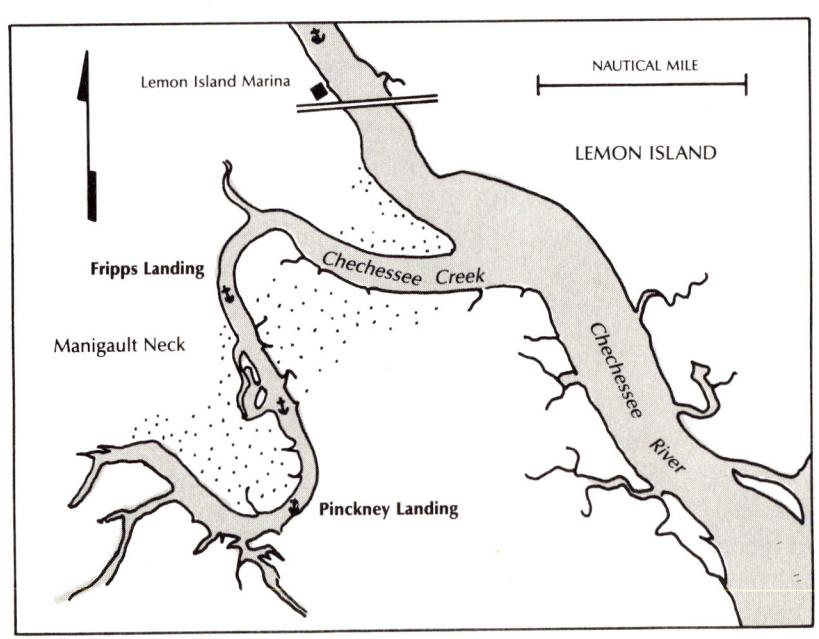

borders the creek's eastern shore at Pinckney Landing. There is only light residential development at the landing, and the island shelters the stream from southerly blows. The creek does narrow somewhat, providing only enough swing room for boats up to 32 feet.

Chechessee River Anchorage

For those who can clear the fixed Chechessee River Bridge (20-foot vertical clearance), the stretch just north of the span narrows sufficiently for anchorage consideration. If the winds are under 15 knots, there should be enough protection for a comfortable evening. The shores are only marsh grass, so you might be obliged to seek better protection if the wind rises.

Hazzard Creek

The Chechessee River splits into two branches, both known as Hazzard Creek, about 1 nautical mile north of the bridge. Both forks offer anchorage opportunities. The westerly branch holds 10-foot minimum depths in its channel, but care must be exercised to avoid several unmarked shallows. The stream briefly borders some high ground on its southern banks at Bellinger Neck. A large pier juts out into the creek at this point. The area just upstream from this dock would be a good place to set the hook.

The western branch of Hazzard Creek pierces a large marsh. The creek eventually becomes shoal and dangerous. However, the stream's lower reaches, from the Chechessee to the area where the creek splits, hold minimum 9-foot depths and could serve as an overnight anchorage in all but heavy weather.

Colleton River

Colleton River splits off from the western shores of the Chechessee at Foot Point. The Colleton's character is in sharp contrast to that of its sister stream. Colleton River is an absolutely beautiful body of water. Wooded shores with light residential development overlook the river from atop Victoria Bluff, and the high land of Spring Island borders a portion of the northern shoreline. The small community of Copps Landing is noted on chart 11519 near the southern tip of Spring Island. Only one lone house is visible from the water. You may spy several shrimpers plying their nets in the river. These classic craft add to the charm of this lovely stream.

The Colleton is free from shoals and other navigational hazards. Depths of 20 feet or more stretch almost from bank to bank. Any skipper would have to be soundly snoring at the helm to run aground on Colleton River.

On the other hand, the river is almost devoid of sidewaters and safe anchorages. One small stream, Sawmill Creek, does penetrate the southern shore south of Spring Island, but minimum depths of 15 feet hold for only a short distance upstream, and there is only enough swing room for boats under 30 feet. It might be possible to anchor in the lee of Spring Island abeam of Copps Landing in northerly blows, but southerly breezes of 10 knots or more would probably raise an uncomfortable chop.

West of Copps Landing the river is bisected by several marsh islands and becomes littered with unmarked shoals. Cruising boaters are strictly advised not to enter this area.

Colleton River is one of those water bodies

cruising boaters encounter from time to time that is a clear case of "good news and bad news." You will have to decide whether the river's great natural beauty justifies a long trip from the ICW without much chance of dropping the hook in a secure place.

Port Royal Area Navigation

As already noted, navigation of Port Royal Sound's tributary streams is not a laughing matter for casual boaters. If you do choose to enter the area, have your compass courses worked out beforehand. Run your intended tracks carefully while measuring your progress with a log. Go slowly, keep an eagle eye on the sounder, and with a bit of luck you may come through without difficulty.

Port Royal Sound If you plan to make use of the Port Royal Inlet channel, simply continue on the marked cut south of flashing buoy #27. The channel is well marked and easy to follow. All other boaters should turn west at #27 and set course to bring flashing daybeacon #246 abeam by some 100 yards to its southerly side. From #246 the cruising boater has many choices available. A cut to the northwest will lead to Broad River and Whale Branch, while a westerly course will bring the boater to the southern mouth of Chechessee River.

Broad River To enter Broad River you must set a northwesterly course from flashing daybeacon #246, which will avoid the large shoal extending south from Ribbon Creek on the Broad's eastern banks. Once abeam of this hazard, set a new course to avoid the shoal guarding the river's mid-width east of Daws Island. After passing this shallow stretch, point for the central pass-through of the Broad River Bridge. There are no further shoals between the Daws Island shallows and the span.

As you are making your run to the bridge you will pass an unnamed creek, west of your course, leading through to Chechessee River south of Rose Island. Do not attempt this stream. It is surrounded by shallow water that holds only 1 foot in some places.

Bend your course a bit to the east after passing through the Broad River Bridge. This maneuver will avoid a shallow spot just west of the pass-through. From this point you need only keep to the mid-width to maintain good depths as far as Whale Branch.

Euhaw Creek makes into the western shores of Broad River through several mouths north of the bridge. This stream, too, should be bypassed. Depths are much too uncertain for visiting boaters.

Boyd Creek Favor the southern banks when entering Boyd Creek but don't approach the shoreline too closely.

Not far into the creek's interior, Cole Creek splits off to the south. If you choose to explore this small sidewater, favor the western banks slightly as you enter; then cruise back to the mid-width. Be sure to stop soon after the stream takes its first jog to port.

To continue upstream on the main body of Boyd Creek, begin favoring the port banks heavily. Follow the shore on around as the creek takes a turn to the north, and continue favoring the port side until the stream takes a sharp turn to the west. As you round this final point, be sure to keep at least 50 feet from the shoreline. Chart 11519 clearly identifies two shoals, which you can bypass by following this procedure. Cruise back to the mid-width and stick to the middle until the creek splits.

Favor the southern shore when entering West Branch Boyd Creek, but do not approach those banks too closely. Cruise back to the mid-width as the creek takes a sharp turn to the north. From here to Deloss Point you can expect good depths *if* you stick scrupulously to the middle of the stream. Don't approach either shoreline. Both banks are shoal and dangerous. Past Deloss Point depths drop off to 4 feet or less.

To cruise East Branch Boyd Creek, simply stick to the mid-width. Discontinue your exploration before the creek enters a hairpin turn to the east, abeam of Pilot Island.

Whale Branch The westerly reaches of Whale Branch join Broad River south of Barnwell Island. Gotton Island divides the entrance into two branches. Both are readily navigable but both require caution.

If you choose to make use of the southern branch, enter the creek on its mid-width. Take care to avoid the finger of shallow water extending north from Port Royal Island on the entranceway's southern quarter. Stick to the middle until the creek takes a sharp turn to the north. Begin favoring the western banks and continue to do so until you enter the main body of Whale Branch at the eastern tip of Gotton Island.

Follow the middle line of the northerly entrance until the stream begins to bend to the east around Gotton Island. As shown on chart 11519, a shoal guards the center of the stream in this area. To avoid this hazard, favor the southern shore until reaching the eastern tip of the island.

Once on the main body of Whale Branch you need simply hold to the mid-width as far as the railroad bridge. Chart 11519 shows a small shoal near the northwestern banks across from Middle Creek. This shallow patch did not show up in on-site research, but to be on the safe side, favor the eastern banks in this area.

To enter the sheltered anchorage area on Cut Off, avoid the point that separates this creek from the main body of Whale Branch. A long shoal extends westward from this marshy point. Otherwise, simply hold to the mid-width and drop the hook anywhere before reaching the railroad bridge.

Begin slightly favoring the southern shore of Whale Branch as you approach the railroad bridge. There is a small shoal on the northern shore. Soon your passage will be blocked by the usually-closed railway span. Discontinue your cruise at this point.

Chechessee River To enter shoal-prone Chechessee River, set course from flashing daybeacon #246 to come abeam of unlighted nun buoy #2, east of Dolphin Head, to the buoy's southerly side. Set a careful compass course to bend your heading to the northwest and enter the deepwater section of Chechessee River. Begin favoring the Daws Island shores after cruising upriver for some 1.5 nautical miles. As shown on chart 11516, a large shoal abuts the western banks south of Foot Point.

At Foot Point the entrance to Colleton River will come abeam to the west. Navigation of this stream will be covered later in this chapter. To continue upstream on the Chechessee, set a new course to pass between the marshes of Spring Island to the west and the small marsh island that bisects the river to the east. Begin working your way slowly back toward the eastern banks as you approach Rose Island. After passing the two marsh islands to the west, set a new course to pass the point south of Chechessee Creek by some 150 yards to port. Study chart 11516 carefully before undertaking this complicated procedure.

Chechessee Creek If you choose to enter Chechessee Creek, favor the southern banks a bit. Shoal water extends out into the creek from Chechessee Point to the north. Once on the main body of the stream, hold to the mid-width. The creek eventually follows a long bend to the south and begins bordering Fripps Landing. Continue on the middle until you approach Pinckney Landing. Here the stream bends to the west; you should begin favoring the eastern shore just before the stream enters a bend to the west at Pinckney Landing. Discontinue your progress before coming abeam of the southern tip of Spring Island's high ground.

On the Chechessee River Hold to the mid-width as you pass the entrance of Chechessee Creek to the west. Slowly cruise toward the eastern banks as you approach the point opposite the southern tip of Chechessee Bluff. Set a new course toward the central pass-through of the Chechessee Bridge.

Once through the span, look to port and you will spy Lemon Island Marina on the western banks. Continue upstream on the mid-width, but begin to favor the eastern banks about .4 of a nautical mile south of the Hazzard Creek split.

Hazzard Creek To enter the western branch of Hazzard Creek, continue favoring the eastern shore of the main body until the mid-width of the creek is directly abeam to port. Then turn 90 degrees to port and enter the creek. As the sharp entrance point comes abeam to port, begin favoring the southern shores heavily. As shown on chart 11516, a large shoal guards the northern banks in this area. Remember to discontinue your cruise before entering the wide stretch of the creek north of Bellinger Neck.

Enter the eastern fork of Hazzard Creek on its mid-width. Good depths continue on the middle with no shoaling problems until the stream splinters south of Hazzard Neck. Stop well short of this area.

Colleton River Avoid Foot Point on the southern quarter of Colleton River's entrance. Otherwise simply stay at least 150 yards from either shore and you will be in deep water all the way to Copps Landing. Remember to stop before reaching Callawassie Creek.

If you pilot a boat under 32 feet and choose to anchor in Sawmill Creek, enter the stream on its mid-width. Don't attempt to cruise past the creek's first bend to port. Depths quickly drop off to 3 and 4 feet.

ICW to Cooper River

South of Port Royal Sound the ICW enters the headwaters of Skull Creek and comes into contact with Hilton Head Island. Hilton Head comprises the eastern banks of the waterway until the route turns south off Calibogue Sound into Cooper River. Six marinas are located on the island and all eagerly accept transients. Nowhere else in coastal South Carolina are so many facilities for the cruising boater concentrated in so small an area.

Skull Creek leads the waterway boater south to Calibogue Sound. Like most open bodies of water, the Calibogue can foster a healthy chop when winds exceed 15 knots. The sound's inlet channel provides fairly reliable access to the open sea. Some markers are not charted, probably because they are frequently shifted. The inlet channel is used by fishing boats from Hilton Head on a daily basis. While not absolutely necessary, local knowledge would certainly be desirable before attempting the inlet. Check on current conditions at one of the area marinas.

May River breaks off to the west near the headwaters of Calibogue Sound and provides beautiful cruising grounds as far inland as the historic community of Bluffton. A well-marked channel and numerous anchorage possibilities add to this lovely stream's charms.

Unlike the Port Royal Sound area, the waters around Hilton Head Island are some of the most heavily used in the state. Their popularity is richly deserved. There are very few shoals or other navigational difficulties. The sound, in particular, is blessed with great natural beauty. The numerous marinas are a real boon to visiting and resident boaters alike. Yet amid all this popularity, there is still the opportunity to cruise isolated waters. Seldom will the cruising boater find a water body so consistently overlooked, yet possessing such a lovely character, as May River. There are even a few creeks off Calibogue Sound that provide sheltered anchorage far from civilization. To summarize, the waters of and around the ICW from Port Royal Sound to Cooper River have just about everything the cruising boater could ever desire.

ICW Through Calibogue Sound

Skull Creek

The ICW enters the northern headwaters of Skull Creek at flashing daybeacon #6. The creek splinters into several branches at this point. The waterway follows the westernmost fork. The marked route is more reliable, but it is worth noting that the easternmost branch does hold minimum 9-foot depths and is readily navigable south to Skull Creek Marina. Boats up to 38 feet will find sufficient swing room to drop the hook in this creek. Be sure to anchor well away from the marina docks.

Skull Creek Marina

Skull Creek Marina is readily visible east of unlighted daybeacon #9A. This large, modern facility gladly accepts transients and features all floating docks with every power and water connection. Gasoline and diesel fuel are available, and two restaurants are located on the premises. The marina offers both mechanical and below-the-waterline repairs. There is also an on-site ships' and convenience store, open seven days a week. Skull Creek struck this writer as an unusually friendly establishment where the visiting cruiser can be assured of a warm welcome.

Outdoor Resorts Yacht Club Marina

Outdoor Resorts Yacht Club Marina is found south of unlighted daybeacon #20. This modern marina provides berths for transients on floating piers with all power and water connections. Both gasoline and diesel fuel can be purchased and the facility maintains a well-stocked ships' store. The marina

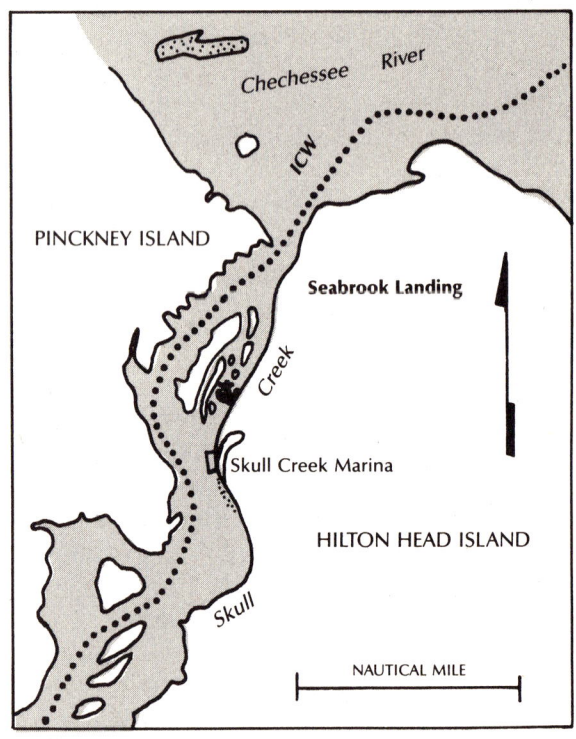

features an on-site gourmet restaurant that is quickly gaining quite a reputation up and down the waterway for fine dining.

Calibogue Sound and Broad Creek Facilities and Anchorages

At flashing daybeacon #24 Skull Creek leads into the northern headwaters of Calibogue Sound. Mackay Creek cuts back to the north and offers prime cruising ground plus several excellent anchorages. Similarly, May River breaks off from the Calibogue west of unlighted daybeacon #2. Both of these water

BEAUFORT RIVER TO GEORGIA 251

bodies will be covered later in this chapter. For now the various facilities and anchorages of Hilton Head Island on Broad Creek and Calibogue Sound will be reviewed.

Jarvis Creek

Jarvis Creek leads northeast into the main body of Hilton Head Island at flashing daybeacon #1, south of Ferry Point. The creek holds minimum 9-foot depths until it takes a sharp jog to port well upstream, but the channel is surrounded by mud flats, which cover at high water. Consequently, it is sometimes difficult to pick out the deepwater passage at high tide. The mud flats also give virtually no protection from hard blows. There is room for boats up to 38 feet to anchor, but it would be an uncomfortable stay if winds exceeded 10 knots.

Bryan Creek

Bryan Creek enters Calibogue Sound west of unlighted daybeacon #30. This stream makes an excellent anchorage for those who prefer an isolated haven for the night. Minimum depths run around 7 feet, with most of the stream being deeper. There is sufficient swing room for boats up to 38 feet.

The creek's entrance is surrounded by shoals and calls for careful cruising. However, there is a broad entrance channel and you should not have too much difficulty. The creek's lower reaches are surrounded by marsh grass, but the higher ground of Bull Island flanks the western banks as the stream takes a turn to starboard. Protection is excellent here.

Bryan Creek eventually splits into two branches. Both branches narrow considerably and depths become uncertain.

Broad Creek Facilities

Broad Creek enters Calibogue Sound at unlighted daybeacon #1 north of Harbour Town. This wide stream leads northeast into the heart of Hilton Head Island. No fewer than three marinas are located along the stream, and all welcome the visiting cruiser.

Outdoor Resorts Yacht Club Marina, Skull Creek

The creek has 8-foot minimum depths, but most of the stream holds more than 15 feet of water. The channel is well marked, though some of the aids are not charted. Just hold to the mid-width and observe all markers carefully. Broad Creek is used on a daily basis by many local craft and you should not have any problems.

Palmetto Bay Marina

Palmetto Bay Marina is the first facility you will encounter on Broad Creek. The marina is located on the creek's southern shore after the stream takes a sharp bend to the east. Palmetto Bay is a large, modern facility that gladly accepts transients. The marina boasts all floating docks with every power and water connection. Gasoline and diesel fuel are readily available. Palmetto Bay features its own travel lift. If you need below-the-waterline repairs, this would be an excellent spot to secure all necessary services. Some mechanical repairs can also be arranged.

There is a ships' store on the premises, and several restaurants are within walking distance. All in all, Palmetto Bay can be unhesitatingly recommended.

Broad Creek Marina

Broad Creek Marina is the second facility you will encounter on the creek of the same name. Located on the stream's northern banks just upstream from Palmetto Bay, Broad Creek is the smallest facility on Hilton Head Island. The marina offers transient dockage on floating piers with all power and water connections. Gasoline (but not diesel fuel) can be purchased dockside. Mechanical repairs are

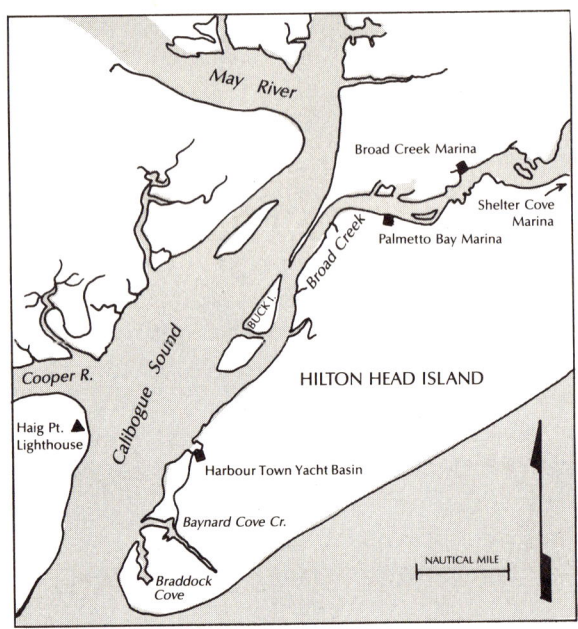

offered, and there is an on-site ships' store where snacks can be purchased.

Shelter Cove Marina

A series of private, unlighted daybeacons leads the boater up Broad Creek to one of the finest facilities on all of Hilton Head Island (or anywhere else for that matter). Shelter Cove Marina is a brand-new facility perched in a man-made cove on the southern shores of Broad Creek. The marina encourages transient business and offers a wide array of services. Minimum dockside depths are a very impressive 8 to 12 feet. The docks are all floating piers and boast all water, power, telephone, and even cable TV connections. Gasoline and diesel fuel are readily available, and the marina maintains a well-stocked ships' store. Some repairs can be arranged.

BEAUFORT RIVER TO GEORGIA

There are two restaurants in the adjacent condo complex, and a grocery store is also within easy walking distance. In my cruising experience I have never come upon a better-equipped marina than Shelter Cove. I encourage my fellow boaters to take advantage of this unusually well-appointed facility.

Harbour Town Yacht Basin

Harbour Town Yacht Basin is certainly the best known of Hilton Head's many boating facilities. Its candy-striped red and white lighthouse is admired by most boaters traveling along the ICW. This very special facility is located east of flashing daybeacon #32. A series of privately maintained flashing daybeacons leads into the man-made harbor. Extreme low tide entrance depths are presently only 5 feet, with dockside depths about the same. Dredging was underway in January of 1985 to raise both entrance and dockside depths to 8-foot minimums.

Harbour Town welcomes the cruising boater with ultramodern concrete floating docks. All slips feature every conceivable power and water connection. Gasoline and diesel are, of course, available, and some mechanical repairs can be arranged.

Harbour Town's docks are grouped in a circular bay around a series of attractive shops and restaurants. There are clothing and gift stores, bookshops, and nautical retailers. Two restaurants stand ready to satisfy the famished cruiser. One, the Cafe Europa, overlooks the sound through its glass walls. This writer particularly recommends the shrimp salad, and for dessert, the cherry torte. A leisurely meal at the end of a long cruising day, with the sun setting across the sound, can be a memorable repast indeed.

Visitors are free to climb the Harbour Town Lighthouse. The view from the light's crown commands a wide panorama of the sound and Daufuskie Island to the west. Eastward, you can see much of Hilton Head. You must ascend many flights of steps to reach the top, but the view is well worth the climb.

Harbour Town remains one of the most

Shelter Cove Marina, Hilton Head Island

popular stops on the entire ICW. It is not difficult to account for its popularity. If you choose to berth here, it would be a good idea to call ahead for reservations to avoid disappointment.

Baynard Cove Creek and Braddock Cove

A series of private markers south of the Harbour Town entrance denotes two channels leading into the western shores of Hilton Head. These channels serve two private dockage areas, which are associated with several condominium projects. At low tide the two cuts carry only some 5 to 6 feet of water. Visiting boaters are advised to bypass both streams.

Hilton Head Island History Hilton Head Island was known as the "Island of the Bears" in early colonial times. The sands of Hilton Head have changed much since the noble bear was its principal resident.

William Hilton explored the region in 1663, and the island was subsequently named in his honor. He described the area in typically glowing terms. "The lands are laden with large tall trees—oaks, walnuts and bayes, except facing the sea it is mostly pines . . . . The country abounds with grapes, large figs and peaches; the woods with deer, conies, turkeys, quail, curlues, plovers, teile, herons, ducks and innumerable other water fowls. Oysters in abundance. . . . The Rivers

Harbour Town Yacht Basin, Hilton Head Island

BEAUFORT RIVER TO GEORGIA 255

stored plentifully with fish which we saw play and leap."

With the danger of Indian attack lessened following the Yemassee Indian Wars, families began to settle on Hilton Head and build plantations. Most of these have vanished with the passing years, but several are remembered in the names of modern resort developments.

During the Revolution the settlers of Hilton Head took a decidedly patriot stand. This contrasted sharply with the loyalist leanings of the Daufuskie Island citizenry across the sound. There were frequent skirmishes on Hilton Head between the two groups.

Hilton Head Island fell to Union forces in the early stages of the Civil War. Fort Walker was hastily constructed by the Confederates to guard the island's southeastern point. The fort was attacked by a huge Union fleet, which landed more than thirteen thousand troops. After its fall, the Northern fleet used the island as a base of supply for their regional operations.

Following the war, Hilton Head was virtually abandoned until the Sea Pines Company, under the leadership of Charles Fraser, pioneered a resort development that began in the 1950s. Today the island hosts the largest collection of condominiums, hotels, restaurants, and marinas in all of coastal South Carolina. Several golf courses, many tennis clubs, and a late fall sailing race known as the Calibogue Cup are among the island's attractions. Happily, most development has been in the best of taste. Hilton Head's future appears unlimited. The island draws larger and larger crowds every year.

Hilton Head Stories Hilton Head Island has its share of buried treasure stories. One tale claims that the Frenchmen of the abortive Charlesfort colony on Parris Island salvaged over one and one-half million dollars in gold recovered from Spanish wrecks by friendly Indians. Tradition holds that the French settlers buried their booty on Hilton Head before beginning their tragic voyage home.

Another old story begins with the successful raiding of Spanish treasure ships by the French navy off the South Carolina coast. The booty was subsequently buried on Hilton Head. When the Spanish conqueror Menendez captured a French colony in Florida, he was offered this treasure as ransom. The offer was refused and the gold was lost. Who knows? Perhaps buried treasure still awaits some young lad with pail and shovel building sand castles on Hilton Head Beach.

ICW Through Calibogue Sound Navigation

Most of the waters between the northern entrance of Skull Creek and Cooper River are well marked and easily traversed. There are some exceptions, but generally the cruising boater can take a welcome break from his constant vigil over the sounder. Proceed warily nevertheless, and don't let the amiable nature of the waters lull you into too great a sense of security.

ICW To Skull Creek Set course from flashing daybeacon #246, south of Parris Island

Spit, to come abeam of unlighted nun buoy #2 by some 25 yards to its southerly side. Set a new course to come abeam of flashing daybeacon #3, north of Dolphin Head, by some 50 to 75 yards to its northerly side. From #3 point to pass unlighted daybeacon #4 by some 50 yards to its easterly side and unlighted daybeacon #5 to its fairly immediate westerly quarter, and to come abeam of flashing daybeacon #6 to its easterly side. From #6 the waterway continues down the westernmost branch of Skull Creek and is easy to follow. Be sure to slow to idle speed when passing the marina.

Skull Creek Anchorage Adventurous boaters can cruise the creek's eastern fork and either anchor there or follow the stream south to Skull Creek Marina. Unless you plan to anchor, it would be better to use the waterway channel. Also, boats over 35 feet may want to use the fork's southern entrance at Skull Creek Marina. This entrance is wider than the northern passage.

If you do choose to enter the eastern branch from the north, avoid the point of marsh separating the side stream from the waterway channel. Cruise on the mid-width until you spy a thin marsh island that divides the stream. Pass the island on its easterly side. The creek now broadens and there is plenty of swing room. If you continue south, hold to the middle until reaching Skull Creek Marina.

On the ICW South of Skull Creek Marina the waterway flows south along a well-marked track. Favor the southern shores a bit between flashing daybeacon #19 and unlighted daybeacon #20. A long shoal abuts the northern shore between the two aids. Abeam of #20 slow to "No Wake" speed when passing Outdoor Resorts Yacht Club Marina.

South of flashing daybeacon #22, the swing bridge shown on the current edition of chart 11507 has been replaced by a new, fixed highrise span. At flashing daybeacon #24 the ICW enters the headwaters of Calibogue Sound. Cruise carefully between #24 and unlighted daybeacon #27. Don't allow leeway to ease you toward either side of the channel. There is shoal water on both sides of the waterway in this section. Past #27 good depths again open out from shore to shore.

South of flashing daybeacon #24, the ICW follows the waters of Calibogue Sound as they hurry seaward. Past unlighted daybeacon #27 the route is well marked and easily followed all the way to Cooper River. However, it is a long run between some markers. You may want to run a compass course down Calibogue Sound to be on the safe side.

Don't approach Middle Marsh Island. It is surrounded by shallow water. Otherwise the sound is pretty much free of shoals all the way to Cooper River.

Jarvis Creek If you choose to enter Jarvis Creek at flashing daybeacon #1, favor the northern shore slightly when entering. Once inside, hold to the middle and good depths will be held until the stream takes a sharp jog to port. Discontinue your cruise before reaching this point.

Bryan Creek Before approaching Bryan Creek, be sure to clear the tongue of shoal water extending south from Middle Marsh Island. Enter the creek on its mid-width but begin favoring the port banks slightly once on the stream's interior. You can expect good depths if you continue to favor this shore as far as the creek's split. Past the forks, depths become too inconsistent for cruising craft.

Broad Creek Leave the waterway route and continue cruising south on Calibogue Sound until the private markers leading to Harbour Town are almost abeam to the east; then curl around to the northeast and pass between unlighted daybeacons #1 and #2, which mark the entrance to Broad Creek. Favor #2 a bit. There is shoal water around #1.

Cruise upstream on the mid-width. Pass unlighted daybeacon #4 to its westerly side along the way. At Bram Point the creek enters a long swing to the east. Many private docks dot the northern banks along this stretch. Watch to starboard as you round the bend and you will catch sight of Palmetto Bay Marina on the southern banks. Be careful of your wake when passing.

Unlighted daybeacon #6 will be sighted just past the marina docks. Pass #6 to starboard. Soon you will spy unlighted daybeacon #7. Pass this aid to port. Broad Creek Marina will be seen to port shortly thereafter.

From #7 you need only pass even numbered aids to starboard and odd numbers to port all the way to Shelter Cove Marina. South of #7 you may spot a series of markers leading in towards the southern banks. These aids lead to a small, private dockage area. Unlike the other markers on Broad Creek, #18 is a flashing daybeacon. Unlighted daybeacon #21 leads the boater toward the marina entrance on the creek's southern shore. This cut is marked by two lighted but unnumbered aids. Pass between the two markers. The gas dock will soon come abeam to starboard. Stop here to inquire about a berth for the night.

Harbour Town Yacht Basin Pass between flashing daybeacons #1 and #4 and between #5 and #6 to enter Harbour Town Yacht Basin. The gas docks will come abeam to port just as you enter the concrete breakwater. If you have not called ahead for reservations, stop here to inquire about slip availability.

Seaward on Calibogue Sound Remember, some of Calibogue Inlet's aids are apparently not charted. It would be best to check at Harbour Town or one of the other area marinas before running the cut. Even better, follow one of the many fishing craft that frequently put out to sea from Hilton Head.

Mackay Creek

Mackay Creek leads north, back towards Port Royal Sound, from flashing daybeacon #24. One fixed bridge with 25 feet of vertical clearance spans the stream. Craft that cannot clear this height must forgo cruising most of the creek.

This is an unusually pretty stream. The high, heavily wooded banks of Pinckney Island to the east contrast pleasantly with marshy shores to the west. The creek is bypassed by most cruising boaters, and this isolation, coupled with the area's undeveloped beauty, can make for a very pleasant cruise.

While there are a few shoals to avoid, most of the stream is readily navigable. A series of uncharted and unlighted daybeacons help the visiting cruiser avoid the shallows. Generally, boats up to 40 feet drawing less than 5½ feet can cruise the creek with confidence.

Several sidewaters offer good anchorage along the passage of Mackay Creek. The first of these is found on a small sidewater west of flashing daybeacon #1. Because a shoal bisects the main body of Mackay Creek south of #1, the small offshoot west of the marker should be approached via the channel running along the creek's western bank. Boats up to 35 feet can anchor in the offshoot with fair protection. However, the mud flats south and west of #1 cover at mid- and high tide. Successful navigation of this area can be tricky at such times. Even when you find the channel, depths drop off quickly as you proceed upstream on the small creek. Be sure to drop the hook before proceeding more than 100 yards.

Further upstream, south of Buzzard Island, a small bubble of deep water shoots off to the northeast. Minimum depths of 9 feet can be held for a short distance from the main channel. Boats of almost any size can anchor here, but protection would not be sufficient for heavy weather. Feel your way along and drop the hook before cruising very far from the main body of the creek.

West of Buzzard Island a small creek branches off to the west. This stream is marked by a series of uncharted and unlighted daybeacons leading to a private dock and country club. There are no facilities for visitors, but anchorage in the stream short of the docks is a very good possibility. The area between unlighted daybeacons #4 and #6 offers enough swinging room for boats up to 38 feet, but this spot is not very sheltered. Further upstream, between #6 and the creek's first sharp turn to starboard, craft up to 36 feet can anchor with somewhat more protection.

Beyond the sharp starboard bend, unlighted daybeacon #8 will be spied to starboard and the private docks to port. High ground fronts onto the port shore in this area. Boats up to 32 feet can anchor between #8 and the private piers. There is not enough swinging room for larger craft. Depths finally begin to drop off past the docks.

Back on the main body of Mackay Creek, the cruising boater can confidently continue upstream with several uncharted markers showing the way. Between unlighted daybeacons #8 and #6 the creek borders higher ground on Pinckney Island to the east. This spot would be a good anchorage for almost

BEAUFORT RIVER TO GEORGIA 259

any size craft if the changeable winds stay under 20 knots.

Mackay Creek eventually enters the southern reaches of Port Royal Sound and Chechessee River. This entrance is currently marked by one lighted, but still uncharted, marker and holds minimum depths of 6 feet. Take care if you should choose to use this passage. Proceed slowly and keep a sharp watch on the sounder.

Mackay Creek Navigation

To enter the southern reaches of Mackay Creek, continue cruising on the ICW until you are 200 yards south of unlighted daybeacon #27; then turn almost 180 degrees back to the north and enter the creek on its mid-width.

If you should be making for the small anchorage near flashing daybeacon #1 on the creek's western shore, begin favoring the western banks soon after entering Mackay Creek. Come abeam of #1 to port, then turn into the small creek to the west. Favor the starboard banks. Don't allow leeway to ease you to the south. Extensive mud banks, which cover at high tide, are found south of #1. Be sure to drop the hook *before* coming abeam of the launching ramp you will spy on the starboard shore. Depths deteriorate to less than 3 feet near the ramp.

Most boats will not be able to continue upstream on the left-hand channel of Mackay Creek that was used to reach the anchorage. The section of bridge crossing this arm of the creek is low and narrow.

To continue upstream on the main body of Mackay Creek, begin favoring the eastern banks as you approach Last End Point, after passing flashing daybeacon #24 well to its westerly side. As shown on chart 11507, a shoal guards the middle of the river in this area. Cruise through Mackay Bridge's central pass-through and continue on the mid-width.

Watch to the east as you begin to approach Buzzard Island. You will quickly spot the large offshoot of deep water that makes off to the northeast. If you choose to anchor here, enter the stream on its mid-width, but be sure to stop before coming abeam of Buzzard Island's southern tip.

A bit further upstream, the marked but unnamed creek leading to the private country club dock will be spied to the west. To enter, cruise between unlighted daybeacons #1 and #2. Continue on the middle, passing unlighted daybeacons #4, #6, and #8 to starboard. Drop the hook anywhere you choose, but be sure to leave plenty of room for passing vessels.

Between the unnamed creek and Port Royal Sound, Mackay Creek is marked by a series of uncharted but very helpful aids. Pass unlighted daybeacon #9 to its fairly immediate westerly side. Don't drift to the west here. As chart 11507 notes, there is a large patch of shallow water along the western banks. Pass unlighted daybeacons #8 and #6 to port and #5 to starboard.

North of #5 Mackay Creek begins its run

> into the southern reaches of Chechessee River and Port Royal Sound. Slow down as you approach the entranceway. Look east and you will see a fairly large marker on several pilings out in the sound. This aid is lighted but does not have any number. Set course from the creek's mouth to come abeam of this marker to its fairly immediate northerly side. Go slow and watch the sounder. Don't attempt this passage if your boat draws more than 4½ feet.

May River

"Picturesqueness and variety, which characterize the lower coast, reach perfection . . . on the River May, lauded by all travelers from Ribault (sic) down." James Henry Rice, Jr., wrote these words in the 1920s, but they are as true today as they were then. This writer was impressed by May River as a microcosm of the many good features of coastal South Carolina. The beautiful shores are undeveloped except for two picturesque communities. Both Brighton Beach and Bluffton look out over the river and provide a pleasant break in the grassy shores. Bluffton is perched atop high earthen banks and is particularly

House at Bluffton, May River

impressive. There are no facilities for boaters at either village.

Viewed in the warm light of a fall afternoon, May River resembles one of those "artist's renditions" of a lovely stream, often seen in boating magazines but seldom discovered in reality. Strangely, few cruising boaters take advantage of the May's charms. I urge you to join the ranks of those fortunate few who have made this extraordinary river's acquaintance.

May River is well marked and easy to navigate. Several unlighted but well-charted daybeacons lead the visiting cruiser to the shores of Bluffton. Past this point depths become too uncertain for large craft.

The river boasts excellent anchorage abeam of Bluffton's high banks, but otherwise the stream's sidewaters are not appropriate for most cruising boats. Bass Creek, north of unlighted daybeacon #4, is surrounded by unmarked shoals, as is Bull Creek southwest of unlighted daybeacon #5. Neither is particularly recommended for those without local knowledge.

Bluffton

Bluffton was settled before 1800 as a summer retreat for the rich planters of the day. Many famous families built residences here, and a study of the old names reads like a *Who's Who* of southern coastal South Carolina history. James Rice once described Bluffton as "retaining enough flavor of the old days to let one know he is within the pale, surrounded by the purple-born, who through storm and stress, war and misfortune, have clung tenaciously to their birthright."

In *Tales of Beaufort,* Nell Graydon relates a description of life in Bluffton before the Civil War as told by a member of the famous Hayward family. "In the days before the war when splendor was in its glory and hoop skirts and tall silk hats held sway, the village was a place of wealth . . . families on surrounding plantations lived in palatial homes . . . . Life and gaiety, old-time formalities and customs ran high. 'Marsuh' and 'Missus' sat in dignity while young sideburn 'Masters' courted young 'Missuses' in bonnets and curls. Tight-waisted, hoop-skirted figures danced and flirted in innocence and mirth."

As the dark days of the Civil War approached, Bluffton strongly favored secession. Some historians claim that the first secession movement in the state was organized here. A fiery speech supporting state's rights was delivered in the village by Dr. Daniel Hamilton, under an old oak tree that is even today known as "the Secession Oak." The movement was carried forward by Barnwell Rhett of Beaufort, who had a summer home in Bluffton. In 1844 Rhett launched the Bluffton Movement for a State Convention. According to Ms. Graydon, his message was direct and left no room for waverers: "I proclaim to you, if you value your rights, you must resist and submit not."

Unfortunately, many of Bluffton's historic buildings are not visible from the water. An exception is the Church of the Cross. This structure dates back to 1854 and can be seen through the trees atop the bluffs overlooking May River.

May River Navigation

Pass well to the south of unlighted daybeacon #2, which marks the easterly mouth of May River. Set course to come abeam and pass unlighted daybeacon #4 by some 100 yards to its southerly side. Watch to be sure that leeway does not ease you to the north after passing #4. As shown on chart 11516, there is shallow water north of the marker.

Continue upstream by setting a new course to come abeam of unlighted daybeacon #5 to its northerly side. Shallow water is located south of #5. Follow the river on around as it makes a slow turn to the south. Favor the northern shores slightly. Pass unlighted daybeacon #6 to its southerly side and come abeam of unlighted daybeacon #8, also to its southerly quarter.

At #8 the marked channel follows a branch of May River that cuts back to the north and leads to Bluffton. After passing #8, follow the cut-through leading off to the west. Pass unlighted daybeacon #10 to starboard. Stick to the mid-width and point to pass unlighted daybeacons #11 and #13 to port.

Past #11 the high cliffs of Bluffton will be sighted on the starboard shores. From here until the river forks, you can anchor abeam of the village with good protection. Do not attempt to cruise past the forks found just past Bluffton. Depths are uncertain and much too treacherous for cruising craft.

ICW to Savannah River

The waters south of Calibogue Sound to Savannah River and the Georgia line are quite different from those of Hilton Head. Gone are the many marinas and condo projects. The cruising boater suddenly finds himself in a wild, mostly uninhabited area, with only a few isolated homes to be seen. Much of the waterway passes through vast saltwater marshes and is not particularly pleasing to the eye.

Portions of the Cooper, New, and Wright rivers, joined by man-made cuts, make up this section of the ICW. Other portions of these streams are abandoned by the waterway. These waters are mostly deep and offer many anchorage possibilities. Unfortunately, the prevailing marsh banks do not give much protection. This is not a good area to ride out a heavy blow.

Those boaters who thrive on cruising waters off the beaten path, but don't wish to stray far from the waterway or contend with too many navigational difficulties, may enjoy this region. Others will find this area to be quite dull and will be glad to reach the wide waters of Savannah River. Whatever your preference, I hope you will enjoy these southernmost waters of coastal South Carolina.

BEAUFORT RIVER TO GEORGIA   263

Haig Point Lighthouse

The old lighthouse at Haig Point has been privately restored and is visible through the trees on the northern tip of Daufuskie Island, across from flashing daybeacon #32. The light was originally built in 1875 to mark the passage from Calibogue Sound to Savannah River. It was used as a range marker until 1936.

Cooper River

Cooper River breaks off from Calibogue Sound at flashing daybeacon #32. The river is mostly free of shoals and is easily navigated. The single shallow spot is marked by unlighted daybeacon #36. Not far into the river's interior, Bull Creek will come abeam to the north.

Bull Creek

Bull Creek, which enters the Cooper north of flashing daybeacon #34, is one of the best anchorages between Calibogue Sound and Savannah River. The creek maintains minimum depths of 12 feet. The lower reaches are bordered by marsh but provide enough swinging room for boats up to 50 feet. Further upstream the high banks of Bull Island line the stream's northern banks. Here boats up to 45

Haig Point Lighthouse, Daufuskie Island

feet can anchor in excellent protection. For those who want to explore further, there is another good anchorage near the overhead power cables noted on chart 11507. Here the creek is sandwiched between the high ground of Bull Island to the east and Savage Island to the west. Unfortunately, you must bypass a large, unmarked shoal to reach this superior anchorage. Craft drawing less than 5 feet should be able to make it with careful navigation. Past the power lines, unmarked shoals become more frequent.

Daufuskie Island

For much of its length, the ICW section of Cooper and New rivers borders remote Daufuskie Island to the east. This body of land is one of the few remaining South Carolina Sea Islands that has not been developed as a resort. It is one of the most remote inhabited regions in all of coastal South Carolina.

"Daufuskie" is an Indian word meaning "the place of blood." The island has lived up to this sinister title throughout its history. Before the Revolution, Daufuskie was a kind of no-man's-land between the English settlers to the north and hostile Indians to the south. There were frequent small battles between the Indians and the colonial militia on the island.

As the Indian threat lessened, English colonists began building plantations on Daufuskie. For some unexplained reason these

Harbour Town channel from lighthouse, Hilton Head Island

settlers took a decidedly loyalist point of view during the Revolution. This was in sharp contrast to the patriot stance of those living on neighboring Hilton Head. The island's ominous name was again confirmed by the many skirmishes that took place between these two groups during the war.

Following the Civil War, Daufuskie Island was virtually abandoned. Its only inhabitants were freed blacks. Today the island's population still numbers only about 100 souls. Some of the residents' small homes can be seen along the eastern shore of the waterway south of Ramshorn Creek, near flashing daybeacon #40.

Lower Cooper River

The ICW abandons Cooper River and runs south on Ramshorn Creek at flashing daybeacon #37. The upriver section of the Cooper holds minimum 6-foot depths with only one or two shoal areas, which are easily avoided. Anchorage possibilities abound. You need only select an area to your liking that seems sheltered from the prevailing winds; then drop the hook for a peaceful evening. Swinging room is sufficient on most areas of the river for boats up to 40 feet.

As the river takes a sharp turn to the west, several power lines cross the water. High ground abuts the river's northern shore at the power lines. This is one of the most sheltered anchorages on the Cooper. Boats up to 45 feet can anchor here with confidence.

Past the power lines two small creeks, shown on chart 11507, break off from the main body of Cooper River. Both streams are

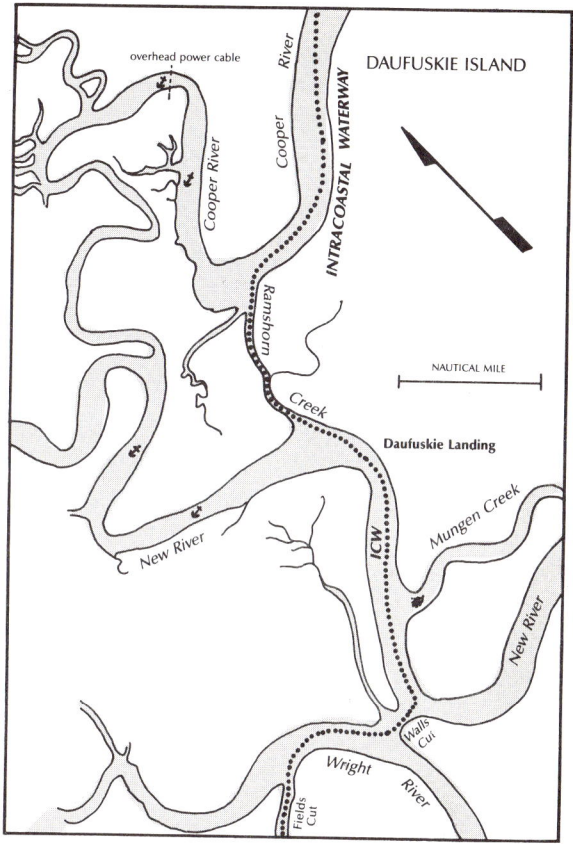

narrow and suffer from unmarked shallows. This writer suggests that you bypass both creeks.

Eventually the Cooper leads into the deep waters of New River. It is a simple matter to follow this stream back to the ICW.

New River

The waterway enters the waters of New River from the southern reaches of Ramshorn Creek at flashing daybeacon #39. This is a tricky area, particularly for northbound boaters. Be sure to read the navigational section on Ramshorn Creek presented later in this chapter.

West of the ICW's entrance, the upper section of New River offers overnight anchorage possibilities. Minimum depths are 6 feet, with most of the stream exhibiting much deeper readings. Both shores are mostly marsh grass and provide only minimal protection. However, in winds under 15 knots, boats up to 50 feet can drop anchor anywhere west of the intersection with Cooper River. Further upstream, unmarked shoals litter the river. Cruising boaters are advised to stop their exploration at the hairpin turn to the west at the Cooper junction.

The ICW leaves New River at flashing daybeacon #42 and follows Walls Cut west to Wright River. The easterly reaches of New River remain deep as far as Bloody Point. This section of the river is open and provides very little shelter indeed. While there is plenty of swinging room for boats of almost any size, this writer advises you to choose the more sheltered upriver section for anchorage.

Mungen Creek

Very adventurous boaters who pilot craft of less than 35 feet that draw less than 4 feet might wish to consider anchoring on the southern reaches of Mungen Creek north of Bloody Point. This stream is well sheltered by the high ground of Daufuskie Island to the north, but successful navigation of the creek is a very tricky business. If you choose to enter, be sure to read the navigational information presented later in this chapter *before* attempting entry. By all accounts you should not cruise past the creek's first sharp turn to port. In spite of soundings shown on chart 11512, depths drop off to 3 and 4 feet past this point.

Bloody Point

Bloody Point, located just below the intersection of New River and Mungen Creek, derives its name from a battle fought nearby during the early days of English colonization. In those uncertain times, Indians from Georgia and Florida often conducted raids on the Beaufort settlers. They would carry off all they could, then hide on Daufuskie Island to enjoy the spoils.

On one occasion an Indian raid so angered the white settlers that the colonial militia set out in hot pursuit of the attackers. The Indians had retreated to the southern point of Daufuskie. Supposing themselves to be safe, they lit cooking fires and fell to enjoying their plunder.

Meanwhile, the militia had learned of the raiders' position from friendly Indians. Landing on the northwest portion of the island, the whites marched overland and surrounded the unsuspecting Indians. A hail of musket balls was the first evidence the Indians had of the militia's arrival. The raiders were cut off from escape and were slaughtered to a man. Ever since, the island's southerly extreme has been known as Bloody Point.

Wright River

The ICW follows Wright River for only a brief distance before entering Fields Cut and hurrying south to Savannah River and the Georgia state line. Abandoned by the waterway, the lower reaches of the Wright, south of unlighted daybeacon #43, carry minimum depths of 7 feet for some distance downstream and boast enough swing room for boats up to 45 feet. The stream is bordered entirely by the usual salt marsh. Winds over 10 knots can give rise to a most unpleasant chop, and anchorage is recommended only in light airs. Eventually depths drop off as the stream approaches a ruined bridge. Be sure to cease exploration well before reaching the old wreck.

West of unlighted nun buoy #44B, the upper portion of the Wright holds minimum depths of 10 feet far upriver until it bends sharply to port east of Turnbridge Lodge. Though both shores are marsh and give minimal protection, there is enough swing room for boats up to 45 feet. However, you must cruise through some 5- to 6-foot depths near #44B to gain access to the deeper portion of the river. In light of these restrictions, the river's upper reaches are recommended only for craft that draw less than 4 feet.

ICW to Savannah River Navigation

There are a few shoal-prone areas on the ICW between the Cooper and Savannah rivers, but most of the route is easily traveled. Similarly, most sidewaters throughout this area are deep and free of obstructions. Of course, there are always exceptions, and areas calling for special caution are discussed below. Observe good piloting practices and you should enjoy these southernmost South Carolina waters.

Cooper River Pass well to the south of flashing daybeacon #32 and enter Cooper River on its mid-width. Look to the south as you pass #32 and you may be able to see the Haig Point Lighthouse on the northern tip of Daufuskie Island.

Begin favoring the northern shore slightly as you approach flashing daybeacon #34. As shown on chart 11507, there is a small shoal on the southern shore, but the channel is quite broad here and you need not have much concern. At #34 Bull Creek breaks off to the north.

Bull Creek Do not approach flashing daybeacon #34 when entering Bull Creek. Pass the aid well to its eastern side and enter the mid-width of the creek. As you approach the stream's first turn to port, begin favoring the port banks slightly.

Shortly beyond this turn the creek follows another loop, this time to the northeast. You may be surprised to note a 60-foot reading on your sounder in one spot while traversing the turn.

Begin heavily favoring the starboard shore as soon as you come out of the northeasterly bend. As shown on chart 11507, there is a large shoal abutting the western shore.

Beyond this obstruction the creek soon

takes a sharp jog to the starboard and then straightens out. The high ground of Bull Island borders the stream's starboard banks in this area. Discontinue your cruise before reaching the next hairpin turn to port. Past this point depths become too uncertain for cruising craft.

On the ICW From flashing daybeacon #34, continue on the mid-width of Cooper River until coming abeam of flashing daybeacon #35 to the south. Begin favoring the southeastern banks and pass unlighted daybeacon #36 to its southerly side. As shown on chart 11507, there is shallow water west of #36. At flashing daybeacon #37 the waterway leaves Cooper River and enters Ramshorn Creek.

Upper Cooper River The upper reaches of Cooper River, abandoned by the ICW, can be easily traversed all the way to New River by holding to the mid-width, with three exceptions. The first comes just short of where the river, bending westward, is crossed by overhead power cables. Just before this bend, chart 11507 correctly notes a small shoal on the port shore. Favor the starboard banks until you round the turn and pass under the cables.

After leaving the cables behind, favor the port banks until the first small sidewater comes abeam to starboard. Cruise back to the mid-width and hold to the middle until reaching the hairpin turn to starboard north of Page Island. As you cruise round the bend, favor the port shore a bit. Return to the middle before approaching the next turn.

On the ICW The southern mouth of Ramshorn Creek is partially obstructed by a shoal and calls for great caution. Pass flashing daybeacon #39 to its immediate westerly quarter and hold course into the deepwater section of New River. Don't let leeway ease you to the west. The shoal on the western point of the creek is building outward. Proceed with just enough speed for good maneuverability. Watch your sounder! If depths start to rise, give way to the east.

The waterway follows the lower portion of New River south to Walls Cut. The upper reaches of the river are also accessible to the cruising boater.

Upper New River Cruising the upper section of New River as far as its intersection with the lower Cooper River is an elementary matter of holding to the mid-width. Be sure to stop after rounding the next sharp turn to port upstream from the junction. Unmarked shoals pepper New River past this point, and the stream soon leaves the chart.

On the ICW Favor the southeastern shore when rounding the turn at Daufuskie Lodge. A small shoal has built out from the opposite banks and has encroached on flashing daybeacon #40. Don't approach this aid closely.

At flashing daybeacon #42 the waterway

follows Walls Cut for a short distance into Wright River. The eastern section of New River offers cruising possibilities for adventurous boaters.

Eastern New River The wide eastern section of New River holds good depths on its mid-width as far as Bloody Point. Don't even think about proceeding further. Depths soon fall off to less than 1 foot of water.

Those daring souls who attempt to enter the southern reaches of Mungen Creek must remember to proceed with the greatest caution. To hold best depths, continue on the mid-width of New River until just before coming abeam of the warning beacon at Bloody Point. Here you may turn north into the creek, favoring the starboard banks. Don't approach this shoreline too closely either. Be sure to discontinue your exploration soon after the creek takes its first turn to port. In spite of soundings shown on chart 11512, depths soon deteriorate.

Lower Wright River South of unlighted daybeacon #43 the lower reaches of Wright River can be cruised to within 1 nautical mile of the ruined bridge guarding the river's seaward mouth. Simply hold to the mid-width and don't go too far.

On the ICW The waterway follows Wright River briefly before cutting south on Fields Cut. The entrance into the man-made canal has chronic shoaling problems and calls for caution. Come abeam of flashing daybeacon #45 to its northerly side and proceed on course for another 50 feet or so; then turn sharply to port, pass unlighted nun buoy #44B to its immediate southeasterly side, and enter the mid-width of the cut.

Upper Wright River To enter the western section of Wright River, abandoned by the waterway, proceed on course as if you were entering Fields Cut until nun buoy #44B comes abeam. Cruise another 20 yards or so on the same course, then cut 90 degrees to the west and pass to the south of #44B. Don't approach the southern shore too closely. A shoal seems to be building out from this bank. Beyond the shoal, favor the southern shore slightly until you approach the stream's first slow turn to starboard. Cruise back to the middle as you enter the bend. Good depths can be held as far as the river's splits, east of Turnbridge Lodge, by sticking to the mid-width. Be sure to give all points a wide berth.

On to Georgia Flashing buoy #48 marks the ICW's entrance into wide Savannah River and the Georgia waters. Watch for swift currents and shoaling problems at the cut's mouth.

I hope you have enjoyed our journey through coastal South Carolina as much I have. I'm sure you will agree it is a land of almost unparalleled opportunity for the cruising boater. Hope you had fun. Good boating!

INDEX 271

Abbapoola Creek, 131, 134–35
Adams Creek, 151, 154
Airy Hall Plantation, 173, 175
Albergottie Creek, 208
Anchorage House, 217–18
Arcadia Plantation, 24
Archer Creek, 240
Ashepoo-Coosaw Cutoff, 172, 174
Ashepoo River, 159, 160, 164, 171–75
Ashley Marina, 83, 122
Ashley River, 81, 105, 106, 121–23
Awendaw Creek, 69, 76

Back River, 110, 113, 115, 117
Bailey Creek, 165–66, 170
Bailey Island, 165, 169
Ballast Creek, 237, 238
Bass Creek (Kiawah River), 133
Bass Creek (Parrot Creek), 184–85, 187
Battery Carriage House, 94
Battery Creek, 234–35, 238
Battery Pringle, 131
Battery White, 49
Baynard Cove Creek, 254
Bay Street Inn, 218
Beaufort, 213–31:
   attractions, 222–29
   history, 218–22
   lodging, 218
   marinas, 215, 216–17
   restaurants, 215–18
Beaufort Downtown Marina, 216, 231
Beaufort Marina, 215, 231
Beaufort River, 233–39
Bella Marina, 5
Belle Isle Marina, 49, 51
Belle Isle Plantation, 49
Belmont Plantation, 108–9
Big Bay Creek, 168–69, 170
Big Hill Marsh, 70
Black River, 29, 41, 45–47
Bloody Point, 266
Bluffton, 249, 260, 261, 262
Bohicket Creek, 142, 149–51, 154–55
Bohicket Marina Village, 150, 155
Bolders Island, 199
Boone Hall Plantation, 120
Botany Bay Marina, 151
Boundary House, 4
Boyd Creek, 240–41, 246–47

Braddock Cove, 254
Breach Inlet, 69, 72–73, 75, 77
Breakfast Creek, *see* Adams Creek
Brickyard Creek, 179, 206, 207–11
Brighton Beach, 260
Broad Creek, 251–53, 257
Broad Creek Marina, 252, 257
Broad River, 239–41, 246–47
Brookgreen Gardens, 11, 17, 21
Bryan Creek, 251, 257
Bucksport, 11, 13
Bucksport Plantation Marina, 15–16
Bucksville, 13, 25
Bucksville Plantation, 13, 25
Bull Creek (Waccamaw River), 16, 25
Bull Creek (Cooper River), 263–64, 267–68
Bull Island, 264, 268
Bull Narrows Creek, 69
Bull River (Coosaw River area), 179, 202–5
Bull River (McClellanville Area), 63, 67
Bulls Bay, 67, 68, 69
Butler Creek, 22, 26
Butler Island, 24
Buzzards Roost Marina, 129, 134

Cafe Europa, 253
Cafe 99, 95–96
Calabash, 4, 8
Calabash Creek, 4, 7–8
Calhoun Mansion, 93
Calibogue Sound, 233, 249, 250–51, 256–57, 262, 263
Cape Romain, 56, 58–60, 65–66
Cape Romain National Wildlife Refuge, 53, 59
Capers Creek, 70, 76–77
Capers Island, 70
Cappy's Seafood Restaurant, 129
Casino Creek, 60–61, 65–66
Cassina Point Plantation, 146–47
Cast-A-Way Marina, 72
Castle, The, 225–27
Castle Pinckney, 94, 103
Cat Island Ferry, 53, 63
Cathou's Boat Yard, 31
Charleston, 81–96:
   attractions, 89–94
   history, 86–89
   lodging, 94
   marinas, 82–83
   restaurants, 95–96

272 INDEX

Charleston Battery, 91–93, 94, 106
Charleston Harbor, 96–106
Charleston Inlet, 97, 106
Charleston Municipal Marina, see George M. Lockwood Municipal Marina
Charleston Shipyard, 108
Charleston Visitors Center, 89
Chechessee Creek, 244–45, 248
Chechessee River, 234, 239, 243–45, 248–49
Childsbury, 113
Chisolm House, 166–67, 170
Chisolm Island, 205
Chowan Creek, 235, 238
Church Creek, 139 40
Citadel, The, 123
Clarendon Plantation, 243
Clouter Creek, 108, 115
Club Bridge Creek, 193, 196
Coffin Creek, 186
Coffin Point Plantation, 182–83, 186
Cole Creek, 241, 246–47
Colleton River, 239, 245–46, 248, 249
Combahee River, 179, 197–98
Conch Creek, 73, 77
Congaree Boat Creek, 60, 65, 66
Conway, 11–13, 24, 25
Cooper River (Charleston area), 81, 105, 106–17
Cooper River (off Calibogue Sound), 233, 249, 262, 263, 265, 267–68
Coosaw Island, 182, 183
Coosaw River, 179, 180, 206, 209
Copahee Sound, 68
Copps Landing, 245, 249
Coquina Harbor, 5
Cork Creek, 54, 64
Cote Bas, 111
Cotton Exchange, 95
Cow House Creek, 21–22
"Cut Off," 242, 247
Cutoff Reach, 133, 135–36
Cypress Gardens, 111

Darby Marine Supply, 97
Datha Island, 182, 183
Daufuskie Island, 264–65, 266
Dawho River, 125, 153, 156, 157
Dean Hall Plantation, 111
Dewees Creek, 70–71, 77
Dewees Island, 70
Distant Island Creek, 235–36, 238

Dodge Plantation, see William Seabrook Plantation
Dolphin Dining Room, 217
Dover Plantation, 50
Drum Island Reach, 114
Duck Creek, 56–57, 64
Dutch Treat Restaurant, 215

East Cooper River, 111–12, 117
Edding Creek, 184, 186–87
Edding Point, 184
Edisto Island, 143–44
Edmondston-Alston House, 90–91, 94
82 Queen, 95
Elliott Cut, 126, 128, 136, 139
Enterprise Landing, 12
Estherville Plantation, 50
Euhaw Creek, 246
Exchange Plantation, 22, 26

Factory Creek, 215, 216, 230, 231
Fenwick Cut, 161, 162, 164, 171, 173
Fenwick Island, 171
Fields Cut, 266, 269
Fields Point, 197
Fishing Creek (Dawho River), 156, 157
Fishing Creek (South Edisto River), 165, 169
Five Fathom Creek, 62–63, 66–67
Flagg Creek, 110, 115
Folly Creek, 133, 136
Folly Island, 129, 134
Folly River, 128, 129, 133, 135–36
Foot Point, 248, 249
Fort Frederick, 234
Fort Johnson, 101–2, 106
Fort Legarre, 130
Fort Moultrie, 69, 73–75, 78, 99
Fort Sumter, 94, 96, 99–101
French Quarter Creek, 112, 117
Fripp Inlet, 188, 191–92, 195
Fripp Island, 179, 188, 192
Fripp Island Marina, 191–92, 195
Fripp's Landing, 244, 248

Garibaldi's, 95
George M. Lockwood Municipal Marina, 82, 122
Georgetown, 29–43:
    attractions, 32–38
    history, 38–42
    marinas, 30–32
    restaurants, 32

INDEX 273

Georgetown Exxon Marina, 30–31
Georgetown Landing Marina, 31–32, 43
Georgetown Lighthouse, 50
Georgetown Rice Museum, 30, 42
Goose Creek, 109, 115
Gotton Island, 247
Grace Island, 65
Graham Creek, 69, 76
Gray Bay, 71
Green Creek, 131
Grove Creek, 110–11, 115–16
Grove Plantation, 110–11
Guendalose Creek, 22
Gulf Auto Marina, 31
Gunboat Island, 197, 198

Hague Marina, 6
Haig Point Lighthouse, 263, 267
Hamlin Creek, 72, 77
Hamlin Sound, 68, 71
Harbor River (McClellanville area), 67
Harbor River (St. Helena Sound area), 179, 180, 188, 189–91, 194
Harbour Town Yacht Basin, 253–54, 257
Hasty Point, 22
Hazzard Creek, 245, 248–49
Hazzard's Marina, 30
Henning-Miller House, 34
Heriot-Tarbox House, 36–38
Heyward-Washington House, 93
Hilton Head Island, 233, 249, 254–55
Hobcaw Barony, 49, 51
Hog Island Reach, 114
"Hole in the Wall," 174
Hopsewee Plantation, 57
Horlbeck Creek, 120
Horry County, 6–7
Horsehead Creek, 60–61, 65–66
Hunting Island, 188, 190–91

Inlet Creek, 72
Intracoastal Waterway:
    Ashepoo River, 171, 172, 173–74
    Ashley River, 121–23
    Beaufort area, 230–31
    Beaufort River to Port Royal Sound, 233–39
    Calibogue Sound to Savannah River, 262–69
    Charleston Harbor area, 96–105
    Elliott Cut to Stono River, 126–28
    Little River to Waccamaw River, 3–10

    McClellanville to Charleston, 67–73, 76–78
    North Edisto River to South Edisto River, 156–57
    Port Royal Sound to Calibogue Sound, 249–57
    Rock Creek, 175–76
    South Edisto River, 162–64
    St. Helena Sound/Coosaw River, 179, 206–11
    Stono River, 134–36
    Stono River to North Edisto River, 136–40
    Waccamaw River, 14–18, 21–24, 25–27
    Wappoo Creek to Stono River, 126, 128
    Winyah Bay, 48–51
    Winyah Bay to McClellanville, 53–67
Isle of Palms, 69, 71, 72

Jack Island, 207, 209–10
James Island, 128, 130
Jarvis Creek, 251, 256–57
Jenkins Creek, 185, 187
Jeremy Creek, 61–62, 66
Jericho Creek, 23–24, 44, 45
John Cross Tavern, 217
Johns Island, 128, 130–31

Kiawah Island, 129, 131, 132–33, 135
Kiawah River, 128, 129, 131–32, 135

Ladies Island Bridge, 231
Lafayette House, 224–25
Lafayette Restaurant, 32
Lake Moultrie, 113
Lands End Restaurant, 32
Leadenwah Creek, 149, 153–54
Leland Marine Services, 62
Lemon Island Marina, 243–44, 248
Lem's Bluff Plantation, 141, 142
Little Papas Creek, 63, 67
Little River, 3
Little River Inlet, 3–4, 7
Little River Marina, 4
Little River Plantation Marina, 4
Little River Village, 4–5
Long Creek, 70–71, 77
Long Island, 75
Lower Toogoodoo Creek, 140
Lucy Point Creek, 185–86, 187–88

Mackay Creek, 250, 258–60
Manigault Neck, 244
Mariners Cay Marina, 133, 136
Marsh Harbor Marina, 215, 230

INDEX

Marshlands, 227–28
Marshlands Plantation, 103, 106
Matthews Creek, 67
May River, 249, 250, 260–62
McClellanville, 53, 54, 61–62, 66
McCleod Plantation, 126
Middle Marsh Island, 256
Minim Creek, 54–55, 64
Minim Creek-Esterville Canal, 53
Moreland Plantation, 111
Morgan Back Creeks, 181, 182
Morgan-Ginsler House, 35
Morgan Island, 180–81, 182
Morgan River, 179, 180, 182–88
Morris Island, 130
Morris Island Lighthouse, 102–3
Mosquito Creek, 173, 174
Mound, The, 168
Mount Pleasant, 98
Mount Pleasant Channel, 97, 105
Mungen Creek, 266, 269
Murrells Inlet, 19–21
Myrtle Beach, 3, 6–7
Myrtle Beach Yacht Club, *see* Coquina Harbor

Nathaniel Russell House, 93
Navy dry-dock facility (Wando River), 120
Neck, The, 168–69
New Chehaw River, 179, 197, 198–200
Net Cut Creek, 137, 139–40
New River, 233, 262, 265–66, 268–69
Nightingale Hall, 44, 45
Nixon Crossroads, 5
North Charleston Port Terminal, 109
North Edisto Inlet, 151–52
North Edisto River, 125, 140, 142–56
North Island, 50
North Santee Bay, 56–57, 64
North Santee River, 55, 57, 64
Northside Marina, 4
Nowell Creek, 119, 120–21

Oak Island Plantation, 147–49
Old Chehaw River, 179, 197, 200–202
Old House Creek, 188, 191–92, 195
Old Island, 192
Old Market (Charleston), 89, 90, 93
Old River, 14
Old Town Creek, 122–23
Orange Grove Creek, 122–23

Oristo, 168
Otter Islands, 171–72
Outdoor Resorts Yacht Club Marina, 250, 256
Oyster House Creek, 138, 140

Palmetto Bay Marina, 252, 257
Palmetto Shores Marina, 5
Papas Creek, 63, 67
Parris Island, 219–20, 221, 222, 234, 238, 240
Parrot Creek, 184, 187
Patriots Point, 103–4, 114
Pawleys Island, 19–20
Pee Dee River, 22, 23, 26, 29, 41, 43–45
Peters Point, 165, 169
Pigeon Point, 209, 211
Pinckney Island, 258
Pinckney Landing, 245, 248
Pine Island Cut, 3, 8–10
Pleasants Point, 208
Pompion Hill Chapel, 112, 117
Port Royal, 218, 222, 238
Port Royal Channel, 237, 238, 239
Port Royal Sound, 86, 233, 234, 239, 246
Presbyterian Manse, 167, 170
Price Creek, 69–70, 76
Prince Creek, 16
Prince George Episcopal Church, Winyah, 32–34
Prospect Hill Plantation, 162–64

Ramshorn Creek, 265, 268
RB's Restaurant, 97–98
Rebellion Reach Channel, 105, 106
Red Store-Tarbox Warehouse, 35–36
Rice Homeplace, 200–201, 202
Rice Hope Plantation, 113, 117
Riverview, 228–29
Robbins Creek, 133, 135
Rock Creek, 159, 160, 174, 175–77
Rockville, 151

Sampit River, 29, 30, 42–43
Sampson Island Creek, 161, 162
Sand Creek, 64
Santee Delta, 53, 56
Santee River, 55–56
Savage Island, 264
Savannah River, 233, 269
Sawmill Creek, 245, 249
Schooner Channel, 203–4, 205
Schooner Creek (Waccamaw River), 23, 26

INDEX

Schooner Creek (Williman Creek), 202
Sea Island Motel, 218
Sea Islands, 125, 126–28, 179
Seaside Marina, 72
Secession House, 225
Sewee Bay, 67, 68
Shelter Cove Marina, 252–53, 257
Shem Creek, 96, 97–98, 105
Shingle Creek, 166
Shipyard Creek, 108, 114–15
Shutes Folly Island, 103
Skrine Creek, 60–61, 66
Skull Creek, 249, 250, 255–56
Skull Creek Marina, 250, 256
Slack Reach, see Yellow House Creek
Socastee Bridge, 9–10
South Edisto Inlet, 170–71
South Edisto River, 159, 160–71
South Santee River, 57–58, 65
Spanish Point, 234
Spring Island, 244–45, 248
St. Helena Episcopal Church, 229
St. Helena Island, 182, 183, 186, 221
St. Helena Sound, 179, 180–82
St. Michael's Church, 90, 93
St. Philip's Episcopal Church, 90, 93
St. Pierre Creek, 165, 169–70
Station Creek, 193–94, 196–97, 237
Steamboat Creek, 144–45, 153
Stono Marina, 129–30, 134
Stono Plantation, 131
Stono River, 125, 126, 128–38
Store Creek, 166–68, 170
Story River, 179, 188, 192–93, 195–96
Stuarttowne, 221, 234
Sullivans Island, 69, 73–75
Sullivans Island Lighthouse, 73, 103
Sunnyside Plantation, 167–68, 170
Swinton Creek, 72

Tee, The, 106, 108, 111, 117
Thoroughfare Creek, 22, 26
Tidalholm, 228
Tomers Cove Marina, 73, 78

Tom Point Creek, 144, 153
Toogoodoo Creek, 140–42
Toomer Creek, 70
Town Creek, 84
Town Creek Boatyard, 107
Town Creek Reach, 108, 113–14
Trenchards Inlet, 188, 193, 196
Two Meeting Street Inn, 94

Vereens Marina, 6
Victoria Bluff, 245
Village Creek, 184, 186

Wacca Wache Marina, 16–18
Waccamaw Neck, 21
Waccamaw River, 3, 11–18, 21–27, 29
Wachesaw Landing, 17
Wadmalaw River, 125, 136
Walls Cut, 266, 268, 269
Wando port facilities, 119
Wando River, 81, 105, 118–21
Wappoo Creek, 106, 126–28
Wards Creek, 190, 194
Warren Island, 199, 200
Waterman-Kaminski House, 34
Watts Cut, 156, 157, 161
Waverly Creek, 22
Westbank Creek, 146–49, 153
West Cooper River, 113, 117
Whale Branch, 206–7, 241–43, 247
White Hall Inn, 215–16
White Point Gardens, 93
Whiteside Creek, 70
Wiggins, 200
Wild Dunes Yacht Harbor, 71
William Seabrook Plantation, 145–46
Williman Creek, 202, 203–4, 205
Wimbee Creek, 202, 203, 204, 205
Windsor Plantation, 46
Winyah Bay, 26, 27, 29, 30, 48–51
Winyah Bay Inlet Channel, 51
Winyah Indigo Society Hall, 34
Wright River, 233, 262, 266–67, 269

Yellow House Creek, 109–10, 115

NAVIGATIONAL NOTES

NAVIGATIONAL NOTES

NAVIGATIONAL NOTES

NAVIGATIONAL NOTES

NAVIGATIONAL NOTES

NAVIGATIONAL NOTES

NAVIGATIONAL NOTES

NAVIGATIONAL NOTES

NAVIGATIONAL NOTES

NAVIGATIONAL NOTES

NAVIGATIONAL NOTES

LEE COUNTY LIBRARY SYSTEM
3 3262 00192 9345
DISCARD

797.1   C 2
Y
Young
Cruising guide to coastal
   South Carolina

DISCARD 11/99

LEE COUNTY LIBRARY
107 Hawkins Ave.
Sanford, NC 27330
GAYLORD S